Gail Hamilton

Summer Rest

Gail Hamilton

Summer Rest

ISBN/EAN: 9783744652926

Printed in Europe, USA, Canada, Australia, Japan

Cover: Foto ©Thomas Meinert / pixelio.de

More available books at **www.hansebooks.com**

GAIL HAMILTON'S WRITINGS.

SUMMER REST. One volume.

SKIRMISHES AND SKETCHES. One volume.

A NEW ATMOSPHERE. One volume.

STUMBLING-BLOCKS. One volume.

GALA-DAYS. One volume.

COUNTRY LIVING AND COUNTRY THINKING. One volume.

The above are published in uniform style, by

TICKNOR AND FIELDS.

SUMMER REST.

BY

GAIL HAMILTON,
AUTHOR OF "COUNTRY LIVING AND COUNTRY THINKING,"
"A NEW ATMOSPHERE," "GALA-DAYS,"
ETC., ETC.

BOSTON:
TICKNOR AND FIELDS.
1866.

Entered according to Act of Congress, in the year 1866, by
TICKNOR AND FIELDS,
in the Clerk's Office of the District Court of the District of Massachusetts.

UNIVERSITY PRESS: WELCH, BIGELOW, & CO.,
CAMBRIDGE.

CONTENTS.

	PAGE
ORCHARD TALK	3
A PROSE HENRIADE	34
LARVA LESSONS	62
FANCY FARMING	100
A COUNCIL ABOUT A COUNCIL	130
GILFILLAN'S SABBATH	153
THE KINGDOM COMING	219
KING JAMES THE FIRST	255
WELL DONE	310

SUMMER REST.

1 A

ORCHARD TALK.

IT is charged that Americans have no repose. We are consumed with energy, and in our eagerness to do have largely lost the power to enjoy. There is some ground for the remark; but possibly we have in our character the elements of repose, though our circumstances have not yet contributed to, or even been tolerant of, its development. Certain it is that there can be no true repose save in connection with right action. Absolute quietude we cannot command, but absolute quietude is not indispensable. A boundless activity may carry along with it all the conditions of perfect rest.

We speak of the quiet of the country, and truly our souls find solace there and peace. But the country seems to be the place of all places where everything is going on. Especially in spring one becomes almost distracted. What is spring in the city? Dead bricks under your feet; dead stones all around you. There are beautiful things in the shop windows, but they never do anything. It is just the same as it was yesterday and as it will be to-morrow. I suppose a faint sense of warmth and fragrance does settle down into the city's old cold heart, and at a few breathing-holes — little irregular patches as we see them, lovely but minute, called "Central Park" or "Boston Common" — Nature comes up to blow. And there are the spring bonnets. Still, as a general thing, it can hardly make much difference whether it be June or January.

But Spring in the country, — O season rightly named ! — a goddess-queen glides through the heavens, and the earth and all that is therein springs up to meet her and do obeisance. We, gross and heavy, blind and deaf, are slow to catch the flutter of her robes, the music of her footfall, the odor of her breath, the brightness of her far-off coming. We call it cold and winter still. We huddle about the fires and wonder if the spring will never come; and all the while, lo, the spring is here ! Ten thousand watching eyes, ten thousand waiting ears, laid along the ground, have signalled the royal approach. Ten thousand times ten thousand voices sound the notes of preparation. Every tiny sleeping germ of animal and of vegetable life springs to its feet, wide awake, girded for duty, vigilant but unhurried, eager, active, and most orderly. Now you must be wide awake too, or you will miss the sights.

And each spring is more lovely than the last. Tenderer green on the earth, intenser blue in the sky, deeper colors, sweeter voices, busier feet, happier hearts, as the Summer comes softly singing through the meadows and pouring her fragrance on the air. Every year it floats into my thought, "I will write something beautiful about the summer," from pure longing to celebrate its loveliness in gratitude for its behests; but I never write the beautiful thing, no, nor ever shall. For the summer absorbs you unawares. The birds and the bees and the buds are so busy; the lambs in the fields, the fishes in the brooks, the cattle on a thousand hills, — with them is no delay nor excusing. And while you are living all these dear dumb lives, gradually the clouds grow leaden, the wind whistles, the leaves shiver and shrivel and fall, and of a sudden you look up to find that the summer is gone. Now, therefore, fair goddess, take, I pray, my speechless enjoyment for meet celebration, and count me no ingrate because I cannot say the thing I would.

But as yet the summer is here, warm and sunny and scented, pouring through the windows and filling house and heart with newness of life; sinking into the brown earth, subtile and sinuous, to rise again in vivid hues and graceful forms. And the birds are here. They came up early from the summer-land, — bluebirds and robins and all manner of winged wonders, familiar and strange, driven northward, so the country folk say, by the long roar and smoke and horror of battle. We have a line of old apple-trees on the south border, marvellously gnarled and unsightly, curiously crooked as one might say, a fat feeding-ground for worms and caterpillars, bearing little fruit, and that untoothsome. A really thrifty and sensible axe would speedily lay itself at their roots; but such is none of ours, and they shall not down. For every spring the faithful old patriarchs go through all the forms of fruitage as dutifully as if they meant to fill our bins with Baldwins. Some secret influence, which our hard humanity cannot discern, but which the vegetable world knows and answers joyfully, floats through the night, a low voice stirs the heart beneath their wrinkled boles, the old sap asserts itself, old ambitions revive, and with the dewy dawn, lo! the apple-trees have thrilled into bloom. What if strength fails them to redeem their promise in some distant, doubtful October? At least the whole air is a sea of perfume now, and the waves come rolling in at all the windows, flooding us with fragrance. You hardly move but some fresh delicate odor smites you softly, waking a new delight. What ravaging axe shall destroy these fountains of incense?

And the old trees, misshapen, uncouth, and well stricken in years, are fireside and forum, temple and theatre, for a community of birds. Little they care for grim bark, or twisted branch, or pre-empted twig. The more bugs the better hunting-ground. Every insect haunt is a well-stocked Faneuil Market ready to hand. In every worm they see a new pinfeather, a sharpening claw, a hardening beak, for some callow darling. I watch them hopping about on the grass in little fits and starts, alighting on the fence and musing there with an air of intense preoccupation, flying up into the trees to some hidden nook among the leafage with a wisp of straw for building, — and I could find it in my heart to pity them. It seems such an endless task to make a nest, straw by by straw, painfully, with only one little bill for all sorts of work. But they seem to like it. Labor is lightened and time shortened perhaps with thinking of the chosen friend who is to share it and the tiny brood that is to be sheltered in it. And they never work hard. It is not dig, dig, dig with the birds. They take life daintily, lords and ladies in their own right. Toil is diversified by game and song and social chit-chat. They will leave their labor for no cause apparently, but just on the spur of the moment, whirl you a wild waltz through the air in a very passion of pastime, then stand a-tilt on a twig and trill out for a second or two a reckless roundelay as if the whole world of the May-time were pouring its joy through their throats, and anon the minstrel is down among the grasses again, no longer a gay Lothario, a Ralph Roister Doister, but a quiet, grave family bird, busily engaged in gathering materials and building himself a local habitation. And what heavenly habitations are theirs! Think of living in a great green overlapping forest, green above, around, beneath you, endless aisles losing themselves in endless arches, the bright sky glimmering far off, the bright sun shining in through a thousand portals and leaving soft wavering shadows everywhere, gentle gales whispering melodies and murmuring sweet lullabys, or sometimes a brave breeze trumpeting some martial air that rouses all the fire in your blood; to be surrounded for days and weeks with great pink and white blossoms bigger than your head, deeps overhead and deeps underfoot, drooping and swinging all through the silent night and the sultry noon and dawn and twilight between; and every crystal cup brimmed and overflowing with pungent delicious odors, — no wonder the birds are drunken with delight and pour forth such mad bacchanal songs as stagger their little frames and set the whole orchard a-tremble!

If they only would be tame, — the shy, nervous sprites! — if they only could discern friend from foe, and let you who love them so draw near to share their pretty secrets! But tame they will not be. Sometimes, in venturesome mood, or thinking perhaps to take a short cut across lots, they dart through an open window and shoot about the room quite bewildered. But if you catch the wanderer, his poor heart throbs so pitifully, and there is such a still, wild terror in his eyes, that you give up trying to make him count you his friend, and bid him back again to tell his open-eared comrades the story of his feather-breadth escape from some savage monster, — *you*. One little swallow slid down somehow between the panes of a window opened from the top and almost beat himself to death in trying to get out. His flattened body, spread wings, and panting struggles were sad to see. We hardly dared move the window lest the sash might give him a fatal injury. We worked over him as carefully as possible full fifteen minutes, and freed him at last, but " Dead, quite dead, poor little thing!" I said, stroking his ruffled feathers as he lay upon my open hand; whereupon he winked his black imp's eye at me, and shot off and out of sight in a second, — the little thankless rogue! Then there is a gray sparrow that has built her nest in the woodbine and a ground sparrow has " squatted " at the edge of the cornfield; but no sooner do you approach than out flutters the one from her quiet bower and up shoots the other from her snug ambush, flying for dear life, as if you could meditate the smallest mischief to their homely, tiny selves, or their tiny speckled eggs. Birds, I was thinking one morning, must be or ought to be thoroughly happy. They have all the conditions of bliss, these orchard birds, enough to eat, stout trees for shelter, everything that the ornithological heart can dream. No bird of prey, no gun nor snare ever comes nigh them. They are a delight to eye and ear. Paradise is here. Every one is their friend. In the wide universe they have no foe. And while the thoughts were yet warm within me, up the porch-steps trotted Rory the cat, with fierce eyes glittering and a dead bird hanging from her jaws. And the very next day another, and not long after a third; and many and many a time since have I seen her crouching and watching, her bones all astir with eagerness, or stealthily creeping on behind an unwary thrush or clawing up into the trees in hot pursuit. Too often a little heap of blood-bedabbled feathers attests her fell success. You can chase her away, but to no moral effect. She takes the chasing for a frolic, and only capers about like a mad creature, scudding atop of the fences, couching on the posts, leaping on the shed-roof and mounting to the ridge-pole of the barn. But Paradise has not yet come, even for the birds. I find they have enemies and are often sore bested. They are like a young author. He flits jauntily into the sunshine and song of the world, pouring forth his own note gayly, never suspecting but he will be as gladly welcomed as he gladly goes. But no sooner is his strain fairly afloat on the air than out springs a surly critic from every corner and rends him in pieces remorselessly.

I said so to my friend Halicarnassus, one morning as we were sitting on the threshold of the back barn-door that opens into the orchard, to which he replied: "Your simile is very touching; but as a sober fact, your young author is not always so innocent and unsophisticated as you represent him. If, instead of pouring his melody on the charmed air he makes his *début* with a sharp stick, poking it into everybody's pet prejudice, stirring up all the settled customs, and thrusting in pell-mell among the creeds, he may reckon on being poked back again. You cannot expect the world, the flesh, and the Devil to sit still and be quietly abolished. If you want smooth sailing, you must not sail in the teeth of the wind."

I. I do not want smooth sailing; and as you and I have never fallen in with literary persons, and must depend entirely upon conjecture in these matters, let me recommend that, in order to avoid the appearance of personality, you substitute "one" for "you." But it is not true, that if you sail with the wind you will always secure smooth sailing. There are many authors who have no sharp stick, who deal only in feathers and honey, and are yet harshly entreated.

H. Stupidity is the unpardonable sin in literature.

I. No: stupidity that is not aggressive might be let alone. There is no harm done when a dull book is published. Why harry the author?

H. It becomes my painful duty to contradict

you, and say that there is often much harm done. A great part of our religious bigotry, for instance, is the direct handiwork of men whose position requires them to think, and the shape and contents of whose skulls incapacitate them for thinking. Their only fault is, that they take the place of leaders when they ought to be followers. Having no capital of their own they borrow, and not being able to grasp large ideas, they possess themselves of narrowness, and prejudice, and tradition, which they deliver over to the masses as gospel. The latter take their religion on trust. Their tastes do not incline them, or their education does not enable them, or their occupations do not permit them, to investigate for themselves. All the more important is it that what is given them should be the truth. But it is not truth, or it is only partial truth, whose effect is falsehood. So mischief is wrought, generation after generation, till the heart of 'he Christian community seems to be so encrusted with intellectual error — let alone its innate weakness or wickedness — as to be wellnigh impregnable. I question sometimes whether it would not be well to have church organizations broken up, church buildings torn down, and the whole religious world fused into one homogeneous mass, to see if it cannot crystallize anew into something better than we have now.

I. I am afraid you would have less fusion than confusion.

H. Chaos was the mother of the world.

I. But God was its Father, and I suspect the Church people generally would think it was quite another being who was to be the father of your new order of things.

H. Well, if you will undertake to undo the wrong that has been done by pious dulness, I will very readily engage to dispose of the evil wrought by brilliant wickedness, and we will let things stand awhile longer.

I. I suppose it is the former that fructifies the seed of the latter. Still I think you are too hard on the stupid ones. As long as the world lasts, there will be bright people who are not good and good people who are not bright; and I for one am not prepared to give the palm to the former.

H. Nor I. It is only when the blind set up to lead the blind that I object, and for the sole reason that they lead us all into the ditch.

I. But I was not thinking so much, after all, of religious or moral as of merely literary writing. There are the daughters of Tupper, for instance, who have printed some verses, — very good, I dare say.

H. Very moral, I dare swear.

I. Yet some of the newspapers have been loading them down with sarcasm as assiduously as if their book was going to be fatal to the British supremacy if it were not speedily suppressed. To what purpose? They have a clear right to publish verses, as well as Milton and Shakespeare.

II. And I have a clear right to publish my opinion that they are spooney.

I. Not necessarily. Why should you not be polite with your pen as well as with your tongue? If Miss Tupper should pay you a morning visit, you would think it very discourteous to ridicule her, though her conversation were ever so foolish. Why shall ninety-nine persons be permitted to talk nonsense all their lives while the hundredth cannot print the nonsense of an hour or two without being publicly executed?

II. The talk dies with the moment, but the printed folly puts in a claim for immortality, which we vociferously deny.

I. But it would soon sink of its own weight, if you would let it alone.

II. Not always. It often happens that some incidental interest of subject, of time, or of puffing gives a book a circulation and reputation which its merits would not secure: it acquires thereby a power to injure the morals, the taste, and the good name of the community; and such books ought to be picked off by the sharpshooters in the interests of virtue.

I. But the Misses Tupper's poetry would do nothing of the sort. It would neither go far enough nor deep enough. I dare say it has no positive faults —

II. Only wants body.

I. If you mean by " body " —

H. Soul.

I. At any rate, it has no mischief-working qualities. It is doubtless good common poetry. But there is a notion that real criticism consists in cutting and slashing. Yet as much stupidity may be shown in censure as in praise, besides all the ill-nature. To find fault is not necessarily to be wise. Criticisms that are meant to be sharp are sometimes only savage. They have what Dr. Newman would call "the provincial note." I think the good-natured, indiscriminate puffs are much better than the ill-natured, indiscriminate growls with which some have attempted to supplant them.

H. Better of the two. But there is something better than either.

I. Of course. Wisdom to discern between the evil and the good, and leisure and patience to point out both. But if you cannot command this, why then give me shallowness that is amiable rather than shallowness that is cross. I would establish it as an indispensable rule, that criticism to be severe needs to be skilful. Let us have the scymitar of Saladin, but no hewing and hacking of a rusty Toledo trusty in the hands of a Hudibras.

H. The author has always this to fall back on, — that the public is a perfectly upright court of appeal. It is a fair fight between him and his critic; and *magna est veritas* and will prevail a bit, generally, as we used to say in college.

I. Not always, for the writer deals only with his subject, while the critic deals with both writer and subject, and therefore occupies a superior position in the eyes of the people; but where the writer does prevail over the critic, it is all the more signal a victory. I remember, for instance, reading some depreciating remarks on "Azarian" in the North American Review. At the time they seemed to have force, to be indeed final. But I read "Azarian" again from mere curiosity, and found its locks entirely unshorn. It had not lost a single charm, — which is a far stronger proof of merit than any first reading could give; but most people will not take the trouble to re-read. They accept the critic's judgment.

II. I recollect that paper. It was unjust not so much in what it said as in what it failed to say. The book has faults in the direction there indicated, only it has merits not there indicated.

I. And merits so great that not to indicate them is to give a false presentation of the book. Nothing can be more unjust than to expend all one's ingenuity and energy on a few surface faults, and entirely pass over the great strength, the solid substance of a book.

II. One cannot include everything, even in a review article.

I. No; but therefore one should not assume to have done everything. If a critic has time or space for only the defects of a book, very well;

but let him state the fact, and make it clear to his reader, that there are merits, and that they stand in such and such relation to the faults. Now "Azarian" has somewhat fine and powerful, something different from and superior to anything else that Miss Prescott has written, which not to see is to be blind. Why, it is as if Undine had found her soul.

H. That is true; and if Miss Prescott goes on working the vein she opened there, and — I have the material for a magnificent metaphor in my head. You might set up in trade for yourself if you could only get at it.

I. And works up the gold she digs out into the beautiful shapes that dazzle and delight us even when the material is soap-suds and the product soap-bubbles, — that is what you mean?

H. Something like that, but far finer.

I. There is this, however, that when you attack a writer of established position like Miss Prescott you take your life in your hands, but you may throw as many sticks and stones at the little Tuppers as you like. Their father makes them a lawful target. But it is very silly and very cowardly to attack Mr. Tupper. In fact he has been so much abused that I begin to suspect he is a far greater man than we have been imagining.

H. Certainly. Contemporary opinion does not go for much. Milton's Paradise Lost, and so forth, Seven Grecian Cities, and so forth.

B

I. Then spare your shafts. Don't force innocent people to suffer the pain of seeing themselves and their verses mocked at in the morning paper.

II. O, if it comes to that, it is not so bad as you think. Everybody has his little clique of admirers, who stand between him and the scorching fire of criticism, just as a drop of water is sheltered by its own steam from the heat of the stove it is dancing round upon. Providence has blessed us all with an inexhaustible fertility of devices to ward off attacks upon our self-love. We can attribute censure to pique or anything but truth, and so take heart again.

I. Yes, and that reminds me of something else. You know Robertson's Life and Letters?

II. I don't know anything else, speaking after the manner of men. Every periodical for the last three months has blossomed and borne Robertson. Doubtless he was a brick, so to say, but one may have too much of a good thing. And the quarterlies have not had their turn at him yet.

I. It only shows that when we have a hero we make the most of him, which is much better than to let him die and (we) give no sign. But I was going to say that I do not understand how with his unquestioned bravery, strength, and grandeur, and all his clearness of perception, he could have suffered so much from opposition and misrepresentation, or even loneliness. All these things were but the natural consequence of his own outspoken words, and to be expected. No misfortune happened unto him but such as is common unto men who battle with popular error, and the more fiercely they give battle, the more clamorous will be the outcry of their foes. But to be moved in one's life by it seems to me unreasonable. One should count the cost before going to war, and if he cannot stand the strain, let him not draw the sword. Robertson's purpose, we must suppose, was to promulgate truth, to promote righteousness. All the malignity he awakened was but the dust of the conflict,— not agreeable, but surely not unprecedented: the smoke and vapor of the valley to him who stands on the mountain-tops. They are to be cleared away because they hide the sun from the lowlands; but they have no power to touch the hidden springs of happiness in his heart who dwells in the eternal sunshine. Truth is so beautiful, so satisfying.

II. Sympathy and approbation and one's fellow-men, and especially women, are very pleasant too.

I. But not indispensable, while there are things which you do from an irresistible impulse. You speak not because you so decide, but a voice utters itself through your lips. If there is a foe in your own heart crying amen to the charges without, you may have misgivings; but when you are sure, hatred and love are one to you. It is not only a better but a happier thing to stand alone clear-eyed, than to consort with the mob blindly groping.

Their outcry is only obstruction to be surmounted. It has nothing to do with your life. To receive the secret of the Lord, to bear the sacred trust, what blessing in all the world can be compared to this? Talk of sympathy! Why, you don't expect sympathy in those whose Dagon you are felling. If they sympathized with you, you would not be talking at all.

H. It strikes me that is just my case.

I. But is n't it so?

H. O yes. I always suspected you would march to the stake and rather like it, if you could but go alone.

I. Never. And I am thankful to live in the days when opposition, at its very worst, takes the shape of paragraphs, and sneers, and coarse personalities, rather than of wheel and thumb-screw and fagot. No; I fear I should recant everything rather than be burnt with green wood. I should confess that the existing order of things is not only the best that has yet existed, but the best that can be dreamed of; that tyranny and sensuality and bigotry and selfishness are pure and sacred, to object to which is immorality and atheism and sour grapes. But I don't know any power at the present day that could make me admit this. As for calling the little *désagrémens* resulting from modern disapprobation trouble, it is for a healthy person simply absurd; while, regarding loneliness, he that is accompanied by the truth seems to me exceeding well companioned. Nay, I would think it better to catch a glimpse of her garments far off, to follow her, and woo and win her to rectify and sweeten the common life that is so bitter and wrong, than sit at ease in the smiles of the wrong-doing multitude.

H.   "In vain the human heart we mock,
      Bring living guests who love the day,
      Nor ghosts who fly at crow of cock.
      The herbs we share with flesh and blood
      Are better than ambrosial food,
      With laurelled shades."

I. I grant it nothing loath; but doubly blessed was Robertson, who could partake of both. Are not husband and wife company?

H. That depends —

I. Depends on what?

H. Times and seasons. Some men's wives are mere housekeepers, and housekeepers are good company when you are cold and hungry; and others are playthings, and playthings are good company when you wish only to be amused: and some women's husbands are watch-dogs, which are the best of company when you are afraid of robbers. The fact is, only a few of us are perfect, and most of our domestic relations savor of the earth if not of sulphur.

I. But our domestic relations are no more sulphurous than our social relations, — though I don't see what the end of your answer has to do with the beginning. A man and his wife are no more imperfect than a man and his friend. But you don't dismiss friendship from the realms of fact with the cavalier remark that we all savor of sulphur. If a man can find sympathy and solace in any human being, he surely ought to find it in the one he has won out of the whole world for the express purpose of being his companion. Now I say no matter how much opposition or obloquy one may encounter outside, if he is married,— married in any such sense as is worthy the name, — it would not be possible for him to be lonely. He might feel the want of support in pushing on his work, but there would be no void in his life. His hard intellectual work would fill his head and his wife would fill his heart. Yet, Robertson writes, "I am alone, and shall be till I die," and I think it was very inconsiderate and wicked in him to say it. A woman might break her heart over a less indignity than that.

H. Hear! hear!

I. O, now you may laugh.

H. I am thankful even for so much.

I. But just ask yourself, how would a man feel if his wife wrote to her female friend, "I am alone, and shall be till I die"; and not once, but repeatedly? It would be just a confession of his failure towards her.

H. Is it not just possible there may have been some failure on her part towards him?

I. No, at least we will not suppose it possible. It would be a monstrosity which may occur in fact, but must not be introduced in fiction. What I suspect and fear and oppose is, that he did not look to her for what he wanted, not imagining the ore that lay there unwrought. If he did, and she withheld her hand, of course there is nothing more to be said; only if men will not explore a mine before they take possession, they have themselves to blame when they find they are bankrupt.

H. But if a woman's gold turns out to be pyrites, she may fill the air with wailing.

I. Well, a man has tracts to "prospect" in so rich and broad, that it would seem to be the most egregious blindness that should blunder, while the gold-field that stretches before a woman is often but a corner lot, where it is pyrites or nothing. And the pyrites glitters, and there is no gold to compare it with; so it is less surprising when she makes a bad investment. No, I am afraid Mr. Robertson did not know what was good for him.

H. What is it that Browning says, —

Tum, tum, "a path of gold for him,
And the need of a world of men for me"?

I. But Robertson had his world of men too. His profession was in the midst of the world. His work was such as one might suppose would bring out everything that was in him of aggressive power. He was in the midst of active, manly vigor. He had just such a life as a wife should round and perfect. I cannot imagine anything in this world better. A good sword to wield, a fierce fight with wrong, and a home for the heart's life, — and yet those dreadful words !

H. On the whole, does it not occur to you that you may be making much ado about nothing? I dare say Mrs. Robertson was more than satisfied, — counted herself a supremely happy woman. Why, then, should you fret?

I. She ought not to have been satisfied.

H. It is a pity that some people will persist in thinking themselves happy in spite of the obstinate endeavors of philanthropy to enlighten them as to the true state of the case.

I. Some people have a way of shutting their eyes to what they do not choose to see.

H. Let us fall back, rather, on the commonplace supposition that the good man's illness and suffering made him morbid and unduly sensitive, or that something was kept back in his life, — some inward jar and shock, — which, if we knew it, would account for his *tremulo*, — which would leave him never again quite trustful. Is not something somewhere said about a "blow, the sudden ruin of a close friendship"? Such a thing might, I conceive, change the whole current of a man's being.

I. Yes, and these causes, too, may excuse the tone of complaint which sometimes rises high in his letters, giving — well, now, it seems almost wrong to say so, but I think there is just a shade of unmanliness.

H. But remember all the complaining we read of was spread over his whole life, though we read it in a few hours. It probably makes an impression greater on us than on his friends, who felt it only at intervals of months, perhaps years.

I. True, and I don't know that one really loves him less for this life of his, but one, perhaps, reverences him less. It makes him a little more common. It shows him only level with the clouds, and not high enough for the eternal sunshine above them. But perfect strength makes no outcry. It is so grand to be calm. It is so heroic to be untouched. It is so godlike to give all things, and crave nothing. Ah well, Robertson was thoroughly noble! — who shall cast a stone at him? — only he was a little unstrung by illness, and so did not take his troubles so cheerily as he otherwise would have done.

H. But if you take your troubles cheerily, how is any one to know you have troubles?

I. What if no one should know?

H. You get no credit for your endurance. What does it profit to be a hero, and nobody know it? Put your annoyances out of sight, and go blithely about your business, and what is the gain? Admiration for your heroism? By no means. People only say you do not mind these things, and keep on inflicting them. Silent en-

2

durance must be blatant, or it will not be counted in.

I. O, I would not have any one bear what can be helped. That is sloth, not fortitude. And if you cannot bear alone what is inevitable, why you must have recourse to others. But it is better to bear it alone. The measure of our weakness is the measure of our strength, — if we conquer it.

H. I admire that sentence, — especially its perspicuity.

I. Why do you sit here idling away your time all the morning? Why do you not go and feed the cows, or pull weeds, or do some such work as is adapted to your capacities?

If you are tired, dear reader, or have something else to do, you can make believe the chapter ends here; but I have nothing else to do, am not at all tired, and shall go on indefinitely.

For the full-blown summer weather is too fine for anything but to sit in the sunshine and shade and enjoy it. When the whole earth is alert, one can afford to be idle, with a most fruitful idleness. Indeed, one can afford nothing else, for the beauty of the month of months is too rare and perfect a thing to miss without grievous loss. It is a pitiable waste to squander May-days and Junes for care and weariness, and gold and dross, that perish with the using. There is plenty of winter for professional uses in a climate like ours. Now let us medicine our pride by laying aside our blundering, blustering busy-ness, and see how rhythmically this old Mother Earth does her work. It is just to loiter and loiter, to listen and linger. It is only to stroll out aimlessly, alone or in such company as deepens and sweetens solitude; to follow the drift of the shadows and the droop of the violets; straying through the orchard, ankle-deep in the dense, purple clover, sweet to sight and smell and taste; — and there stands soft-eyed Mooly, her head well stretched over the orchard wall, smelling the tempting smells, and wishing she were in your shoes. Stroke her long nose, pressing up to meet your hand. Beautiful Mooly, with your lovely longing eyes, do not be impatient. It is all going to be yours by and by, the honey-sweet clover and the buttercups and the juicy rich grass. It is not so bad a thing to be a cow, after all. And this Mooly cow, mild as she looks, loves her fat pastures and has a will of her own. I go after her sometimes at night, and though she has nothing to do but eat and drink all day long, it is almost impossible to get her past the clover-banks in the lane. An affectionate pat on her back and sides moves her but a single step. I take hold of a horn and pull. I might as well pull at the bow of the Great Eastern. I go up the bank and push against her with all my might, as if she were aground on the slope. She turns her head back upon me with a look which says, "Is it a fly you are trying to persuade off me? Thank you!" I try what virtue there is in stones, like the old man in the spelling-book; she walks leisurely to the other side and resumes her craunching. I am tempted to bang her faithful old bones with the knotted head of my pilgrim's staff, but never yield to the temptation, and we gradually work our passage home in very good humor with each other, thinking one time is about as good as another, when it is all summer evening.

And if we stroll far enough down the sloping orchard, where

"Ripe grasses trammel a travelling foot,"

we come out upon the knoll beyond and the cow-path under it; and the pond and the pine-trees and the swamp, odorous with wild-honeysuckle, azalia, which shall be swamp-apples in their season, tender, rich with tropical hints; and here are the blackberry vines smothering the gray wall, and secretly ripening the pulpy fruit whose saucy black beauty shall soon laugh out from every chink and crevice; and on the hillside a grove of oaks dearer than Dodona, — a little wood, but dense and deep enough to lose yourself in as it creeps up and around to the other side of the hill, defying winter and the north-wind there, here welcoming summer and the south, a whole choir of breezes humming through the tree-tops, and a troop of fairies flinging shadows on a little pool at the foot of the grove. And do you know how grasshoppers grow? I do, for I have seen them. Come out here some warm evening and you will see little clots of foam on the grass. Stir one open, and all covered up inside will be a baby grasshopper, green and delicate; and that is all I know about it. Down here in the oak wood there is a sunny spot where we almost always find ourselves sooner or later. It seems somehow as if the Mays and Junes distil a more subtile essence here than elsewhere. The tenderness of the one and the fulness of the other meet and melt into a warmth of wooing, into a gracious fervor and welcome, which there is neither wish nor will to resist. The songs of the old poets sing themselves through these shadowy places. Life is a sunny south sea, that buoys you and rocks you and wraps you about with a delicious rest. All sounds of the world without come robbed of their dissonance, and blend into a low melody, less heard than felt. To Tennyson

"The individual withers, and the world is more and more,"

but here the world is far off. Its sights fade out of view and thought, and you only sit among the shadows, recline along the sward, toying with the wild columbines and the geraniums and the rank grasses, and all the spirit of the woods breathes into the very penetralia of the soul. It seems you would hardly care ever to hear another voice or do a deed again. Passivity is so much better than activity. Let us receive, and be content to give nothing where our all is so little. This multiform life, gentle, continuous, harmonious, so puts to shame our harsh, crude efforts. The grace of the woods mocks the world's awkward gait. There was a man once planted (" *Nam Polydorus ego!* "), and pious Æneas found it no laughing matter to root him up. I wonder if these old fables, — fables of Narcissus and Danae and the wondrous loves of earth and heaven, — are not the graceful Greek way of draping what our harsh Saxon speech lays bare in the skeletons of science, or what our eyes, that love less these earth-forces, have as yet failed to discern.

> " Danae in a golden tower,
> Where no love was, loved a shower."

More precious than golden showers the warm April rains that descend on these swells and dimples of verdure, and precious as any fabled Perseus the fruit they bear. Is it hard to believe that one might dwell in the woods away from men, and live so deep down in the secret of the forest, of rock and tree and water-flow and fall, that their individualities should intermingle, there should be a kind of out-go and in-come, so that one should hardly know where the human ended and the earth-born began?

There is a real and wondrous influence astir in that world which we call nature, whose deathless life endures spite of all our feeble prating about it. But prate we must, for puny love is just as exacting towards a puny soul as a great passion to the great. The bright-hearted Greeks have painted and sculptured and sung, for all succeeding ages, the beauty of their wave-washed home. Every grove and fountain, vine-clad hill, mountain-pass and shady valley has its story of passion, of struggle, or of fate. Here a hero was born, here a virgin slain. Green islands rise from the sea, thick studded with the footprints of the gods. Ears that never heard the surf washing against a foreign shore have heard the thunders of Jove rolling around the brow of Olympus; and sitting on a pleasant slope in this young Western world, I see across three thousand years and twice three thousand miles the smile and sparkle of the blue Ægean Sea.

The Greeks are gone. Gone dryad and hamadryad, nymph and naiad. Gone faun and satyr from the Latin groves. Gone elf and fay from the sombre northern wilds. Druids no longer deepen the gloom of the awful forest; the tricksy fairies have ceased their dance, and there is no glitter of English armor, no dart of daring English outlaw gleaming in the gay greenwood. But the gay greenwood has not lost its spell; for it lay in none of these. Deeper than haunt of nymph or fairy is the secret place where its soul abideth. You cannot linger in its recesses without feeling its mystical charm. Rests upon you a calm content. Your spirit is set to a more peaceful melody. You lose yourself in the twitter and chirp and whirr of the unconscious multitudes around you. Vexations, pleasures, hopes, disappointments, ambitions, anxieties, are all dissolved in the magic alembic which distils the one elixir peace. Yesterday, to-day, and to-morrow are but the present moment, unending. The

"Queen and Huntress chaste and fair"

might chase her flying hart past your hiding-place, Robert of Huntington might glide from behind a tree, bravely bedight, and share his hard-fought gains with faithful Little John, or the white wings of a visitant from some upper world, that goes sailing through the night, might wave athwart your dream, and you would feel no shock and scarcely a surprise. In the wide world none know this spot but the birds and the squirrels, the insects, the wood-cutters, and just ourselves. Yet here the vintage pours its choicest wine. Sweet, wise words spoken long, long ago are woven in with the wild vine's teasing tangle. Minstrel and troubadour over the sea, dead now these many generations, live again in the

"Lisp of leaves and ripple of rain."

Dust is the hand that wrote, dust the lips that sung, but, vivid with the vigor of immortals, the spirit of the past dwells forevermore in these whispering woods, and, loving the greenwood and the May of its own lusty time, scorns not to light up a wild American jungle with the light of other days.

And over all this sunny scene broods the spirit of a deeper past. Far back in the twilight of eternity, what life was it that lounged through the lazy centuries? What rank trees, never blossoming, yawned up to the dun skies and stretched their indolent arms in the hot moist air? What slow-souled lizards, huge and harmless, trailed their giant length through the succulent thickets? Great solemn eyes that smiled upon no flower, heavy ears that heard no voice of bird nor any music softer than the swirl of the restless sea, or the moans of the laboring land, — wild monsters paddling through the warm dark waters, or waddling over the jellied earth, — the treacherous quicksands engulfed them, the pit opened her mouth and swallowed them; but their story is not untold. The molten continent took it and declared it to the listening ages. The listening ages heard it and graved it on the rock forever. A little cloud sailed across the sky, flung its largess to the ground, and went on its way most evanescent of all the children of Nature. And the perpetual hills have no surer record to-day than that scurrying cloud that hurled its drops slantwise on the mud a million years ago.

A PROSE HENRIADE.

NOT only is the time of the singing of birds come, but the time of the cackling of homely, honest barn-yard fowls, that have never had justice done them. Why do we extol foreign growths and neglect the children of the soil? Where is there a more magnificent bird than the Rooster? What a lofty air! What a spirited pose of the head! Note his elaborately scalloped comb, his stately steppings, the lithe, quick, graceful motions of his arching neck. Mark his brilliant plumage, smooth and lustrous as satin, soft as floss silk. What necklace of a duchess ever surpassed in beauty the circles of feathers which he wears, — layer shooting over layer, up and down, hither and thither, an amber waterfall, swift and soundless as the light, but never disturbing the matchless order of his array? What plume from African deserts can rival the rich hues, the graceful curves, and the palm-like erectness of his tail? All his colors are tropical. With every quick motion the tints change as in a prism, and each tint is more splendid than the last: green more beautiful than any green, except that of a duck's neck; brown infiltrated with gold, and ranging through the whole gamut of its possibilities. (I am not sure that this last is correct in point of expression, but it is correct in point of sense, as any one who ever saw a red rooster will bear witness.)

Hens are not intrinsically handsome, but they abundantly prove the truth of the old adage, "Handsome is that handsome does." Lord Kaimes describes one kind of beauty as that founded on the relations of objects. And surely the relation of a hen to a dozen white, fresh eggs, and the relation of those eggs to puddings and custards, and the twenty-five or fifty cents which they can have for the asking, make even an ungainly hen, like many heroines in novels, "not beautiful, but very interesting." "Twenty thousand dollars," said a connoisseur in such matters, "is a handsome feature in any lady's face." And the "cut-cut-cut-ca-D-A-H-cut" of a hen, whose word is as good as her bond for an egg a day, is a handsome feather in any bird's cap. Once, however, this trumpet of victory deceived me, though by no fault of the hen. I heard it sounding lustily, and I ransacked the barn on tiptoe to discover the new-made nest and the exultant *mater-familias*. But instead of a white old hen with yellow legs, who had laid her master many eggs, there, on a barrel, stood brave Chanticleer, cackling away for dear life, — Hercules holding the distaff among his Omphales! Now, — for there are many things to be learned from hens, — mark the injustice of the tyrant man. From time immemorial, girls, — at least country girls, — have been taught that

> "A whistling girl and a crowing hen
> Always come to some bad end":

but not a word is said about a cackling rooster! Worse still, a crowing hen is so rare a thing that its very existence is problematical. I never heard of one out of that couplet. I have made diligent inquiry, but I have not been able to find any person who had heard, or who had ever seen or heard of any one who had heard, a crowing hen. But these very hands have fed, these very eyes seen, and these ears heard a cackling rooster! Where is manly impartiality, not to say chivalry? Why do men overlook the crying sins of their own sex, and expend all their energies in attempting to eradicate sins which never existed in the other?

I have lived among hens lately, and I know all about them. They are just like people. Not a few only, but the whole human race, are chicken-hearted.

Hens are fond of little mysteries. With tons of hay at their disposal, they will steal a nest in a discarded feeding-trough. With nobody to harbor an evil thought against them, they will hide under the corn-stalks as carefully as if a sheriff were on their track. They will not go to their nests while you are about, but tarry midway and meditate profoundly on fixed fate, free-will, foreknowledge absolute, till you are tired of watching and waiting, and withdraw. — No, you did not know it all before. The world is in a state of Cimmerian darkness regarding hens. There were never any chickens hatched till three weeks from a week before Fast Day. How should you, my readers, know anything about them? Be docile, and I will enlighten you.

Hens must have a depression where the bump of locality should be, for they have no manner of tenderness for old haunts. "Where are the birds in last year's nests?" queries the poet; but he might have asked quite as pertinently, "Where are the birds in last month's nests?" Echo, if she were at all familiar with the subject, would reply, "The birds are here, but where are the nests?" Hens very sensibly decide that it is easier to build a new house than to keep the old one in order; and having laid one round of eggs, off they go to erect, or rather to excavate, another dwelling. You have scarcely learned the way to their nook above the great beam when it is abandoned, and they betake themselves to a hole at the very bottom of the haymow. I wish I could tell you a story about a Hebrew prophet crawling under a barn after hens' eggs, and crawling out again from the musty darkness into sweet light with his clothes full of cobwebs, his eyes full of dust, his hands full of eggs, to find himself winking and blinking in the midst of a party of ladies and gentlemen who had come lion-hunting from a farre countrie. I cannot tell you, because it would be a breach of confidence; but I am going to edit my Sheikh's Life and Letters, if I live long enough, and he does not live too long, and then you shall have the whole story.

Another very singular habit hens have, — that of dusting themselves. They do not seem to care for bathing, like canary-birds; but in warm afternoons, when they have eaten their fill, they like to stroll into the highway, where the dust lies ankle-deep in heaps and ridges, and settle down and stir and burrow in it till it has penetrated through all their inmost feathers, and so filled them, that, when they arise and shake themselves, they stand in a cloud of dust. I do not like this habit in the hens; yet I observe how a correspondence exists in all the Vertebrata; for do not fine ladies similarly dust themselves? They do not, indeed, sit in the road *à la Turque*. They box up the dust, and take it to their dressing-rooms, and, because Nature has not provided them with feathers, ingenuity more than supplies the deficiency with the softest of white down brushes, that harbor and convey the coveted dust. O I doubt not through the races one resembling purpose runs; and many a stately matron and many a lovely maiden might truly say unto the hen, "Thou art my sister."

Did I say I knew all about hens? The half was not told you; for I am wise in chickens too. I know the tribe from "egg to bird," as the country people say, when they wish to express the most radical, sweeping acquaintance with any subject, — a phrase, by the way, whose felicity is hardly to be comprehended till experience has unfolded its meaning.

When hens have laid a certain number of eggs, — twelve or twenty, — they evince a strong disposition, I might almost say a determination, to sit.* In every such case, it is plain that they ought to be allowed to sit. It is a violation of nature to souse them in cold water in order to make them change their minds; and Marcus Antoninus tell us that nothing is evil which is according to nature. But people want eggs, and they do not care for nature; and the consequence is, that hens are obliged to undergo "heroic treatment" of various kinds. Sometimes it is the cold bath; sometimes it is the hospital. One I tied to the bottom of one of the standards; but, eager to escape, and ignorant of the qualities of cord,

---

* I say *sit*, out of regard to the proprieties of the occasion; but I do not expose myself to ridicule by going about among the neighbors and talking of a *sitting* hen! Everywhere but in print hens *set*.

she flew up over the top rail, and, the next time I entered the barn, presented the unpleasing spectacle of a dignified and deliberate fowl hanging in mid-air by one leg. Greatly alarmed, I hurried her down. Life was not extinct, except in that leg. I rubbed it tenderly till warmth was restored, and then it grew so hot that I feared inflammation would set in, and made local applications to check the tendency, wondering in my own mind whether, in case worse should come to worst, she could get on at all with a Palmer leg. The next morning the question became unnecessary, as she walked quite well with her own. The remaining hens were put in hospital till they signified a willingness to resume their former profitable habits, — except one who was arbitrarily chosen to be foster-mother of the future brood. Fifteen eggs, fair and fresh, reserved for the purpose, I counted out and put into her nest; and there she sat day after day and all day long, with a quietness, a silent, patient persistence, which I admired, but could not in the least imitate; for I kept continually prying her up to see how matters fared. Many hens would have resented so much interference, but she knew it was sympathy, and not malice; besides, she was very good-natured, and so was I, and we stood on the best possible footing towards each other. As we say in the country, "A hen's time is not much to her"; and in this case the opinion was certainly correct.

One morning I thought I heard a faint noise. Turning out the good old creature, that I might take an observation, eggs still, and no chickens, were discernible; but the tiniest little, silvery, sunny-hearted chirp that you ever heard, inside the eggs, and a little, tender pecking from every imprisoned chick, standing at his crystal door, and with his faint, fairy tap, tap, tap, craving admission into the great world. Never can I forget or describe the sensations of that moment; and, as promise rapidly culminated in performance, — as the eggs ceased to be eggs, and analyzed themselves into shattered shells and chirping chickens, — it seemed as if I had been transported back to the beginning of creation. Right before my eyes I saw, in my hands I held, the mystery of life. These eggs, that had been laid under my very eyes as it were, that I had at least hunted and found and confiscated and restored, — these eggs that I had broken and eaten a thousand times, and learned of a surety to be nothing but eggs, — were before me now; and, lo, they were eyes and feathers and bill and claws! Yes, little puffball, I saw you when you were hard and cold and had no more life than a Lima bean. I might have scrambled you, or boiled you, or made a pasch-egg of you, and you would not have known that anything was happening. If you had been cooked then, you would have been only an omelet; now you may be a fricassee. As I looked at the nest, so lately full only of white quiet, now swarming with downy life, and vocal with low, soft music,

"I felt a newer life in every gale."

O, no one can tell, till he has chickens of his own, what delicious emotions are stirred in the heart by their downy, appealing tenderness!

Swarming, however, as the nest seemed, it soon transpired that only seven chickens had transpired. Eight eggs still maintained their integrity. I remarked to the hen, that she would better keep on awhile longer, and I would take the seven into the house, and provide for them. She assented, having, justly enough, all confidence in my sagacity; and I put them into a warm old worsted hood, and brought them into the house. But the hood was not a hen, though it was tucked around them almost to the point of suffocation; and they filled the house with dolorous cries, — " yopping " it is called in the rural districts. Nothing would soothe them but to be cuddled together in somebody's lap, and brooded with somebody's hand. Then their shrill, piercing shrieks would die away into a contented chirp of heartfelt satisfaction. I took a world of comfort in those chickens, — it is so pleasant to feel that you are really making sentient beings happy. The tiny things grew so familiar and fond in a few hours that they could hardly tell which was which, — I or the hen. I could do everything for them but cluck. I tried that, but the experiment was not satisfactory to myself, and as regards deceiving the chicks it was a dead failure; otherwise they accepted the situation gracefully. They would all fall asleep in a soft, stirring lump for five seconds, and then rouse up, with no apparent cause, but as suddenly and simultaneously as if the drum had beat a reveille, and go foraging about in the most enterprising manner. One would snap at a ring, under the impression that it was petrified dough, I suppose; and all the rest would rush up determinedly to secure a share in the prize. Next they would pounce upon a button, evidently thinking it curd; and though they must have concluded, after a while, that it was the hardest kind of coagulated milk on record, they were not restrained from renewing the attack in squads at irregular intervals. When they first broke camp, we put soaked and sweetened cracker into their bills; but they developed such an appetite, that, in view of the high price of sugar, we cut off their allowance, and economized on Indian meal and bread-water. Every night they went to the hen, and every morning they came in to me; and still Dame Partlet sat with stolid patience, and still eight eggs remained. I concluded, at length, to let the eggs take their chance with another hen, and restore the first to freedom and her chickens. But just as I was about to commence operations, some one announced, that, if eggs are inverted during the process of incubation, the chickens from them will be crazy. Appalled at the thought of a brood of chickens laboring under an aberration of mind, yet fired with the love of scientific investigation, I inverted one by way of experiment, and placed it in another nest. The next morning, when I entered the barn, Biddy stretched out her neck, and declared that there was no use in waiting any longer, and she was determined to leave the place, which she accordingly did, discovering, to my surprise, two little ·dead, crushed, flattened chickens. Poor things! I coaxed them on a shingle, and took them into the house to show to a person whose name I have often had occasion to mention, and who, in all experimental matters, considers my testimony good for nothing without the strongest corroborative evidence. Notice now the unreasoning obstinacy with which people will cling to their prejudices in the face of the most palpable opposing facts.

"Where did these come from?" I asked.

"Probably the hen trod on them and killed them," he said.

"But there were seven whole eggs remaining, and the insane one was in another nest."

"Well, he supposed some other hen might have laid in the nest after the first had begun to sit. Hens often did so."

"No, for I had counted the eggs every day."

Here, then, was an equation to be produced between fifteen original eggs on one side, and seven whole eggs, seven live chickens, two dead chickens, and another egg on the other. My theory was, that two of the eggs contained twins.

"But no," says Halicarnassus, — "such a thing was never known as two live chickens from one egg."

"But these were dead chickens," I affirmed.

"But they were alive when they pecked out. They could not break the shell when they were dead."

"But the two dead chickens may have been in the same shell with two live ones, and, when the live ones broke the shell, the dead ones dropped out."

"Nonsense!"

"But here are the facts, Mr. Gradgrind, — seven live chickens, two dead chickens, seven whole eggs, and another egg to be accounted for, and only fifteen eggs to account for them."

Yet, as if a thing that never happened on our farm is a thing that never can happen, oblivious of the fact that "a pair of chickens" is a common phrase enough, — simply because a man never saw twin chickens, he maintains that there cannot be any such thing as twin chickens. This, too, in spite of one egg I brought in large enough to hold a brood of chickens. In fact, it does not look like an egg; it looks like the keel of a man-of-war.

The problem remains unsolved. But never, while I remember my addition table, can you make me believe that seven whole — But the individual mentioned above is so sore on this point, that the moment I get thus far he leaves the room, and my equation remains unstated.

There is a great deal of human nature in hens. They have the same qualities that people have, but unmodified. A human mother loves her children, but she is restrained by a sense of propriety from tearing other mothers' children in pieces. A hen has no such checks; her motherhood exists without any qualification. Her intense love for her own brood is softened by no social requirements. If a poor lost waif from another coop strays into her realm, no pity, no sympathy springing from the thought of her own offspring, moves her to kindness; but she goes at it with a demoniac fury, and would peck its little life out, if fear did not lend it wings. She has a self-abnegation as great as that of human mothers. Her voracity and timidity disappear. She goes almost without food herself, that her chicks may eat. She scatters the dough about with her own bill, that it may be accessible to the little bills, or, perhaps, to teach them how to work. The wire-worms, the bugs, the flies, all the choice little tidbits that her soul loves, she divides for her chicks, reserving not a morsel for herself. All their gambols and pranks and wild ways she bears with untiring patience. They hop up by twos and threes on her back. They peck at her bill. One saucy little imp actually jumped up and caught hold of the little red lappet above her beak, and, hanging to it, swung to and fro half a dozen times; and she was evidently only amused, and reckoned it a mark of precocity.

Yet, with all her intense, absorbing parental love, the hen has very serious deficiencies, — deficiencies occasioned by the same lack of modification which I have before mentioned. Devoted to her little ones, she will scratch vigorously and untiringly to provide them food, yet fails to remember that they do not stand before her in a straight line out of harm's way, but are hovering around her on all sides in a dangerous proximity. Like the poet, she looks not forward nor behind. If they are beyond reach, very well; if they are not, all the same; scratch, scratch, scratch in the soil goes her great, strong, horny claw, and up flies a cloud of dust, and away goes a poor unfortunate, whirling involuntary somersets through the air without the least warning. She is a living monument of the mischief that may be done by giving undue prominence to one idea. I only wonder that so few broken heads and dislocated joints bear witness to the falseness of such philosophy. I am quite sure that if *I* should give the chickens such merciless impulses, they would not recover from the effects so speedily. Unlike human mothers, too, she has no especial tenderness for invalids. She makes arrangements only for a healthy family. If a pair of tiny wings droop, and a pair of tiny legs falter, so much the worse for the unlucky owner; but not one journey the less does Mother Hen take. She is the very soul of impartiality; but there is no cosseting. Sick or well, chick must run with the others, or be left behind. Run they do, with a remarkable uniformity. I marvel to see the perfect understanding among them all. Obedience is absolute on the one side, and control on the other, and without a single harsh measure. It is pure Quaker discipline, simple moral suasion. The specks understand her every word, and so do I — almost. When she is stepping about in a general way, — and hens always step, — she has simply a motherly sort of cluck, that is but a general expression of affection and oversight. But the moment she finds a worm or a crumb or a splash of dough, the note changes into a quick, eager " Here! here! here! " and away rushes the brood pell-mell and topsy-turvy. If a stray cat approaches, or danger in any form, her defiant, menacing " C-r-r-r-r ! " shows her anger and alarm.

See how, in Bedford jail, John Bunyan turned to good account the lessons learned in barn-yards. " 'Yet again,' said he, 'observe and look.' So they gave heed and perceived that the hen did walk in a fourfold method towards her chickens.

1. She had a *common call*, and that she hath all day long; 2. She had a *special call*, and that she had but sometimes; 3. She had a *brooding note;* and, 4. She had an *outcry*. 'Now,' said he, 'compare this hen to your king, and these chickens to his obedient ones. For, answerable to her, himself has his methods which he walketh in towards his people: by his *common call* he gives nothing; by his *special call* he always has something to give; he has also a *brooding voice* for them that are under his wing; and he has an *outcry* to give the alarm when he seeth the enemy come. I chose, my darlings, to lead you into the room where such things are, because you are women, and they are easy for you.'" Kind Mr. Interpreter!

To personal fear, as I have intimated, the hen-mother is a stranger; but her power is not always equal to her pluck. One week ago this very day, —ah me! this very hour,— the cat ran by the window with a chicken in her mouth. Cats are a separate feature in country establishments. In the city I have understood them to lead a nomadic, disturbed, and somewhat shabby life. In the country they attach themselves to special localities and prey upon the human race. We have three steady and several occasional cats quartered upon us. One was retained for the name of the thing,—called derivatively Maltesa, and Molly "for short." One was adopted for charity,—a hideous, saffron-hued, forlorn little wretch, left behind by a Celtic family, called, from its color, Aurora, contracted into Rory O'More. She had a narrow escape one day last winter. I happened to pass through the kitchen in the afternoon and detected her taking an after-dinner nap in the stove-oven, lured evidently by the genial warmth of the fading fire. I know it was not exactly a proper place for a cat, but she looked so cunning and comfortable, I had not the heart to disturb her, and, not disturbing her, there was no harm in increasing her comfort, so I shut the oven door to retain the heat as long as possible. At dusk, I went to give her her supper and send her to bed in the barn as usual, but she did not make her appearance. Forgetting the episode of the oven I called at all the doors, but no kitty responded, and as she was a cat of an eminently social turn of mind, I concluded she was visiting the neighbors and gave her no further thought. Next morning a fine fire was built and breakfast preparations were going on merrily when a stifled "mew" began to be heard. There was another search in closet and cupboard to no purpose, when of a sudden my wits came back to me. I flung open the oven door and out leaped kitty, out and out and never stopped till she had buried herself in a snow-bank. I was very sorry, and consoled her with brimming bowls that day; but apart from the slight discomfort of the process, I never could see that her baking did her the least harm. The third was a fierce black-and-white unnamed wild creature, of whom one never got more than a glimpse in her savage flight. Cats are tolerated here from a tradition that they catch rats and mice, but they do not. We catch the mice ourselves and put them in a barrel, and put the cat in after them; and then she is frightened out of her wits. As for rats, they will gather wherever corn and potatoes congregate, cats or no cats. It is said in the country, that, if you write a polite letter to rats, asking them to go away, they will go. I received my information from one who had tried the experiment, or known it to be tried, with great success. Standing ready always to write a letter on the slightest provocation, you may be sure I did not neglect so good an opportunity. The letter acknowledged their skill and sagacity, applauded their valor and their perseverance, but stated, that, in the present scarcity of labor, the resident family were not able to provide more supplies than were necessary for their own immediate use and for that of our brave soldiers, and they must therefore beg the Messrs. Rats to leave their country for their country's good. It was laid on the potato-chest, and I have never seen a rat since!

Short colloquy between the principal actors in this drama: —

H. Had you ever seen one before?

I. Well, — perhaps, — no!

While I have been penning this quadrupedic episode, you may imagine Molly, formerly Maltesa, as Kinglake would say, bearing off the chicken in triumph to her domicile. But the alarm is given, and the whole plantation turns out to rescue the victim or perish in the attempt. Molly takes refuge in a sleigh, but is ignominiously ejected. She rushes with great leaps under the corn-barn, and defies us all to follow her. But she does not know that in a contest strategy may be an overmatch for swiftness. She is familiar with the sheltering power of the elevated cornbarn, but she never conjectures to what base uses a clothes-pole may come, until one plunges into her sides. As she is not a St. Médard Convulsionist, she does not like it, but strikes a bee-line for the piazza, and rushes through the lattice-work into the darkness underneath. We stoop to conquer, and she hurls Greek fire at us from her wrathful eyes, but cannot stand against a reinforcement of poles which vex her soul. With teeth still fastened upon her now unconscious victim, she leaves her place of refuge, which indeed is no refuge for her, and gallops through the yard and across the field; but an unseen column has flanked her, and she turns back only to fall into the hands of the main army, — too late, alas! for the tender chick, who has picked his last worm, and will never chirp again. But his death is speedily avenged. Within the space of three days, Molly, formerly Maltesa, is taken into custody, tried, convicted, sentenced, committed to prison in an old wagon-box, and transported to Botany Bay; greatly to the delight of Rory O'More, formerly Aurora, who, in the presence of her overgrown contemporary, was never suffered to call her soul her own, much less a bone or a crust. Indeed, Molly never seemed half so anxious to eat, herself, as she was to bind Rory to total abstinence. When a plate was set for them, the preliminary ceremony was invariably a box on the ear for poor Rory, or a grab on the neck, from Molly's spasmodic paw, which would not release its hold till armed intervention enforced a growling neutrality. In short, like the hens, these cats held up a mirror to human nature. They showed what men and women would be, if they were — cats; which they would be, if a few modifying qualities were left out. They exhibit selfishness and greed in their pure forms, and we see and ought to shun the unlovely shapes. Evil propensities may be hidden by a silver veil, but they are none the less evil and bring forth evil fruit. Let cats delight to snarl and bite, but let men and women be generous and beneficent.

Little chickens, tender and winsome as they are, early discover the same disposition. When one of them comes into possession of the forequarter of a fly, he does not share it with his brother. He does not even quietly swallow it himself. He clutches it in his bill and flies around in circles and irregular polygons, like one distracted, trying to find a corner where he can gormandize alone. It is no matter that not a single chicken is in pursuit, nor that there is enough and to spare for all. He hears a voice we cannot hear, telling him that the Philistines be upon him. And every chicken snatches his morsel and radiates from every other as fast as his little legs can carry him. His selfishness overpowers his sense, — which is, indeed, not a very signal victory, for his selfishness is very strong and his sense is very weak. It is no wonder that Hopeful was wellnigh moved to anger, and queried, " Why art thou so tart, my brother ?" when Christian said to him, " Thou talkest like one upon whose head is the shell to this very day." To be compared to a chicken is disparaging enough ; but to be compared to a chicken so very young that he has not yet quite divested himself of his shell must be, as Pet Marjorie would say, " what Nature itself can't endure." A little chicken's greedy crop blinds his eyes to every consideration except that of the insect squirming in his bill. I watched once a bill-to-bill conflict for the possession of an overgrown earth-worm. One held it by the head, one by the tail, and then they just braced themselves back and pulled ! It was a laughable affair for the observer, but very awkward for the worm. When one, exhausted, let go his hold, the other ran; but the worm dangled under his feet and impeded him, and then a fresh little bill would seize it and scud in the opposite direction. The unhappy worm changed bills repeatedly and dragged at each remove a *shortening* chain, till it was at length gobbled up piecemeal, and on the whole very fairly distributed. But they fought just as furiously and ran just as frantically for its last inch as they did for his whole length. They snatched it from each other so quickly that the pursued would fly quite a distance after it had been plucked away before he discovered his loss, when, with a half-second's bewilderment, he would turn about and become pursuer. Apparently they never detected the deterioration in their prize, nor do I think it was ever quite clear to them what finally became of the worm. One might pity their victim, but I believe that kind of beast is somewhat indifferent to dissection, — on the whole rather likes it.

A chicken is beautiful and round and full of cunning ways, but he has no resources for an emergency. He will lose his reckoning and be quite out at sea, though only ten steps from home. He never knows enough to turn a corner. All his intelligence is like light, moving only in straight lines. He is impetuous and timid, and has not the smallest presence of mind or sagacity to discern between friend and foe. He has no confidence in any earthly power that does not reside in an old hen. Her cluck will he follow to the last ditch, and to nothing else will he give heed. I am afraid that the Interpreter was putting almost too fine a point upon it, when he had Christiana and her children " into another room, where was a hen and chickens, and bid them observe awhile. So one of the chickens went to the trough to drink, and every time she drank she lift up her head and her eyes towards heaven. 'See,' said he, 'what this little chick doth, and learn of her to acknowledge whence your mercies come, by receiving them with looking up.'" Doubtless the chick lift her eyes towards heaven, but a close acquaintance with the race would put anything but acknowledgment in the act. A gratitude that thanks Heaven for favors received, and then runs into a hole to prevent any other person from sharing the benefit of those favors, is a very questionable kind of gratitude, and certainly should be confined to the bipeds that wear feathers.

Yet, if you take away selfishness from a chicken's moral make-up, and fatuity from his intellectual, you have a very charming little creature left. For, apart from their excessive greed, chickens seem to be affectionate. They have sweet social ways. They huddle together with fond caressing chatter, and chirp soft lullabies. Their toilet performances are full of interest. They trim each other's bills with great thoroughness and dexterity, much better indeed than they dress their own heads, — for their bungling, awkward little claws make sad work of it. It is as much as they can do to stand on two feet, and they naturally make several revolutions when they attempt to stand on one. Nothing can be more ludicrous than their early efforts to walk. They do not really walk. They sight their object, waver, balance, decide, and then tumble forward, stopping all in a heap as soon as the original impetus is lost, — generally some way ahead of the place to which they wished to go. It is delightful to watch them as drowsiness films their round, bright, black eyes, and the dear old mother croons them under her ample wings, and they nestle in perfect harmony. How they manage to bestow themselves with such limited accommodations, or how they manage to breathe in a room so close, it is difficult to imagine. They certainly deal a staggering blow to our preconceived notions of the necessity of oxygen and ventilation, but they make it easy to see whence the Germans derived their fashion of sleeping under feather-beds. But breathe and bestow themselves they do. The deep mother-heart and the broad mother-wings take them all in. They penetrate her feathers, and open for themselves unseen little doors into the mysterious, brooding, beckoning darkness. But it is long before they can arrange themselves satisfactorily. They chirp, and stir, and snuggle, trying to find the warmest and softest nook. Now an uneasy head is thrust out, and now a whole tiny body, but it soon re-enters in another quarter, and at length the stir and chirr grow still. You see only a collection of little legs, as if the hen were a banyan-tree, and presently even they disappear, she settles down comfortably, and all are wrapped in a slumberous silence. And as I sit by the hour, watching their winning ways, and see all the steps of this sleepy subsidence, I can but remember that outburst of love and sorrow from the lips of Him who, though He came to earth from a dwelling-place of ineffable glory, called nothing unclean because it was common, found no homely detail too homely or too trivial to illustrate the Father's love, but from the birds of the air, the fish of the sea, the lilies of the field, the stones in the street, the foxes in their holes, the patch on a coat, the oxen in the furrow, the sheep in the pit, the camel under his burden, drew lessons of divine pity and patience, of heavenly duty and delight. Standing in the presence of the great congregation, seeing, as never man saw, the hypocrisy and the iniquity gathered before Him, — seeing too, alas! the calamities and the woe that awaited this doomed people, a god-like pity overbears His righteous indignation, and cries out in passionate appeal, "O Jerusalem, Jerusalem, thou that killest the prophets, and stonest them which are sent unto thee, how often would I have gathered thy children together, even as a hen gathereth her chickens under her wings, and ye would not!"

The agriculturist says that women take care of young chickens much better than men. I can easily believe it. One of our chickens seemed to be drooping awhile ago, and I reported the fact to a man who lives on the farm. "Sick, eh? Better give him some Richardson's Bitters." That is all a man knows! I suppose my face said something of the sort, for he added, "Or perhaps take him out to drive with you for a change of air." I did neither, only let him diet a little, and he was well in a day. In fact, my experiments with chickens have been attended with a success so brilliant that unfortunate poultry-fanciers have appealed to me for assistance. I have even taken ailing chickens from the city to board. A brood of nineteen had rapidly dwindled down to eleven when it was brought to me, one even then dying. His little life ebbed away in a few hours; but of the remaining ten, nine, now in the third week of their abode under my roof, have recovered health, strength, and spirits, and bid fair to live to a good old age, if not prematurely cut off. One of them, more feeble than the others, needed and received especial attention. Him I tended through dreary days of east-wind and rain in a box on the mantelpiece, nursing him through a severe attack of asthma, feeding and amusing him through his protracted convalescence, holding him in my hand one whole Sunday afternoon to relieve him of home-sickness and hen-sickness, and being rewarded at last by seeing animation and activity come back to his poor sickly little body. He will never be a robust chicken. He seems to have a permanent distortion of the spine, and his crop is one-sided; and if there is any such thing as blind staggers, he has them. Besides, he has a strong and increasing tendency not to grow. This, however, I reckon a beauty rather than a blemish. It is the one fatal defect in chickens that they grow. With them, youth and beauty are truly inseparable terms. The better they are, the worse they look. After they are three weeks old, every day detracts from their comeliness. They lose their plump roundness, their fascinating soft down, and put out the most ridiculous little wings and tails and hard-looking feathers, and are no longer dear, tender chicks, but small hens, — a very uninteresting Young America. It is said, that, if you give chickens rum, they will not grow, but retain always their juvenile size and appearance. Under our present laws it is somewhat difficult, I suppose, to obtain rum, and I fear it would be still more difficult to administer it. I have concluded instead to keep some hen sitting through the summer, and so have a regular succession of young chickens. The growth of my little patient was not arrested at a sufficiently early stage to secure his perpetual good looks, and, as I intimated, he will never, probably, be the Windship of his race; but he has found his appetite, he is free from acute disease, he runs about with the rest, under-sized, but bright, happy, and enterprising, and is therefore a wellspring of pleasure. Indeed, in view of the fact that I have unquestionably saved his life, we talk seriously of opening a *Hôtel des Invalides*, a kind of Chickens' Home, that the benefits which he has received may be extended to all his unfortunate brethren who stand in need.

LARVA LESSONS.

ABOUT this matter of June there is a great deal to be said on both sides. June has a great reputation, — June, beloved of youth and maidens, — June, dear to poets.

 "What is so rare as a day in June!
 Then if ever come perfect days,"

or something like that, sighs the knight of Launfals, and all June-lovers swell the chorus; but June has another side to her shield that shines with a different and a less lustrous light. June roses have woven wreathes for many a lay, but I went out to my rose-bushes this morning, after a few days' absence, and behold! havoc and ravage; for delicate green leaves, only wiry skeletons, from which life and loveliness had departed. Near the ground, to the brown, mottled stalk clung the cause, — a great gluttonous caterpillar, full to the brim of pulpy parenchyma, and dreaming his dull larvic dreams in stupid satisfaction. A whisking stick soon snapped him off into space; but will my rose-buds be able to grow into full-blown beauty with lungs so frightfully diseased? Over against the rose-bush stands a young apple-tree, faint and feeble with the repeated charges of a battalion of canker-worms. The other night a high wind blew, and the old elm-tree was depopulated; at least, if one might judge from the population that suddenly appeared around it and beneath it. The canker-worms, flung off by the wind, spun down from the window-frames, looped up the door-posts, spanned along the fences, tormenting us before the time. They knew it, too. They felt in their gelatinous frames that their hour was not yet come; so, instead of scooping out their little graves, they began a toilsome "homeward bound!" up, up, up into the old elm-tree, if possible, but, at all events, up, by such slow, painful, intermittent lunges and loops, that one could but pity while he loathed. Rudely disturbed in their cradles, rudely ousted from their homes, they hang around, bewildered and disgusting, heart-sick and home-sick. Their meek brown ugliness looks up from every surface. We have lived on carbon and nitrogen for several days; for no sooner was a window opened than a stray little fellow would look in, bow, throw forward his head, bring up his tail, and there he was! They fringe the closed blinds, and speckle the gray door-stone. There is no comfort in church, because there is always a canker-worm on the woman in front of you, just at the edge of her collar, balancing himself on his hind legs and gazing around wildly in doubt whether to set his fore and four hundred horrid feet down on her bare neck or somewhere else, and while you are dreading what to do you feel one looping over your own wrist. Poor things! it is to be hoped they do not know how disagreeable they are, but go on rearing their helpless little ones with serene self-complacence, unsuspecting that they are not the very pink of the universe.

Their existence is a living monument of circular justice, an ever-recurring proof of the inevitableness of the laws of compensation. I walk past an orchard, shrivelled, red, dry, dead, and mourn over the ruin, — juice and flavor and tang of luscious apples, sweetness of marmalade and jellies, homely hospitality of pan-dowdies and dumplings, all withered away, leaving only an arid waste. " Whence and wherefore comes this destroying army?" I sigh; and from the savans comes answer, Because ye have hewed down the forests which were their natural homes, the forests whose broad expanse gave them ample room and verge enough to increase and multiply; the forests wherein they could feed without devouring, and flourish without destroying; because, madder yet, ye have lifted up your hands against the birds; for grudge of the few cherries which they took, taxes rather than booty, nay, even out of wanton and wicked lust of blood and fierce greed of taking life, ye have shot and snared the birds, your foresters, which kept the balance true, and insured the preservation of God's own game-laws, restraining increase and multiplication within natural and harmless limits." " Live and let live," I begin to think is the watchword of creation. Nature evolves her myriads, but with such nice adjustments that interference mars her proportions, and creates fatal disturbance. We have all read how a new centre-table introduced discord and discontent into an old and formerly peaceful and harmonious room, so that time-honored furniture withdrew to attics, and finer reigned in its stead; walls retreated, ceilings soared, and the unhappy owner found no rest till an entirely new house squared itself around the new table, unconscious cause of all his woe. With just such exact dovetailing has Nature grouped her arrangements, and one disjointure makes the whole system rickety. We have felled the forests that should have fed the canker-worms, we have shot the birds that should have eaten them, and now they swarm in our gardens, and spin down before our faces, and we vex our souls in vain to mend our losses. Yonder goes a man in blue blouse and overalls, with a long hooked pole in his hand. Responsive to his soft, sonorous call, a troop of motherly "biddies," proud young pullets, and even a few inexperienced chickens, cluck and scamper at his heels. What is the man going to do with the hooked pole, and why do the chickens run? (if I may adopt the style which seems to be in vogue among the later novelists.) The man is going to hook his hook into the tree, and shake the limbs, and the poultry sees with prophetic eye a fat repast; with the first jar, and with each succeeding jar, the startled denizens of the apple-tree will come tumbling down into the very jaws of death. Seed-time of canker-worms is harvest-time of hens. Corn and moist meal and the loved potato-parings have lost their charms for the brood that loiters coop-ward with distended crops. Many will be the desolated homes on the green leaves to-night, and sweet the dreams of Dame Partlet on her peaceful perch, — not knowing that, like the suppression of the Rebellion, " it is but a question of time," and the same solace that has been administered to her by her articulated sisters she shall one day administer to her vertebral kinsmen.

But hens are not the only foes that lie in wait. Unclean beasts, — that noisome race into which the devils entered eighteen hundred years ago, and of which they have held possession ever since, — prey on these defenceless creatures. Horrid snouts root into the warm little caves, wherein the tender chrysalids lie, and bring inexorable fate. Or in their long spring journeys up the difficult bark, the virgins are submerged unawares in a boundless sea of oil, or mired in vast bogs of tar. Nay, human hate does not confine itself to human ingenuity, but shamelessly has recourse to the very nature which it has outraged.

"Call for the robin redbreast and the wren,"

despairing nurseryman. Hither lure the angry wasp that stores her cellars with vermes-steak, well salted down. Hither let the beetle wheel his droning flight, and hither come the winged epicures that regale themselves on omelets of canker-worm eggs. With all our appliances, surely there shall be none left to tell the tale. That which the unclean beasts have left the tar hath swallowed, and that which the tar hath left Jenny Wren hath eaten, and that which Jenny hath left Chanticleer hath devoured. But boast not thyself, O man. Though canker-worms be little upon the earth, they are exceeding wise. For all your tar and your poles, it shall go hard but in your teil-tree shall be left a tenth, — two or three in the top of the uppermost bough, four or five in the outmost fruitful branches thereof; and when you reflect that a single moth will lay a hundred eggs, you need not be surprised next year to feel a dozen or two swinging into your face as you walk to and fro in your orchard.

There is a comforting tradition that canker-worms have a seven years' lease of life, and then die out. But do not set your heart and stake your property upon it. The damsel who remembers all along

> "From when she gambolled on the green,
> A baby-germ, till when
> The maiden blossoms of her teens
> Had numbered five from ten,"

and five more, has not outlived the dynasty of the canker-worms. They come and go when and where they list. Your trees are leafless and barren, your neighbors' are green and fruitful; and though in the multitude of words that are used to account for this there wanteth not wisdom, he that refraineth his lips is the wisest; for the burden of the knowledge of the nineteenth century may be found in the book of the vision of Nahum the Elkoshite, written now these five and twenty centuries: "The canker-worm spoileth, and flieth away."

There is also a tradition that caterpillars eat canker-worms, and so make themselves partially useful; but they do not. They eat everything else. It is as Joel says, "That which the canker-worm hath left hath the caterpillar eaten." Some one looking over my shoulder says the tradition is, not that they eat canker-worms, but *eat them out*, — so destroy the herbage that there is nothing left for their smaller brethren. I question whether there is much truth in either report, except what lies in the radical fact, that they eat. They leave their nests among the birds in the morning, and crawl up and down seeking what they may devour. At noon they withdraw to their homes for a nap. Towards evening again they take their walks abroad, evidently, but very inconveniently, sharing mortal delight in the cool of the day. But they pay the penalty for presuming to mimic their betters. If they kept themselves dispersed like canker-worms, they might as easily elude capture; but by spontaneous concentration they prepare the way for that difficult military operation known as "bagging." Lovely Lulu looks longingly from her lattice towards the green quiet of the country, and fancies June to be all roses and nightingales. But this noon a beautiful orchard, responsive to gentle solicitations, yielded up a bucketful of caterpillars. Yes, Mr. Robert Browning, that is

"What's in the blossom
June wears in her bosom,"

I regret to be obliged to admit, — a bucketful of caterpillars! And then Halicarnassus comes in gleefully, and says they have made a clean breast of it. There is n't a caterpillar left on the farm! By way of comment, I point to one just rolling up the door-step. "Yes," he says, winking very hard, "that is one of the neighbors' caterpillars running over to make a call on ours."

But there is small good in cleaning out your own borders unless the community make common cause with you. Why does not America, like France, pass a law constituting it a penal offence to harbor caterpillars?

One can hardly walk through the street without bringing home on his clothes enough to found a flourishing colony. You climb up a stone-wall, and barely save yourself from descending into half a dozen nests on the other side. They gather in squirming squads under the heads of the gate-posts, and creep, creep, creep, with slow persistence up the sides of the house. Last evening I found in the lane a shattered nest. The occupants had evidently been rudely torn from their home and greatly disturbed,—quite put out, in fact; but they had rallied, organized their forces, drawn up in line, sent out scouts, stationed pickets, and were *en route* for the place where their Troy was. From the wheel-rut in the road to the grassy sidewalk — more than a yard — they formed a solid column; marching in a straight line at an acute angle with the road in a tolerably regular rank and file, from two to four abreast, with two active, energetic leaders, who were continually striking out right and left and returning to report. I passed that way again in about half an hour, to find them still moving. A wagon had gone by meanwhile, but there were no traces of disaster. Their bodies were scarcely half-grown, but the emergency seemed to have ripened their souls prematurely.

The other day there might have been seen a caterpillar coming down the gravel-walk in a ludicrously eager hurry. He was a singular looking creature,—much more elaborately finished off than the rest of his kind, for his tail tapered and terminated in a curious black bead. He made such an impression on me, that after I had reached the house I turned back again to examine him. Minute investigation resolved the black bead into a terrible little vixen of a huge black ant that had fastened upon him and was putting him to the torture. The caterpillar would plunge ahead a few wriggles, — which I take to be Caterpillaree for paces, — dragging the ant with him. Then losing patience, he would halt, double himself back into an O, and butt off the ant. The latter would make a side-leap and keep away till the caterpillar started, then fasten upon his side, perhaps, and away they would go again. Then would come another halt, another hit, another leap, grapple, race. The energy of that ant cannot be described or surpassed. He evidently knew no such word as fail. Thrust aside, he would take breath, push up his wristbands, — in a figure, — and begin afresh. He had all the persistency that belongs to a fight and all the agility that belongs to a frolic. The caterpillar labored under the same disadvantages that attended our commerce in its conflict with the late Rebel navy: he presented a broad frontier for attack, and had but small opportunity for reprisals. I followed in their wake till they disappeared beneath a rose-bush. Do you think I ought to have separated them? How do I know which was to blame? Perhaps the caterpillar had mobbed the ant's house or murdered all his brood at one fell swoop, and was only reaping his meet reward. A little power does not generally attack a large power without extreme provocation; and Nature must adjudicate in her own courts. Besides, I have heard that there is a natural hostility between black ants and caterpillars, and that you can at any time have all the excitement and pleasure of a bull-fight by offering them to each other.

Caterpillars are a melancholy race. They have no vivacity, no song, no sport, no seeming interest in anything but some mysterious, far-off errand. They lie about hopeless and heavy; nor, indeed, can it well be otherwise, if they eat, as is asserted, and as the poor rose-bushes and apple-trees seem to indicate, seven hundred times their own weight in a day. Spiders, loathsome though they be, are ever on the alert; but caterpillars hang to the posts or squirm aimlessly about each other till they have arrived at maturity, and then, with constant restlessness, they creep, creep, creep slowly to their graves. Nobody sees what becomes of them; only you notice a belated and bewildered wayfarer wandering about like one who treads alone some banquet-hall deserted, or a brilliant black and red creature, large enough for a child's muff, hurrying in great waves across the road; then you wake suddenly to the fact that the caterpillars are gone.

We have speculated much this summer, and

about caterpillars as well as other things. Halicarnassus is disposed to take a desponding view of the matter. "What right or reason have we," he asks, "to endow ourselves with an immortality which we deny to them? They are to us a disagreeable incident, which we quietly put out of the way as fast as possible; regarding only our own convenience, and often only our own feelings, and not at all their pleasure or profit. Why may it not be that we hold to a higher race of beings the same relation which this holds to us? Why may it not be that our lives are relatively as transient and unimportant, and that we perish as entirely and as unregarded?"

"Well," I answer, "I don't know why, only we don't."

"But are you so sure of that? As far as we see, man goeth to the grave, and where is he?"

I. But he goes to his grave by the law of his own nature. He dies or is killed by his kind. He is not brought into contact with any higher race, and the caterpillar is. His higher race is close about him. He sees it and feels it. Our higher race, if we have any, is invisible and impalpable. It never gives any sign, and I don't believe in you (defiantly, in case any of them should happen to be within hearing).

H. Very just reasoning; yet if that group of caterpillars yonder should happen to be a debating-society, in which two philosophers like us are discussing the question of a higher race, they use, unquestionably, the same arguments which you have advanced, and will arrive at just as decided a negative.

I. You mean that they do not see us nor hear us?

H. They do not see us as *us.* To them we are only obstacle, danger, accident, not beings.

I. Very true. When I crush an insect under my foot, I suppose he does not suspect it is the foot of his superior that crushed him.

H. Certainly not. He will always think he died in a fit.

I. When we kill them by the bucketful, they do not know it is " we " or a " bucket."

H. No, they probably call it an earthquake, an avalanche, the operation of natural laws. And when the French soldiers were writhing in Victor Hugo's pit at Waterloo, they called it a pit, and not a higher power.

I. But they knew they rushed in, and the caterpillars must have known, if they knew anything, that they did not walk into that bucket by any will of their own, even if they did not perceive the existence of any higher will.

H. Some higher power may have acted on our circumstances just as directly, if not just as perceptibly, as we act on a caterpillar's. Perhaps, when we grope out among the stars, or feel down into the earth after the fossils and the fire and all the old time's secrets, we crawl into their domain just as obnoxiously as the caterpillars do into ours, and so they contrive ways to rid themselves of us.

I. But we have faculties, feelings, thoughts, entirely above and beyond them. They have not even the germ of what we have in full flower, and there is no analogy between us. We are an entirely distinct race, and you cannot reason from them to us.

H. So is the dog and so is the cat an entirely distinct race from the caterpillar; they have thoughts and feelings which the most cultivated and highly developed caterpillar never attained to. Yet their great sagacity does not immortalize them.

I. But they have no intellect, no conscience.

H. Pardon me, I think we have evidence of both. They reason, and they distinguish right from wrong. When Rory is sleeping on the kitchen mat before the fire, she does not stir for your approach; she only raises her head sleepily, or perhaps puts up her nose for a caress. But when she has surreptitiously crept up stairs and bestowed herself on the best bed to take her after-dinner nap, no sooner does she hear an approaching footstep than she leaps off and scuds down the back stairs. There, it seems to me, you have memory, conscience, reasoning, and prudent action; and often dogs and cats show these and other high human qualities in far more intricate forms.

I. Yes, but their reasoning never goes beyond a certain limit. It is confined to concrete personal matters. They never reason on abstractions, and even their conscience is, I apprehend, a purely physical one. They have no notion of right as right. They know that such a thing is followed by punishment and such a thing by caresses. That is all.

H. And that is all a small child knows. He distinguishes right from wrong, but has no conception of right or of God, while in point of intellect he is far beneath the dog.

I. But he is susceptible of unlimited cultivation, while no dog was ever educated into a knowledge of holiness or of mathematics.

H. Certainly there is a difference in degree, but it still remains that you have in the dog the germs of his master's qualities. Now the point is, why do we affirm that those beings in whom the germ exists must die, while those in whom it is a little more developed shall live? What element of life exists in a quart of intellect that does not inhere in a thimbleful? If the cultivation of faculties is the crucial test, many a man will be in evil case as compared with his dog. With a capacity of becoming godlike, he does meaner things than even his dog can do. His dog is faithful to his bad master; his master is faithless to his good wife and his innocent children. The dog lives an honest and enlightened dog life. The man perverts his powers to brutal and worse than brutal uses. Why is he to be permitted to live forever, — a blot upon creation, — while the high-hearted dog must go back to darkness and dust?

I. Yet Dr. Kane, who must certainly have seen very low if not the lowest types of human kind and some of the highest types of animal, said he considered the lowest man higher than the highest brute.

H. We should need to inquire what precisely he meant by "low" and "high."

I. My dear, this is all nonsense. You know perfectly well that there is an essential difference between brute and man; and that this — whatever you call it, — soul, spirit, heart, — this in which the essential difference consists, — is indestructible.

H. How do I know it?

I. You know it from the Bible.

H. Where does the Bible say so?

I. I do not know that there is any one verse where it is said in so many words; but the whole Bible goes upon the assumption that the soul is immortal. The incarnation of Christ is presumptive evidence of it. The means would be disproportionate to the end, if the Son of God had died to redeem creatures whose lives were to stretch over but a few years, — a mere point of time compared with the boundless eternity.

H. Pardon me again, but you are speaking from the midst of confusion. You are mixing up theories which are entirely separate. You say, first, that man and beast are essentially different, and therefore man is immortal. I dispute your major premise. Man may have an element of character or of nature, if you will, entirely distinct from, and indisputably higher than, the animal; but it need not, for that reason, be immortal. What the essence of immortality is, what that quality is whose very existence is its guaranty of eternity, I do not know. I certainly do not see any reason for supposing that humanity, which in its naked infancy is visibly but *earthiness*, is that quality. If the Bible should, as you think, give us God's word for it, that would be enough. But, so far from assuming any such thing, it seems to me to assume quite the contrary. The Bible continually represents the soul, not as inherently, but only as contingently immortal. Eternal life is not spoken of as an inheritance, but as a boon. "By grace are ye saved through faith, and that not of yourselves: it is the gift of God." Immortality is something to be sought after, and that which is to be sought is not a thing which we should have in any case. "To them who by patient continuance in well-doing seek for glory and honor and immortality, eternal life."

I. But in the converse, it does not promise to the bad eternal death, but "indignation and wrath," tribulation and anguish.

II. It does not, however, deny eternal death;

and you must distinguish between a non-assertion and a denial. God's indignation and wrath, man's tribulation and anguish, are not incompatible with final death. Rather, we might suppose death must result from them. At any rate, the Bible predicates immortality of God alone. "Who only hath immortality." Now, supposing man to have been originally made capable of living forever, but by some sin to have forfeited this ability, would it not be a most divine work, one worthy of the

"Strong Son of God, immortal Love,"

to devise a scheme by which this forfeited life might be restored? Does it seem a little thing for millions of beings, with so great capacities, to be rescued from nothingness and redeemed to bright and ever-brightening life, becoming more and more like Him, and enjoying Him and themselves forever? I rather think, if it was a glorious thing for God to make the world, it was a far more glorious, as it was a far more difficult, thing for Him thus to make it over.

I. Yet the belief in immortality is universal. Not only the educated and the religious, but the low and vile, savages and barbarians, to whom the Gospel has never been offered, who, certainly, according to your theory, must have forfeited their immortality for their own selves, even if Adam had never done it for them, and who have never so much as heard that there is a chance for its recovery, and who therefore ought to know nothing about it, — even they have their theory of a future life. No nation or tribe has ever been found, I have read, so degraded as not to have some notion, however gross, of a God and of immortality; and this instinct of immortality is, I should surely think, a premonition of immortality. And besides this inborn instinct you have the creeds of all Pagandom and all Christendom. It is impossible that a belief so wide-spread should be utterly baseless.

H. I do not know which will be the strongest answer, — to deny your facts or to account for them. You may have your choice.

I. I will have both, first one and then the other.

II. First, then, I will deny them, and declare that the belief in immortality, so far from being universal, is rare. Even at the present time our own people hardly believe in it, let alone the old Pagans. Religious persons think it is wicked to talk of a future state out of meeting. Speak of heaven as a place where there is real life, actual talking and walking and working and playing and planning and laughing and loving, and they are shocked, and think you irreverent. In a future solemn, pale, passionless dream they believe, perhaps, but not in a future life. For a life without functions is no life. If you have not the same capacities in another world that you have in this, you are not the same being, and if you are not the same being, it is not a resurrection that has occurred, but a new creation. Most of the persons whom you and I know do not entertain a belief in heaven or hell sufficiently vivid to influence materially or apparently their dealings with their fellow-men.

I. There I think you cannot judge. You only see how people live. You do not know how they would live if they had no such belief. You might say people do not believe in law, because there is so much thieving; but if they believed there were no law, there would be nothing but thieving.

H. Your case is not quite parallel, but it can easily be made so, and it will at once turn against you. The point on which a thief is doubtful is, not the existence of law, but the possibility of eluding the law. The point on which the world is doubtful is, not the possibility of eluding unending wretchedness, but its existence. All agree that if it is, there is no escape for him who is doomed to it. If a thief should avow that he believed there was no escaping the law, and yet after a theft he should seek to escape it, we should at once infer that he believed it might be escaped. So when men say they believe there is a future life, yet act as if there were none, shall we not believe their acts rather than their words? The price of gold is a much better national barometer than fine theorizing about prosperity. And if we who have lived under centuries of the Church doctrine of inevitable immortality have so faint a belief in it, I question whether it is so deep-seated or so wide-spread in Pagandom as is generally supposed. The old poets, indeed, describe a posthumous life with great minuteness; but undoubtedly they intended it should be received as a work of imagination, not a narrative of fact. Milton would not wish his account of Pandemonium or the battles in Heaven to be taken as parts of his creed, nor did Virgil intend Octavia to receive the account of Marcellus as a truthful narrative. When the Greek and Latin poets express their own actual, every-day belief, it is chilling and uncomfortable to the last degree. And even their poetical conceptions were scarcely attractive. Their future life was but the ghost of life, — viewless shades, realms of night, unsubstantial all. It was

"Death, and great darkness after death."

All that Patroclus's sad shade could ask of Achilles was proper burial, that he might pass through the gloomy gates of Hades. Nothing is more touching than the calm, hopeless bravery of the ancient men, looking upon death as the end of all, yet cheering each other on to meet it as brave men should. It was according to nature; it was inevitable. To fear it was unmanly; and so they gathered their mantles around them, and slept the iron sleep. But there was no joy, no hope, no anticipation.

"Ἄπαξ θανόντος οὔτις ἔστ' ἀνάστασις."

The sole consolation that Horace could bring to Mæcenas was, not a prospect of future reunion, but that the same day should bring death to both, — *ruinam*, how meaning a term! and all beyond the tomb were but *fabulæ manes*. Cicero was to find comfort for Tullia's death in remembering that there were no youths in Rome worthy of being her husband. Christ seems never so bright and blessed as when he brings life and immortality to light through his Gospel, — brings the warm sun of heaven for the ghostly, ghastly twilight of these old sepulchral worlds. The best and wisest among the ancients seem never to have got beyond a *perhaps*.

I. Plato had arrived at the doctrine of immortality.

H. Plato reasoned out a doctrine —

I. We have good authority for saying that he reasoned well.

H. Poetical, not logical authority. Because the soul does not depend upon the body, he inferred that it could exist without the body, — which it may do abundantly, and yet not be immortal. But he assumed that it held within itself the principle of life, — a groundless assumption, though a wise man made it. For no man knows what the principle of life is.

I. Still, death is the greatest shock that we know of; and if death does not destroy the soul, if, as you admit, the soul is independent of the body, how do you know that Plato was not right in predicating of it immortality? If it survive death, why may it not survive anything? If it live after that, why may it not live forever?

H. Plato *was* right in reasoning thus from what he knew. I should be wrong, because I have light that Plato never had. Plato saw only by his inward light. I have the word of God, saying the soul that sinneth, it shall die. There is another hero of the old world, Marcus Aurelius, the noblest Roman of them all; yet he can only say " about death: whether it is a dispersion, or a resolution into atoms, or annihilation, it is either extinction or change," and, at best, his change is only every part of him being reduced into some part of the universe, and that again changing into another part of the universe, and so on forever. And when his great heart stoops to take in some "vulgar comfort" for the dread doom, it is not in considering the goodness of those he is going to meet, but the badness of those he is to leave. Do you find here any such belief in immortality as you can well build a system on? And these, you must recollect, are the high-water marks. These are the opinions of the foremost men of all their time. Where, then, will you be likely to find the rank and file?

I. In Valhall and Vingolfa I should be sure to find them.

H. Sipping mead, not to say blood, from the skulls of the foes they had slain in battle.

I. Still, inadequate, gross, grotesque, and horrible as these conceptions are, you have under them all the one idea of future unending life.

H. But so distorted as to be a mockery, a humiliation, a sorrow, — apart from the fact that we do not know how firm or broad a hold it had upon the common people. But see now, we all admit that man is capable of being made immortal, and that without any organic change. Christ only redeems from sin; he does not make an angel. Man, then, must have been originally adapted to immortality. He sinned, and thereby forfeited it. But is it strange that the tradition of his lost estate still clings to him, the ghost of his forfeited immortality haunts him, — no longer an angel to comfort, but a demon to vex? Is not this phantom of immortality which has always flitted around the grave, — at best a cold, shadowy, eluding shape, a horror, and never a hope, — is it not just such a phantom as we might suppose man's disordered brain would evoke? It was the Devil who first taught man the doctrine of his immortality, and that in God's despite. "Ye shall not surely die." Satan tempting and man tempted put their heads together, and Hades and Valhall, the transmigration of souls, haunted houses and churchyard wraiths, are the pleasant fruits of their copartnership.

I. But does it not seem something like a waste to have so many souls made and so few come to anything?

H. Apparently that is the Divine way. A thousand seeds are formed for one that fructifies. Destruction walks hand in hand with production. Besides, is it any more a waste for souls to die out than it is for them to live in ever-increasing and hopeless wretchedness? Here I think the old Pagans had the advantage of us. Their belief was more cheerful than ours. Their future existence was indeed only a *perhaps;* but future misery was involved in the uncertainty of this *perhaps,* for which we Orthodox have substituted — for the greater part of the world — a fearful certainty.

I. But we do not impose it upon the world; we open wide to all the gates of Heaven.

H. Knowing that the greater part will never enter. What inroads does the Church make upon the World? How much larger a part of the population of the earth is Christianized now than was Christianized ten, twenty, thirty years ago? And how much more is the Christianized part spiritualized? Remember, the point is not now by whose fault men are reduced to eternal misery, but the fact of their being so reduced. And I maintain that the pagan no-faith here left life more comfortable than our faith. The pagans, moreover, fell back on nature. They reasoned that death was natural, and therefore ought not to be dreaded; and that whatever should come after it would be natural, and need give them no concern. They trusted the unknown God. There is something touching, sometimes almost sublime, in this sturdy if rather blind reliance, — this tenacious clinging to the best they knew or could devise.

I. Yet Orthodox society is very cheerful and often merry, and in its religious life and aspiration not seldom exultant, while nothing can be more sad than "heathenesse," if we may judge from certain signs, — "Atalanta in Calydon," for instance: —

> " Thy limbs to the leaf,
> Thy face to the flower,
> Thy blood to the water, thy soul to the gods who divide and devour."

And Marcus Aurelius you confess yourself has an " o'ermastering sadness."

H. Atalanta is neither here nor there, — being but a modern's imagination of the ancient, — if it were not far too tragic to be a representation of the ordinary mood of the Greeks. Nor am I saying that the ancient was less cheerful than the modern, but that ancient orthodoxy as a faith was less terrible than modern orthodoxy. Believers in the latter are happy, just as far as we do not believe or do not comprehend our creed, — which gives a large enough margin for the exigencies of ordinary society.

I. Do you mean to say that we are hypocrites?

H. Not at all. Undoubtedly we think we believe. Undoubtedly some do believe it, and the joy of life has died out of them. But the great majority believe only on the outmost thin surface of their minds, with the merest hem of their soul's garments, — believe so slightly that it scarcely colors their thoughts, not to say influences their life.

I. Your positions seem to have some force, but probably it is only phenomenal. It is but an inglorious victory you can get over me; say these things to a minister, or some one who knows a great deal, and I dare say your argument would be torn into shreds.

H. I dare say.

I. Tell me, now, honestly as a man, and not cautiously as a controversialist, do you believe this doctrine yourself? When you began, I thought you were only arguing as a gymnast, — just to show how much might be said on the side of an absurdity, but you seem to be quite serious.

H. I am quite serious, though I do not say that I believe the doctrine for which I have been arguing. But, on the other hand, neither do I disbelieve it. I will say this for it, that it offers the most satisfactory solution of the great problem that I have ever yet seen. It is the easiest way out of the difficulty. It shows how God may be just to the souls he has made, and yet it does not attempt to wash away the sins of the world with rose-water. It seems to me a doctrine perfectly natural and reasonable. It is at one with God's judgments as we see them executed. It only carries on into another world the same laws which we see operating in this. The tendency of sin is to destroy the sinner. Vice is suicidal. Evil is fate. Crime pulls down the whole man. It is not the intellect, nor the physical strength, but the character, which is the man. It is the spiritual nature which is to stand before the judgment-seat of Christ, and it is this spiritual nature which sin wars against and plots against, and perpetually and insidiously destroys. Immortality! Why, how many people one constantly sees, concerning whom the wonder is, not that they should finally perish, but that they should have been suffered to live at all. Have you not met persons who seemed to be mere chemical compounds? There is no individuality in them, no strong flavor of a soul. When their chemistry fails, they disappear. Take away the salts and gases, and there is nothing left. Their souls are but nebulæ, — a fine spiritual film, which at death one imagines must simply exhale. There are others, more pronounced, but with so pungent an earth-smell that we must conclude they are not yet developed out of the gnome-state into full manhood. What use they subserve, what glory they bring to their Maker beyond the beasts of the field, it is difficult to see. They are mere earth-worms. All their thoughts, hopes, plans, are confined to the earth, — very often to one little corner in the earth. Shrewdness they may have, and industry and all the earthly virtues. Perhaps they grow rich; perhaps they become known; but of the qualities that do not pertain to earth, of those which raise the soul into a similitude of its Maker, they have no more, to all appearance, at life's end than at its beginning. Now, if a man lives seventy years without having made a start in godliness, what reason is there to suppose he will make a start in seventy-thousand years? And if a man is good for nothing in this world but to convert grain into tissue, what is there for him to do in a world in which is neither grain nor tissue? Why *should* they live again? It would seem to be more economical to make new beings than to make these over. I see much more reason for the resurrection of a sagacious and faithful dog than for that of his foolish and faithless master.

I. If he could rise no longer foolish and faithless, but wise and loyal to God and man, that would be a justification.

II. But I see no ground for hoping that, either in reason or revelation. When a man has resisted all the promptings to good which this world offers him, I do not know that there is a prospect of his yielding to any promptings to good. If Christ's sacrifice does not move him, nothing will, to my thinking.

I. But the poor people who know nothing about Christ's sacrifice?

H. We can very safely leave them in the hands of their Maker.

I. It seems to me we are getting into deep waters.

H. That supposition is creditable to your penetration, for we are, and should speedily be — if we are not already — beyond our depth. So we may as well make for dry land again; but you cannot fail to see that this doctrine of eternal death marshals on its side arguments enough, both from nature and the Bible, to give it an honorable claim on every man's respect. One may not feel called upon to investigate it, but only ignorance or bigotry can revile it.

I. Now how strange it is! The caterpillars led us into all this talk of death, and yet the butterfly, Psyche, has been the symbol of immortality for thousands of years.

H. My dear, are you tired?

I. Tired of what?

H. O, walking, for instance.

I. Not that I know of. Why should I be?

H. Perhaps you would not mind running into the house and bringing me Whately's Bacon. I had it yesterday, and you will find it lying about somewhere.

As I was curious to know what he had in mind, I brought the book, and he read the following extract from Whately's annotations to the essay "On Death."

"Most persons know that every *butterfly* (the Greek name for which, it is remarkable, is the same that signifies also the *Soul*, — *Psyche*) comes from a grub or caterpillar; in the language of naturalists, called a *larva*. The last name (which signifies literally a *mask*) was introduced by Linnæus, because the caterpillar is a kind of outward covering, or disguise, of the future butterfly within. For it has been ascertained by curious microscopic examination, that a distinct butterfly, only undeveloped and not full grown, is contained within the body of the caterpillar; that this latter has its own organs of digestion, respiration, &c., suitable to its larva-life, quite distinct from, and independent of, the future butterfly which it encloses. When the proper period arrives, and the life of the insect, in this its first stage, is to close, it becomes what is called a *pupa*, enclosed in a chrysalis or cocoon (often composed of silk; as is that of the silkworm which supplies us that important article), and lies torpid for a time within this natural coffin, from which it issues, at the proper period, as a perfect butterfly.

"But sometimes this process is marred. There is a numerous tribe of insects, well known to naturalists, called ichneumon flies, which in their larva state are *parasitical;* that is, inhabit and feed on other larvæ. The ichneumon fly, being provided with a long, sharp sting, which is, in fact, an *ovipositor* (egg-layer), pierces with this the body of a caterpillar in several places, and deposits her eggs, which are there hatched, and feed, as grubs (larvæ), on the inward parts of their victim. A most wonderful circumstance connected with this process is, that a caterpillar which has been thus attacked goes on feeding, and apparently thriving quite as well, during the whole of its larva-life, as those that have escaped. For, by a wonderful provision of instinct, the ichneumon grubs within do not injure any of the organs of the larva, but feed only on the future butterfly enclosed within it. And consequently it is hardly possible to distinguish a caterpillar which has these enemies within it from those that are untouched. But when the period arrives for the close of the larva life the difference appears. You may often observe the common cabbage-caterpillars retiring, to undergo their change, into some sheltered spot, — such as the walls of a summer-house; and some of them — those that have escaped the parasites — assuming the pupa state, from which they emerge butterflies. Of the unfortunate caterpillar that has been preyed upon nothing remains but an empty skin. The hidden butterfly has been secretly consumed.

"Now is there not something analogous to this wonderful phenomenon in the condition of some of our race? May not a man have a kind of secret enemy within his own bosom, destroying his soul, *Psyche*, though without interfering with his well-being *during the present stage* of his existence; and whose presence may never be detected till the time arrives when the *last great change* should take place?"

I. That is very significant, but I have seen it quoted to enforce the doctrine of eternal woe.

II. It might be quoted to enforce direct taxation, or universal suffrage, or the high prices of butter, or anything else with which it has nothing to do.

I. I wonder what the consequences would be, if a belief in annihilation were substituted for that of unending misery?

II. I suppose you know that question is not relevant.

I. I know that it does not concern the truth of the doctrine, but I have a right to ask it as an independent question. I fancy the first impression would be, that a restraint had been removed and that sin would revel unchecked.

II. Probably the impression would be a wrong one. It depends, of course, ultimately, upon the facts. If eternal life in suffering is the fate of the unrepentant, then we must suppose the preaching of that doctrine to be the most effectual. But as that is the very question at issue, we must judge from other considerations. There is this first to be taken into account, — that the human mind is unable to contain the doctrine of eternal woe. You may see a community where it has been preached from time immemorial, where the contrary has never been preached, where everybody believes it; and that community has no more received it as a part of its real faith than an infant of days. It lives in a state of soggy indifference to it. As the ancient drew calmness from nature, so the modern draws calmness from a certain dogged trust that he shall do as well as his neighbors. His belief in eternal torments produces no appreciable change in his life. He does not think himself a Christian, but believes he shall somehow get to heaven when the time comes. A congregation will listen to a sermon of the most solemn warning, one that points out with tenderness, with real power, and perhaps in a truly Christian spirit, the sure doom that awaits the sinner. There will not be a word of cavil, nor a thought of opposition. The congregation will be attentive and hushed, — and will go home in an hour's time as "chirp" as crickets, and look after their farms and merchandise, next day, as eagerly as if hell was not supposed to yawn before them.

I. Yes, I remember such sermons when I was little, and they generally ended with the terrible assurance that some one of us might die that very day. Nobody could tell who, but I always thought it might mean me, and was sadly scared. I remember how I used to watch the clock, and think every time it struck, "Well, I'm not dead yet." Every hour I lasted over was so much clear gain, and I was always so glad to wake Monday morning and find I was alive after all As I found I never did die on these occasions, I rather got used to it after a while, and took it as a matter of course.

H. I suspect that is the general result of preaching righteousness through fear of death. But suppose any member of this congregation knew that his wife or his neighbor was, in the next house, burning in a fierce fire, yet never to be consumed, would he be able to eat his dinner and drive his team and be interested in prices? Yet we profess to believe, and fancy we do believe, that a very large number of our kinsmen, neighbors or acquaintance are in this condition. Rev. Justin Doolittle, who ought to know, says that a few hundred individuals, actuated by the love of money, are annually doing very much more to demoralize and destroy the Chinese, than all the millions of Christian believers in Christendom, constrained by the love of Jesus, are doing to benefit and save them. A few gentlemen in New York make up a purse of a hundred thousand dollars for General Grant, and we hardly hear of it; but all the Congregational Christians of the North, after beating the drum and blowing the trumpet for months, after appealing to all the power that lies in simultaneous action and in the associations of a great historic day, can barely raise a hundred thousand dollars to build up the waste places of Zion in our own country.

I. We do more than any other denomination, though.

H. That is not to the purpose. Notice what we do in connection with what we declare ourselves to believe, — how much of faith in eternal torment we show by the efforts we make to snatch the world from it.

I. O, we are so constituted that we cannot realize the idea. There would be no living if we could.

H. That is just what I say. And the question is, then, Is that doctrine likely to be true, which is so dreadful as to be intolerable? Is not the fact that the human mind instinctively, though unconsciously, rejects it, dulls its edge, gets over it or round it in some way, an indication, at least, that it is not the true doctrine? How can that have a practical bearing on life which must be dismissed before life can be endured? In human society it is well known that undue severity defeats itself. If a too heavy penalty is affixed to a law, the jury fails to convict, and guilt and innocence go alike free. A moderate punishment, sure to be inflicted, is far more efficacious in repressing crime than an immoderate one from which there is a probability of escape. So here the punishment is so overpowering that the mind is forced to reject it, and rejects along with it all punishment whatever. Add to this a something arbitrary and extrajudicial in the popular notion of future punishment and you have at once an explanation of its futility. But let men be taught, with a stern simplicity, that the laws which they see working around them and in them are eternal laws; that if they live like beasts they shall die like beasts; that where their treasure is their hearts are; and if they set their hearts on things of time and sense only, time, sense, and heart will perish together, — and I think they would begin to reflect; for love of life is strong, and loss of life a most bitter loss.

I. Yet if all this is true, how comes the popular doctrine to have been the popular doctrine so long? Would God let the truth lie lost and error so prevail?

H. He let the good and gentle Queen Isabella, a lover of truth and of her country, crush the one and curse the other for centuries, with the yoke of the Inquisition. Why was the good and great Marcus Aurelius suffered to approach only to repress that Christianity whose spirit was so in unison with his own, and of which he was so eminently fitted to be the apostle before the world?

I. Matthew Arnold asks the same question.

H. But does not answer it, I venture to say, for it cannot be answered. It concerns some principle of the Divine economy which we have not yet discovered. All our attempts to explain it reveal the limits of our own powers, but cast no light on the unknown footsteps of God. In His name must be our final trust, — God the Good.

I. Caterpillar, how little you know what a commentary you furnish on a great man's words. If you could but understand Latin now, what comfort you might take, as you roll along, in repeating Cicero's dictum, — "*Etenim omnes artes,*" — what is the rest of it, "have as it were a common chain"? I recollect the sentiment, but forget the words.

H. *Quæ ad humanitatem pertinent* — a little far-fetched, still — *habent quoddam commune vinculum; et, quasi cognatione quâdam, inter se continentur;* but you might have said it yourself, without calling up Cicero.

I. It would not have sounded half so learned. Never say anything in English when you can say it in Latin.

H. Or get anybody else to say it for you.

I. I wonder where the caterpillars get their name?

H. *Cat* for their fur, *pillar* for their shape, and *er* for euphony.

I. Halicarnassus, one cannot easily decide whether your turn for exegesis or etymology is the more remarkable. If you are weighty in the one, you are brilliant in the other.

FANCY FARMING.

 WENT out one morning to build a barn. Not that I knew exactly how to build a barn, but I knew very well how to keep up a clatter till some one should come that did know, which amounts to the same thing. There was, indeed, already a barn on our plantation. It was there many years before we were. I ought to say, a part of it; for the barn is a conglomerate, — the farther end stretching far back into antiquity, and the hither end coming down to a period which is within the memory of men still living. Of course its ancient history is involved in obscurity; but as we read in the rocks somewhat of the earth's otherwise unwritten story, so in our barn are many marks which point out to the curious student the different eras of its creation. The main line of demarcation comes in the centre, and consists chiefly of a kind of bulge. That part of the front which dates back to the Lower Silurian epoch ran south-southwest, but at some time during the Drift

period it turned to the right about and drifted to the north-northeast. The result is a bold front, subtending an obtuse angle. People who have nothing else in the world to annoy them might afford to be annoyed by this departure from a right line; but, unless one is reduced to such straits, he will do well to call it a bow-window, and be at rest, — which, indeed, it is, only the window is a little to the windward of the bow.

Viewed in certain aspects, an old barn is far superior to a new one. If you build a new barn, you have no resources. It is all finished, and you know where you are. There is a place for everything, and everything in its place. There is no use in looking for anything. If it is not where it belongs, it will not be anywhere. An old barn, on the contrary, is a mine of wealth. It has nooks and corners full of rubbish waiting to be turned to all manner of beautiful use. Do you want a shingle, a board, a door, a window, a log, a screw, a wedge? There are heaps and piles of them somewhere, if you do not mind cobwebs. The old barn has a sort of sympathy with you, welcomes you to secret recesses, and never snubs you with primness when you are at a pinch: not to mention the dove-cotes, and the martins' nests, and the mouse-holes, and the lurking-places loved of laying hens.

I will tell you a very romantic story, too, about this old barn. Once, a great many years before any of us were born, there lived on this plantation a charming young princess, beloved by all who knew her. One day the king sent word that he was coming down to sup with her. But it so happened that on the day the king was to come to supper the princess and all her household were to be away on an excursion, which was called, in the somewhat homely language of that day, a "clam-bake." However, the princess concluded to go to the clam-bake, and come home in season to sit with the king at supper. So they cooked mightily beforehand; for it was the fixed law of royal suppers in that day to have cream-toast, the cream flowing in rivers, cheese and jelly, pound-cake, and plum-cake, and cranberry-tart, and three kinds of pie, mince, apple, and squash, or die! Whereat the people of other countries laughed; but they ate the suppers, for all that, — the starvelings, — and came again. So the pies were all made with elaborate scalloped edges, and the hoar-frost of the cake; and all was set carefully away, awaiting the eventful hour, and the princess and her household went forth and locked the doors behind them. And when the time was fully come, the princess left the clam-bake, and waited by the roadside till the king came by, and then they both went together to the princess's house. And as they went up the steps to the house, the charming young princess, who never drank tea herself, said seductively to the king, "Do you mind, if you don't have tea? It is a great trouble every way, and the self-denial will do you good." And the king, lured into a wrong story by the music of her voice, suppressed a rising sigh, and said no, it was no matter. And then the princess unlocked the door, and essayed to go in; but though the door was unlocked, it refused to open. And suddenly the unhappy princess bethought herself that she had locked the door upon the inside, and bolted it, and herself passed out through the postern-gate, of which her lord high-steward still held the key. So there they were. Then, troubled, they marched hither and thither around the house with stately and majestic step, trying every door and window, and finding every avenue of approach barricaded except the sink-nose, which Libby prisoners might try, intent on getting out, but not a constitutional monarch, however anxious to get in. As two mice, lurking near the full cheese-safe, prowl around the crevices, braving cold and darkness in the middle of the night; safe on the shelf the cheese reposes, unmindful; they, fierce and heedless with anger, rave against it out of reach and emit a squeal; a rage for eating, collected from a long fast, and throats dry from curd, urge them on: not otherwise anger inflamed the king and princess surveying the walls, and anguish burned in their bones; by what way they might obtain access; in what manner they might dislodge the rations shut up in inaccessible places. *Nequicquam!* They could only look at each other with a wild surmise, and then, unfriended, melancholy, slow, betake themselves to the rude shelter and frugal fare of the barn. Then the scene suddenly changed. The westering sun came serenely in. The dreamy mist of graceful cobwebs, festooning and fantastic, and many a tiny window all adust, softened his brilliancy to a dim, religious light. The brown old rafters shone, amber-hued, in that mellow glory. The rough floors were fretted gold. A hundred summer sunsets glowed in the yellow corn that lay massed in ridged and burnished splendor. Mounds of apples, ruddy and round, loaded the air with their rich fragrance. Innumerable clover-blossoms, succulent with evening dews and morning showers, impurpled in the dusky silence of June nights, and cut down with all their sweetness in them, treasured up their dense deliciousness for balm-breathed cows, but did not disdain to flood our human sphere with tides of pleasant perfume. Meeting and mingling with these dear home-scents came gales from far Spice Islands and Araby the Blest, breathing over wild Western seas, to be tangled in pungent grasses and freight with welcome burden our rustic gondolas. (I mean English hay and salt hay.) And there, soothed into exceeding peace by Nature's lullaby, borne into ethereal realms on her clouds of unseen incense, all through the golden afternoon sat the king and princess, discoursing dreamily of the time

> " when men
> With angels may participate, and find
> No inconvenient date, nor too light fare;
> And from these corporal nutriments perhaps
> Our bodies may at last turn all to spirit."

While ever and anon a squat old hen or an elegant young rooster would hop up the steps and tread into the rooms, looking curiously at the unwonted sight, whereat the king would rise from his throne on an old cider-cask, and make a right royal speech, " Go to! base intruder!"—emphasizing his peroration by hurling an ear of corn at his visitors, which, as our wayward sisters were wont to say, when our generals had done them a particularly bad turn, was just what they wanted. So the afternoon sang itself peacefully away; only the princess was of an evil mind, and would mar the king's pleasure, when he was solacing himself with a remainder-biscuit brought in the princess's basket from the clam-bake, by saying, " Do you see that window? There is the closet where the cake is kept. Just behind that clapboard stands the jar of jam. Two feet to the right, I should think, reposes a cranberry-tart, the crust flaky and fantastic as a January snow-wreath, the jelly rich and red as the curve of Fantasima's lip"; and then the king would roll his eyes around at her in a fine frenzy, and gnaw his crust with a still more wrathful despair. And that is the end of my romance of the barn.

Still, it must be confessed, an old barn is not without its disadvantages, which the impartial historian must not pass silently by. It shakes wonderfully in a high wind. You hardly dare drive a nail anywhere, for fear the whole edifice should rattle down over your head. We desired to set up in the loft one of Dr. Dio Lewis's jumping-machines; but, upon minute investigation, Halicarnassus said no, — with the first antic we should find ourselves in the barn-cellar. In short, an old barn, in an advanced stage of disintegration, must be treated as tenderly as a loveress. (There seems to be a movement now-a-days towards the introduction of feminine nouns; so I venture to make my contribution.)

When the seeds were to be sown, it became necessary to shut up the hens, — necessary, but difficult. I closed the door myself every night with unwearied assiduity, but bright and early every morning came the homely hens and the stately-stepping rooster, treading and pecking as innocently as if they had never suspected they were on forbidden ground. I instituted a search one day: and no wonder they got out! We might have barricaded the door to our heart's content, and they would have tossed their crests in scorn. For there, directly under their perch, was a great hole in the side of the edifice. Hole do I say? It was many holes run into one. Hole was the rule, and barn the exception. It was vacancy bounded by a rough, serrate-dentate coast of decayed boards. It is little to say chicken, — a condor might have contemplated imprisonment there undismayed. Of course reparation must be made, or farewell, dream of early peas! At the same time, the evil to be remedied was so overgrown, and a monster evil to be disposed of is so much greater an undertaking than a mere new measure to be carried, that I think it no exaggeration, but at worst only what we classic writers call synecdoche, to say, as I did at the beginning of this paper, that I went out to build a barn.

What brilliant success would have crowned heroic effort, if knowledge had been, as the old copy-books used to say it was, power! It was clear enough what needed to be done, and there was abundance of material to do it with, — plenty of boards, — a little rough, to be sure, — and plenty of nails, — a little rusty. But boards are so uncommonly heavy! and a ladder affords a footing at once so contracted and so uncertain! and a hammer has such a will of its own, coming down with ill-timed fervor in the most unexpected places! And when a board has been lifted and pulled by main force into position, it takes both hands to hold it there; and then how are you going to drive in the nails to make it stay, I should like to know, especially with your ladder continually threatening a change of base ? I am confident, moreover, that our boards were made of mahogany, or some other impenetrable substance; for when, by dexterous manipulation, by close crowding up against them, and holding them up with my elbows, I at length proceeded to strike an effective blow, do you think the nail went in ? Not in the least. It did everything else. It doubled up, it snapped short, it plunged about frantically whenever it was touched, to say nothing of the not innumerous occasions on which the stroke aimed at its unprincipled head fell with crushing force — elsewhere. Then my strength would begin to fail, and the board would slowly, slowly slide away from me, till I let it go, and it dashed with a crash to the ground.

Here, to use the language of the poet, —

> "A man I know,
> But shall not discover,
> Since ears are dull,
> And time discloses,"

was aroused to unwonted activity by the pounding, and sauntered out into the midst of the *mêlée*. I do not know how long he had been watching me; for I was so absorbed in my architectural problem as to be dead to the outer world; but into the recesses of my complications penetrated a sound which seemed very much like what the world's people call a — a — a — snicker! I looked around, and there he was. Very sober, very blameless, having very much the air of being just arrived; but could my ears deceive me? Then up spake I, cheerily, "O Halicarnassus, you are just in time to hold this board steady while I hammer it on," — as if I had that moment adjusted it for the first time. He took his stand under the ladder, and held on as I told him, with a beautiful docility. I did not hurry in selecting a nail; for he was strong, and I thought it would do him good to be in an uncomfortable position a little while, particularly as I was not quite satisfied about the — half-suppressed, broken laugh (definition of *snicker* given by "The Best").

Carpentry was far easier after this, yet progress was not what you could call rapid. The ladder was short, and I had to reach up painfully; but I should not mind my arms aching, I informed my apprentice, if it were not that all the splinters and dust and rubbish that my hammer struck from the old boards marched straight into my uplooking eyes.

"You might keep your eyes shut," suggested he.

"But then," I responded, "I could not see how to strike."

"Never mind," said he, tenderly; "you would hit just as well."

"Oh, that way madness lies!"

The upshot of it was, that he bestirred himself, and turned that barn into a marvel of art. It had been a barn: it became a villa. An immense wooden sarcophagus, — only nobody had ever been deposited in it, — perhaps it was a horse-trough in its day, — was set up " on end," and turned into a three-story house. Fresh, sweet-smelling hay was piled on each floor, and such attractive little nests were scooped out therein, that a hen of a domestic turn of mind would go there and lay, just for the fun of it, you might suppose. Then the porticos, and the sliding-doors, and the galleries, and the hospital, and the vistas, and the palisades, and the inner and outer courts, — every arrangement that heart of hen could wish, both for seclusion and for society, — why, those fowls might have dreamt they dwelt in marble halls every night of their lives, and not have been very far out of the way! And the summer residences that he made for them, — little Gothic cottages built for a single family, with all the modern conveniences, and a good many more improvised on the spot, and with this signal advantage over similar structures at Newport and Nahant, — that you can take them under your arm, and carry them wherever you please.

Before finally leaving my hen-coop, will a generous public pardon me for recurring to the subject of crowing hens? It may possibly be remembered that a little while ago I hazarded a doubt as to the existence of any such *lusus naturæ*. Since that time proof has accumulated upon me from different quarters that crowing hens do exist. But let it be noted, that the gist of my remarks was the inconsistency of the tyrant man. Now see whether an admission of the disputed fact relieves him from the guilt charged upon him.

Observe once more the couplet, —

"A whistling girl and a crowing hen
Always come to some bad end," —

a couplet which, I affirm without fear of contradiction, endeavors to affix a stigma upon the character of crowing hens; for what sinister and ulterior purpose I scornfully refrain from designating. Fourteen crowing hens have reported themselves to me: one from Maine, two from New Hampshire, three from Massachusetts, one each from Connecticut, New York, New Jersey, and North Carolina, and four from Pennsylvania. Of these fourteen, —

Number One is "Bobby, an excellent Biddy. Lays nice large eggs, and brings up her families well."

Number Two, named Queen Mab. Always crows to the music of a sweet-voiced Steinway. Is in all other respects an amiable and exemplary hen.

Number Three is a black hen, now three years old. Has laid eggs.

Number Four crowed regularly every morning,

when the cock did. When she was a little over a year old, she and her seven babes were stolen from a wild-cherry-tree, where they went to bed, by a fox, who came up on an old log.

Number Five crowed irregularly. Raised several broods of chicks. Lived to be four or five years old.

Number Six crowed chiefly in the fall, when the young chicks were practising (no doubt to encourage them). Lived to the remarkable age of nine years, and was then decapitated.

Number Seven raised a large brood of chickens. Their papa was killed at about the time for them to begin to crow, and one morning she flew up on the fence and crowed with all her might. Continued it until they had learned, and then stopped. Was called Old Sam. Her end was the soup-pot.

Number Eight, an old speckled hen. Took to crowing after a raid on the poultry-yard had deprived it of every rooster. Crowed as well as anybody.

Number Nine lived twenty-five years ago. Witness has forgotten whether she ever did anything but crow. Had a wicked name, which I shall not give.

Number Ten laid eggs.

Number Eleven crowed repeatedly and often spunkily after the roosters had been killed, never while they were alive.

Number Twelve crows sometimes in the presence of the rooster, chiefly when alone. Most energetic in crowing.

Numbers Thirteen and Fourteen have simply the fact of their existence recorded.

Now, mere proverb-mongers, bear in mind: In the whole country only fourteen well-defined crowing hens, — at the worst, not a very crying evil.

Of the fourteen, only one is recorded as having come to a bad end, and that end had no connection with the crowing, but occurred while she was engaged in the faithful discharge of her maternal duties.

Seven are reported as bearing an excellent domestic character, a blessing to the society which they adorned. Against the remaining seven not a syllable of reproach is breathed; but if there had been any evil thing in them, who believes it would not have been learned and conned by rote and cast into our teeth?

In the case of five, their crowing was not only innocent, but a pre-eminent virtue, a manly crown set upon every feminine excellence.

Inconsistency? It is a white and shining word for the black quality to which I applied it.

Men, the indictment is quashed. You are ruled out of court. Take your couplet and depart, giving thanks that you are not prosecuted for defamation of character.

While the architect and the hens were thus

revelling in the halls of the Montezumas, I turned my attention to the more modest purpose of providing accommodations for the tomatoes. All our efforts in that line hitherto had been comparative failures. "It is a good thing to take time by the forelock," I had remarked to a subordinate, as early, I should think, as February, perhaps January, and begun planting a great many seeds in boxes, which were set in the sunshine under the kitchen windows. A great many shoots came up, and then a great many flocks and herds of little green things oozed out of them and began to creep over them, evidently with the design of eating them up. This would never do. I borrowed a bound volume of the old "New England Farmer," from a young New England farmer, — the worst thing in the world to do, let me say to all amateur farmers. Use every lawful means of perfecting yourself in your profession, but on no account touch an agricultural journal. They bewilder an honest heart into despair. They show the importance and the feasibility of so many things, every one of which is full of interest, profit, and pleasure, that you know not where to begin; and instead of doing one thing, you dream of a dozen. I sent the "New England Farmer" home, and, according to advice, bought a handful of tobacco, put it on a shovel and set fire to it, and smoked the young shoots thoroughly, — as well as the house and all that therein was. The experiment succeeded perfectly. Any way, it killed the tomatoes. I am not so sure about their colonists, but I do not believe they long survived the destruction of their Arcadia. "It is just as well," I said, to encourage one whose spirits depend upon me. " It is, indeed, far better. There are many kind people in cities, who will sow the seeds, and tend the plants, and take all the trouble, and give us as many plants as we want, for fifty cents." Which, indeed, they did,— and I set the plants out duly in a square. But they are delicate, and need protection from untimely summer frosts. Thriftless people put up stakes, bushes, and such hand-to-mouth contrivances, and perhaps throw an old apron or a fragment of a table-cloth over them. Practical, but prosaic people, cover them with pots and pans during their fragile infancy; all of which makes an unsightly feature in a landscape. I built a conservatory. And here let me say to all my young friends who may design to devote themselves to rural pursuits, Do not be narrowly content with the utilities, nor count the hours spent upon the beautiful as time lost. For aught we know, the fields might be just as fruitful, if they put forth only a gray and dingy sedge. Instead of which, we have their green and velvet loveliness starred all over with violet and daisy and dandelion. A hen-house is no less serviceable because built in the Gothic style with suites of rooms. A rough, nomadic tent of poles and rags gives no surer protection to your tender herbs than the stately and beautiful conservatory. That is why I built a conservatory. The walls were of brick: there was a pile of bricks in a corner of the barn. The roof was of glass: there was a pile of superannuated windows, ditto, ditto. The edifice was not quite so firm as might be desired, owing to the fact of there being no underpinning nor cement; nor did its sides not sometimes deviate from strictly right lines, as they were obliged to yield to the undulations of the soil; but it was at least classical, — brick and windows. The only serious trouble with it was, that one fine morning it ceased to be conservative at all, but became revolutionary to the last degree, — utterly subversive, in fact, of the existing order of things. Why, the calves got in over night and turned everything topsy-turvy. Their hoofs crushed in the walls and roof, and the walls and roof between them crushed the tomato-plants, so that architecture and horticulture were involved in a common ruin. We knew it was the calves, because their juvenile tracks were all about. Besides, there were the calves. It turned out to be of no account, for that proved to be a bad year for tomatoes, so we should have had none in any event, and were saved all the trouble of cultivating them, while the calves had a free frolic, poor things. To be sure, they have a fine court-yard for exercise, a vestibule for noonday lounging, and snug quarters for sleep and shelter; but as it was in the beginning, is now, and ever shall be,

> "Fredome is a noble thing!
> Fredome mayss man to haiff liking:
> Fredome all solace to man giffis:
> He levys at ess, that frely levys!
> A noble calf may haiff nane ess,
> Na ellys nocht that may him pless,
> Gyff fredome failyhe: for fre liking
> Is yharnyt our all othir thing.
> Na he, that ay hass levyt fre,
> May nocht knaw weill the propyrte,
> The angyr, na the wrechyt dome,
> That is cowplyt to foule thyrldome.
> Bot gyff he had assayit it,
> Than all perquer he suld it wyt:
> And suld think fredome mar to pryss,
> Than all the gold in warld that is."

And if these wayward children of the earth could find any way of escape from their gilded fetters, and wander out under the beautiful star-sown heavens into the wilderness of night to taste the sweets of liberty, and, if you please, of license, who can find it in his heart to blame them? Farmers ought not to restrict their thoughts to human motives. We should endeavor sometimes to look at things with the eyes of a cow, an ox, a chicken, and so learn to have more consideration for and sympathy with these younger brethren of ours, — these children of a common Father. The earth is theirs as truly, if not as thoroughly, as it is ours. The good God makes grass to grow for the cattle as well as herb for the service of man. All the beasts of the field are His. Undoubtedly He enjoys the happiness of every lamb frisking on the hillside; and not a bluebird flashes through the morning, not a swallow twitters on his spray, but the Creator smiles on its glistening beauty and listens lovingly to its song. "Doth God take care for oxen?" asks Paul; and looking into the Bible, as well as abroad over the fertile fields, we can but answer, Yes; though Paul himself seems to incline to the negative, and to consider the command not to muzzle the ox when he treadeth out the corn as given altogether for our sakes. Partly for our sakes, no doubt, but partly also for the comfort of the toiling, patient oxen; and so, probably, would Paul say, were the question fairly put to him from the bovine side. So, indeed, in effect he does say, when writing to Timothy with another end in view. Perhaps that "Original Greek," to whom commentators and expositors are so fond of appealing in an emergency, may yet be found to help us out of our difficulty by proving, past a cavil, that *no* means *yes*. At any rate, the Bible shows that God does take care of all dumb, uncomplaining lives, and all humble human creatures, — and shows it so conclusively, so minutely, and so practically, that we can hardly be said to need any supplementary revelation on that point, though a reverend gentleman, evidently thinking otherwise, has written what he modestly terms "a scripture" about Timid Tom and Old Gurdy, — very tender and touching, yet he will pardon me for saying I still think Matthew rather better adapted to the rural districts.

So we will remember that to the birds our cherry-trees are a true Promised Land, where Nature herself invites them to enter in and take possession. We will ever bear in mind that Mooly and Brindle have no forecast of full granaries to console them for present deprivation, and that the waving corn-field rustles for them, and for them the rich rye quivers, and they do but obey their highest law, when they pass through the carelessly swinging gate and feast on the fatness of the land.

In fact, our three little calves always wrought their mischief with such winsome grace as disarmed anger and amply repaid us in amusement what they cost us of trouble. They were a source of unfailing interest and wonder, —

> "A phantom of delight,
> When first they gleamed upon our sight,
> A lovely apparition, sent
> To be a moment's ornament."

And every day heightened their charms.

Mr. Henry James, illustrating some false conception of the relation between God and man, somewhere says, " You simply need to recall the relation of irksome superintendence on the one hand, and of utter indifference on the other, which vivify the intercourse of a farmer and his calves."

Now to Mr. Henry James, as a general rule, it would be difficult to award too much praise. The river of his speech, rippling through summer shadows, or rushing over rocky ways, still flows, like Siloa's brook, fast by the oracles of God. And though it winds sometimes through inaccessible places, and you tell its course only by its music, and not by its sparkle, and though it channels a path sometimes through murky valleys whose every vapor is laden with pestilence, yet you know that, pure and purifying, singing through its leafy solitudes and shining heavenly clear in Tophet as in Tempe, the burden of its song is, Peace on earth, good-will to man, while it hastens on to mingle its crystal stream with the waters of the river of life.

But, Mr. Henry James, good and wise as you are, I am certain you never owned a calf. At least, you never stood in confidential relations to one. "Irksome superintendence?" You did not witness the welcome we gave our poor little favorite, torn all trembling from its mother's side by the stern demand of some greedy purse; how we stroked him, and patted him, and — begging your pardon — scratched his head, and so soothed away his sorrow ere he was aware; how we stayed his staggering limbs, and because he was too young, and knew not how to drink, but only stared at the basin and at us and vacancy, in an uncertain, moonstruck way, did I not put my own fingers into the milk and draw his mouth down to them, and, deceived by the pious fraud, did not the poor little hungry innocent, like Dido of old, drink large draughts of love, in happy ignorance that it was not Nature's own arrangement for such case made and provided? No, Mr. James, — where it is a question of absolute philosophy, ordinary cosmology, noumenal force, instinctual relegation, and the fundamental antithesis of Me and Not-Me, you shall have everything your own way; but when it comes to livestock, you must ask me first!

Such a mistake, however, is not unaccountable. Farming, it must be conceded, is in some respects a hard-hearted business, little calculated to cherish the finer feelings. Separation of families is so common a thing among farmers that the sight of sorrow ceases to sadden. Calves are taken from their mothers at a tender age, to the great trial of both mother and child; and a sufficient excuse for this trampling upon Nature is supposed to be concentrated in the one word, *Veal*. All last night the air reverberated with the agonized lowings of a bereaved cow in a neighboring pasture, and with the earliest dawn there she stood forlorn, pressing her aching breast against the cold, dew-damp gate, and gazing with mournful longing up the road last trodden by her darling's lingering feet. But it is all right, because—*veal!* A hen may be suddenly wrested from her infant brood and brought back from her private nest into the dreary phalanstery, because Mr. Worldly Wiseman thinks the laying of eggs a more important thing than the cultivation of domestic virtues. To the exigencies of "profit" everything else must give way. The result can but be deleterious. The peach-bloom of sensibility is presently rubbed off by constant trituration of harsh utilities. Only yesterday I received an invitation from a gentleman of standing and character to visit a famous farm; and one of the inducements expressly held out was the pleasure of seeing a hundred sheep from Canada, with a hundred little lambs, all their respective little tails cut off short. What a request was there, my countrymen! For why were those little tails cut off, in the first place? and if they were cut off, why should any humane person be invited to see such a spectacle of man's rapacity? It must have been sheer wantonness. You sometimes prune away sundry branches of a tree, to make the rest of it grow better; but will there be any more to a leg of mutton because it had no tail? No, sir. When I go a sheep-gazing, I want to see the sheep walking about with dignity and comfort, and coming home, as little Bo-Peep wanted hers, bringing their tails behind them.

What we can we do to stem this tide of demoralization. We have never set our hearts upon taking the first prize at any fair for anything. We do not count upon deriving great pecuniary strength from contact with our Mother Earth. But upon this one thing we have determined, — that every creature on our plantation, which is allowed to live at all, shall live as far as possible in the enjoyment of every bounty which Nature bestowed upon him. No dumb life shall be the worse for falling into our hands. We do not disdain to study the nature of our calves, nor to gratify their innocent whims. One refuses milk and chooses water: water is always provided. Another exults in apples, bread, and fried potatoes, and eats them from your hand with most winsome confidence. They dislike the confinement of their parade-ground, yearning to roam over the grassy knolls, to snuff the scent of the clover-blossoms, to drink the dew from buttercups, to lie on the velvet turf and let the summer soak through their tough hides and penetrate their inmost hearts. How calm then are their beautiful mazarine blue eyes! What deep content relaxes every fibre of their breathing bodies! How happily the days of Thalaba go by! They seem to have attained to a premature tranquillity, the meditative mood of full-grown kine. But if sometimes the morning wine of June leaps through their veins with a strange vigor in its pulse, you shall see how bravely their latent youthfulness asserts itself. Frisking with many an ungainly gambol, they dash across the orchard, bending their backs into an angle, brandishing their tails aloft, jerking, butting, pushing, and jostling each other, in joy too intense for expression.

In truth, Nature is fond of her little joke as well as the rest of us, though the actors in the comedy do not always discern the comic element in it. Strange how ridiculous anything may be, and yet not have the smallest suspicion that it is ridiculous. As when, for instance, one of these little "Bossy calves," fumbling and smelling around a chair, got his head between the rounds of the lower part and could not get it out again. He did not see the point of the joke at all, but stumbled about, shaking his head wildly, and wedging it in more firmly with every struggle. It was no easy matter to get near enough to help him; and, in spite of his terror and impatience of the situation, one could but laugh at the figure he made. I remember once seeing a pretty little yellow-bird on the fence looking as if he had three legs. A three-legged bird!—this must be attended to. I crept near enough to resolve the third leg into his tail, on which he had settled himself, leaning backward in a persistent determination to swallow a huge worm, which was just as persistently determined not to be swallowed. Birdie gulped and wormie wriggled. Birdie looked very solemn, and wormie very angry. Birdie would not give up, and wormie would not go down. There was a good deal of fun, but I had it all to myself. Once a caterpillar hung his cocoon to my window-sash, and I determined to keep my eye on him and see him begin life as a butterfly. I watched him week after week without detecting any change, and upon consulting the text-books of Natural History, found that he had probably reached middle age, as butterflies count time, before I began to suspect he had been born at all. But did the little sprite know I was watching him? Did he creep out on the farther side, and shut the door behind him carefully, and steal slyly around the corner of the house for his wings to dry, and come peeping down from the roof every day, laughing in his sleeve to see me watching that empty nest? And did he tell the story to his friends at some butterfly dinner-party, and did they laugh at me till the tears ran from their wicked little eyes, and say, in butterfly jargon, what a "sell" it was, and pat him on the shoulder, and call him "a sad dog"?

Driving in Natick one day, I observed, in some of the pleasant grounds which ornament that town, a very nice little contrivance; — a coil of fence you might call it, made of iron wire, capable of being rolled and unrolled, and so enabling you to make an enclosure when and where you chose. Set your fence down on one part of the lawn, turn in your lambs, and, when they have cropped all the grass, remove the establishment to another place. I represented very ably and vividly to my prime minister the advantages of such a fence to our calves and to ourselves. It gives them at once the freedom of the turf, yet does not loose them beyond our control. And then it looks so picturesque!

"Yes," said he, briskly, "we must have one."

"That we must!" I responded with enthusiasm, delighted at his ready acquiescence. Not that a non-acquiescence would have made any difference in the result, but the process would have been more tedious.

The next morning he called me out, with great flourish of trumpets, to see The Iron Fence.

"It is not possible," I said, in astonishment. "You have had no time to send."

"No, — I made it," he replied, boldly.

"You!" still more astonished. "I knew there was a tangle of iron wire in the barn, but it looked rusty."

He made no reply, only whistled me on as if I were his dog, — he often does that, — and I followed, musing. The iron fences that I had seen showed a fine tracery, delicate and graceful, seemingly, as the cobwebs on the morning grass: could they, like these, be woven in a single summer night? The sequel will show. I appeared upon the scene. A single slender iron pole was driven into the ground: one end of a piece of rope was fastened to it, the other end encircled the neck of our little black, woolly calf, Topsy, who was describing great circles around the pole, in her frenzy to escape.

"Sir," said I, after a somewhat prolonged silence, "it is the old crow-bar."

"No," said he, confidently, "it is an Iron Fence,—such as they have in Natick. Only," he added, after a short pause, and as if the thought had just occurred to him, "perhaps theirs is the old-fashioned centripetal kind. This is the New Centrifugal Iron Fence!"

Kindness to animals is, like every other good thing, its own reward. It is homage to Nature, and Nature takes you into the circle of her sympathies and refreshes you with balsam and opiate. We, too, delight in green meadows and blue sky. Resting with our pets on the southern slope, the heavens lean tenderly over us, and star-flowers whisper to us the brown earth's secrets. Ever wonderful and beautiful is it to see the frozen, dingy sod springing into slender grass-blades, purple violets, and snow-white daisies. The lover deemed it a token of extraordinary devotion, that, when his mistress came by, his

> "dust would hear her and beat,
> Had I lain for a century dead;
> Would start and tremble under her feet,
> And blossom in purple and red."

But no foot so humble, so little loved, so seldom listened for, that the earth will not feel its tread and blossom up a hundred-fold to meet her child. And every dainty blossom shall be so distinctly wrought, so gracefully poised, so generously endowed, that you might suppose Nature had lavished all her love on that one fair flower.

As you lie on the grass, watching the ever-shifting billows of the sheeny sea, that dash with soundless surge against the rough old tree-trunks, marking how the tall grasses bend to every breeze and darken to every cloud, only to arise and shine again when breeze and cloud are passed by, there comes through your charmed silence — which is but the perfect blending of a thousand happy voices — one cold and bitter voice, —

"Golden to-day, to-morrow gray:
So fades young love from life away!"

O cold, false voice, die back again into your outer darkness! I know the reaper will come, and the golden grain will bow before him, for this is Nature's law; but in its death lies the highest work of its circling life. All was fair; but this is fairest of all. It dies, indeed, but only to continue its beneficence; and with fresh beauty and new vigor it shall blossom for other springs.

Fainter, but distinctly still, comes the chilling voice, —

"Though every summer green the plain,
This harvest cannot bloom again."

False still! This harvest shall bloom again in perpetual and ever-increasing loveliness. It shall leap in the grace of the lithe-limbed steed, it shall foam in the milk of gentle-hearted cows, it shall shine in the splendor of light-winged birds, it shall laugh in the baby's dimple, toss in the child's fair curls, and blush in the maiden's cheek. Nay, by some inward way, it shall spring again in the green pastures of the soul, blossoming in great thoughts, in kindly words, in Christian deeds, till the soil that cherished it shall seem to seeing eyes all consecrate, and the Earth that flowers such growths shall be Eden, the Garden of God.

A COUNCIL ABOUT A COUNCIL.

WE had been talking of the National Council. I shall not explain what that is, though there are people who affect not to know. I would only suggest modestly, and in an undertone, that the National Council can much better afford not to be known by any person, than any person can afford not to know it. Rarely is there witnessed a scene óf more deep, wide, and overpowering interest than that which happened one June day in the Mount Vernon church, in Boston, when America met England in open court, and with calm voice read out to her the list of her wrongdoings. It was an old story. It had rung across the sea a thousand times, and returned to us void; but heard on our own soil, heralded by the cheers of a victorious army, three hundred thousand strong, it sounded after quite another sort. The England that had sinned cried *peccavi;* the better England, that had fought side by side with us bravely against the sin, joined in our *jubilate;* and then Christian America, too noble to overlook an unrepented or to remember a repented wrong, gave, amid tears and cheers, — fierce outburst of an excitement that would not be suppressed, — the right-hand of forgiveness and Christian fellowship.

There was another hour not to be easily forgotten, or lightly remembered. Two hundred and forty years and more after the landing of the Pilgrims on Plymouth Rock, with winter and the Indian in front, two unknown foes, and deadly as unknown, there met on the same rock a goodly company, the flower of men gathered from the Atlantic and the Pacific shores, from the continent stretching between, and from beyond the seas, —

> "The sons of sires who conquered there
> With arm to strike, and soul to dare,
> As quick, as far as they";

and on that rock, the sacred shrine of Liberty in this young Western world, they gave in their joyful adhesion to the principles which had borne the fathers through their long agony to the glorious end.

The appearance of the Council was altogether impressive. I had no disposition to quarrel with any of its decisions, or if I had, it was overborne by the weight which their deliberation and ability carried. But a friend of mine, who is less impressible, was not so disposed to assent, and persisted in asking, Was I *quite* satisfied with *all* the proceedings, — with the "Declaration of Faith," for instance?

I. I thought I was. I am certainly profoundly satisfied with its promulgation at Plymouth Rock.

H. That is, you are pleased with the dramatic element; but as it was mainly a theological and ecclesiastical council, convened only once in two hundred years, is it not rather desirable that its theology should be of no uncertain cast?

I. I find no fault with its theology. The Declaration of Faith seems to me simple and sublime.

H. I have no quarrel with its sublimity, but I am not so sure on the simplicity side. We declare our adherence to the faith and order " which the synods of 1648 and 1680 set forth or reaffirmed." Have the goodness to tell me what that faith and order are.

I. Goodness, indeed! How should I know? Are they published in Webster's Spelling-Book, that I should have them at command?

H. Exactly. Why, then, did not these reverend seigniors state our own points of faith, and let every one judge for himself, rather than refer back to something which ninety-nine persons in a hundred have no means of reading, and which nine hundred and ninety-nine in a thousand never will read.

I. I suppose it was done partly to save time and trouble, and partly for the express purpose of showing the world that the faith has not changed.

H. So far as saving time and trouble is concerned, it would have saved still more if the Council had not met at all. It is poor economy for a Council to save time by not doing what it was expressly convened to do; and if the faith of the fathers is not changed, so much the worse for the sons. To adhere to their faith can hardly but be to depart from their spirit. To be like our fathers is not to do what they did, but as they did, — not to wear their clothes, but to be moved by their spirit. They searched the Scriptures, and tried to frame their creeds, and guide their lives by the light they found therein. But we have been searching the Scriptures for two hundred years more, and with such assistance as they could not command. Bible literature has been wonderfully improved and increased since their time. Geography, philology, history, travel, criticism, have all made the sacred text a focus of their light. It would be very strange if all this illumination had brought out no new meaning, — if our fathers saw as much in their darkness as we in our light. The Reverend Assembly of Divines at Westminster were undoubtedly an able body of men, but probably less able than the body assembled in Ashburton Place. The former were chosen at random, every member of Parliament selecting his man. The latter were chosen deliberately, each man by the community around him, who knew its best man, and would have every motive to elect him its delegate. These men, the flower of all the churches, would have done an act much more worthy of the character, and suitable to the dignity of the Council which they composed, had they drawn up as simply and comprehensively as possible a Declaration of Faith which should have expressed the present belief of the churches in the present language of the people, instead of pinning their faith to the sleeves of the Westminster and other Divines.

I. I don't recollect that there was anything said about Westminster in the "Declaration."

H. The first draft, read by Dr. Thompson, mentioned the Westminster Confession and Catechism. No member of the Council made any opposition to it, that I know of. Probably most of them agree with it. Why these names were left out of the final draft by the skilful managers of the Council I do not know. But the thorough authentication of them is there under the innocent-looking declaration of adherence to the faith and order, "which our synods of 1648 and 1680 set forth or reaffirmed."

I. You speak as if there were something sinister in the matter, which I do not believe. It is not the way of our people to do things under the rose. Besides, what motive was there? We all believe the Westminster Catechism, so that there could have been no intrinsic objection to having it inserted bodily into the Declaration.

H. You subscribe to it, do you?

I. Certainly I do, from turret to foundation-stone, — "as I understand it": which is not saying much, to be sure.

H. Did you ever happen to read that document?

I. I happened to learn it by heart when I was a child, and repeated it to the minister, and got a Bible for my pains.

H. Then perhaps you can answer the question, "What is the work of creation?"

I. Just as easy as nothing! "The work of creation is, God's making all things of nothing by the word of his power, in the space of six days, and all very good."

H. You believe, then, that God did make all things in six days?

I. Not exactly, no; that is, not as we now use the word day. But the Bible says "six days," and whatever the Bible means by that we believe. The only question is as to what the Bible does mean.

H. But there is no question as to what the Westminster Divines meant by six days. And what they meant we do not mean. Therefore we cannot subscribe to their statement.

I. But this is a mere side-issue. These old Divines knew nothing of Geology, and took the words as they appeared on the face of them, just as I suppose the Jews did.

You know we are not obliged to take the Catechism with strict verbal adherence, but only for "substance of doctrine," which is not affected, whether the world were made in six days or six ages.

II. Not at all; but why adopt a two-hundred-year-old creed, which contains and must contain all the incorrectness of its age? Our own generation has errors enough of its own. Why should it adopt also those of its ancestors?

Here is another question that trenches hard upon even the "substance of doctrine."

"What did God at first reveal to man for the rule of his obedience?"

I. "And so forth, — the moral law."

II. "Where is the moral law summarily comprehended?"

I. "Ditto. In the ten commandments."

II. Yet St. Paul says that when the Gentiles, which have not the law, do by nature the things contained in the law, they are a law unto themselves; so that, in spite of the Westminster Divines, we believe that God did not leave himself without witness, even before the ten commandments were issued, or where they had never been heard of.

But again, "What is required in the fourth commandment?"

I. "The fourth commandment requireth the keeping holy to God such set times as he hath appointed in his word, expressly one whole day in seven, to be an holy Sabbath to himself."

H. "Which day of the seven hath God appointed to be the weekly Sabbath?"

I. Dear! dear! "From the beginning of the world to the resurrection of Christ, God appointed the seventh day of the week to be the weekly Sabbath, and the first day of the week ever since to continue to the end of the world, which is the Christian Sabbath." Now do not ask me if I believe that, because you know I do not. But in truth I did not think anything about it. I forgot the Catechism said anything about Sunday, and so I dare say did the rest of the Council.

H. "The *rest* of the Council!" But so much the worse if a deliberative assembly subscribed to they knew not what.

I. They only subscribed to the "substance of doctrine." Justification and sanctification and the atonement, and such things, were what I suppose they had chiefly in mind.

H. What I have in mind is, that a fly is not a proper ingredient in a pot of ointment, and that those who publish a recommendation of the ointment ought first to take out the fly. If there were as much untruth, implied and direct, in the Westminster Catechism about the atonement as there is about this matter of the "Christian Sabbath," would you think it well to accept the Catechism by wholesale, and say nothing about it?

I. No, and I do not think it was well as it is. I am sorry they did it. I am sorry they did not make a declaration of their own faith. But I do not believe that there was any underhand work about it. I believe the framers and the receivers of this declaration were scrupulously honest and upright, and that they had no design whatever to foist any doctrine into the Church.

H. Neither do I think they had; but it is a pity they did not avoid the appearance of evil. The worst I think or suspect is, that under cover of the old synod they hoped to avoid discussions which might promise to be unprofitable and interminable. But it seems to me that there are discussions which ought to be held, unless certain matters quietly change themselves. For instance, this very one of Sunday. I suspect the reason why the Catechism passed muster in its Sabbath doctrine was, not simply, as you say, that the Council did not think of it, — though that fact may be true, — but that they would have found no fault with it if they had thought of it. Probably every member of the Council teaches in his own pulpit, and has taught in his Sunday school, that God commands us in the Bible to keep the first day of the week as a Sabbath. It is not discussed, and would not have been discussed had it been brought up, because it is a settled matter. But since it is settled wrong and settled mischievously, it ought to be unsettled.

I. I do not believe you, it is my painful duty to declare. I am an Orthodox Congregationalist born and bred, and *I* do not believe that God anywhere commanded us to keep the Sabbath, or ever did command anybody but the Jews to keep it.

H. Then you do not believe as you were taught.

I. If I have changed the faith to which I was born, the change has been so gradual that I have not perceived it.

H. If you would go into your next "teachers' meeting" and state your views, I presume the change would at once become palpable.

I. No, I thank you.

H. And "No, I thank you" say others on whom such a course lies as a duty. I have no doubt that in the aggregate there are many who see the inconsequence of the popular mode of reasoning, but say nothing about it. There is not in the whole range of fallacies a more absolute *non sequitur* than that which imposes the Sabbath upon Christians, but many have been brought up in that habit of thought, and pay no attention to the thought itself; others who do consider it, look at it with their traditions, not with their eyes, and many who do see it, do not care to take the trouble and incur the obloquy of opposing and exposing it. As for the religious newspapers, they are conducted, not in the interests of truth, but of a denomination, with as much truth as that denomination may happen to have embraced. So that the fallacy for a while has it all its own way. In this

Sunday question, that is taught as a duty which is not a duty. The lesson is enforced by arguments that are fallacious, but they are accepted by the people partly through an inaptitude for thinking, and partly through a blind confidence in their teachers, who are supposed to think for them. These arguments are defended by "proof-texts," the majority of which prove nothing to the purpose, have indeed no connection, or but an incidental one, with the matter in hand, but have verbal resemblance enough to a proof to deceive the unwary or the inexpert. A jumble of Old and New Testament is served out from pulpit and press as Christianity. But while this medley is diffused throughout our religious literature, in Sunday-school book, tract, and periodical, no fair statement of the opposite side is permitted to appear.

I. O no, no, that is not true. You overstate.

II. Crede experto.

I. But doubtless your expert-ing was with a long, belligerent, metaphysical paper, too unwieldy for use, whatever its doctrine may have been.

II. Vastly complimentary.

I. Just you write, or I will write, a short, incidental article, touching the question lightly, but not uncertainly, making not so much an attack as a suggestion, and I have no doubt we should find ample room and verge enough.

H. Try it if you like.

I. I will try it.

I did try it, sending my short paper to various respectable religious newspapers. Some formally and freezingly replied, and some said by their silence, Better stay at home. They thought the tendency of the paper "would be to *unsettle* the minds of many readers." They " would use cheerfully that which relates to the importance of setting forth our belief in the language of to-day, but it would be with the greatest reluctance we could consent to publish what you say about the Sabbath." They did not " believe that one in ten of our readers would agree with you, and its publication would tend strongly to the secularization of the Sabbath." They could not publish this paper, but would be glad " to publish an article from you in which you and we could agree." But if people agree, what is the need of saying anything? There is no use in going further, is there? I asked.

H. Not the least in the world. You would be served with the same sauce by the Monthlies and the Quarterlies as by the Weeklies. Boston Review, New Englander, and the majestic Bibliotheca Sacra, — not one of them all will suffer you to lay a finger's weight on the Sabbath. No strange thing has happened to you. It is a matter of course, that where you diverge from a sect, you must go on your own account. They will not lend you their organs to refute their own arguments. No matter how well you can prove that you have the Bible on your side, *their* readers shall never see the proof. They are the teachers of the people, and if they choose to teach the traditions of the elders instead of the Gospel of Christ, they will not help you to publish anything impugning those traditions. You will be shut out from their columns, and you cannot possibly get your statements before the mass of their subscribers.

I. Of course if they believe it is error, they will not turn to and promulgate it. And I can very clearly see that there is danger in that direction. To strip from Sunday its false sanctity may seem to be plundering it of its true. That is to be guarded against.

II. But not by letting it keep its borrowed or stolen feathers.

I. No. And it seems to me cowardly and unphilosophical, and not at all in the true spirit of inquiry, to be so afraid of what a thing may lead to. The question is, not what a truth is going to do, but what is truth. We are not put here to keep the universe in motion, but to find out what is its principle of motion, and to put ourselves in harmony with that. Besides, truth is always safe and conservative; falsehood, never. There is no such thing as arriving at right conclusions, if you are always to be hampered by the clamor of some craft that is in danger. It is absolutely indispensable that we take to investigation a pure heart, an open mind, ready to receive what is, without fear or favor, or respect of persons or prejudices or interests.

H. But many minds have lost this receptive power. They have become callous. No argument touches them. They never come into contact with another mind. There is a sort of mental paralysis.

I. It is very sad.

H. It is the saddest of all mental conditions short of insanity, for it is the stoppage of growth. It is death in life. It is the old fable of the Medusa's head come true. And the worst of it is, that the persons suffering from it are profoundly unconscious of their condition. For it consists with great apparent activity. The present state of the Sunday question is largely due to this want of sensitiveness to the truth, yet there is a vigorous effort now making to diffuse these unscriptural and untruthful notions. All the Presbyterian, and I believe all the Baptist ministers, are to be supplied with a copy of Gilfillan's book on the Sabbath. It is very plausible, and its arguments will be received honestly by many of both teachers and taught. People have been so educated and accustomed to look upon the Bible as one dead level of doctrine that they are easily led blindfold by such fellows as this Gilfillan.

I. Do not call him "fellows." It is bad enough to be a man without being men in general. That is spiteful, is it not? But you are really growing quite cross, and I shall have to "fight fire with fire."

H. When one man or men in general spice a sufficient quantity of pious language with a little holy horror of the impiety of their opponents' teachings, and fortify their positions with a dozen or twenty Old Testament texts on the sanctification of the Sabbath, asserting or assuming that those texts are as conclusive for the first day of the week to the Americans as they were for the seventh to the Jews, and closing up the argument with a twang of Q. E. D., the state of Biblical knowledge is such that nineteen out of twenty will think he has made out his case.

I. Now I really must interfere. I do not so much wonder at your bitterness; for to have one's articles rejected by everybody is enough to provoke a saint, which you were never accused of being. But it is sad to see you losing not only temper and manners, but logic. What a contradiction it is to say the state of Biblical knowledge is so low, when, only a little while ago, you arrogated to our day a vast superiority in Biblical knowledge over that of our ancestors. Or do you think that you alone are versed in Biblical knowledge, and that all wisdom will die with you? Really, you talk about the Sunday question as if you thought so!

H. You have a lovely way of charming one unconsciously out of ill-temper, if one should ever happen to be in it! But you may rest assured it is quite possible for Biblical knowledge to be much further advanced than formerly, and yet nineteen out of twenty have very little of it. I fear our congregations generally know no more about the Bible than did the congregations of fifty or a hundred years ago, — if indeed they know as much. But if they are disposed to study it, they can learn a great deal more than could have been learned then.

I. I tell you what I will do. Have you read this book of Gilfillan's?

H. No; nor any man of woman born, I suspect. I have read at it several times.

I. You have it?

H. In some boundless contiguity or other. I carted it round several days last winter in town.

I. Say you took it with you. That would be much more civil. Don't you think I might write out a sort of exposition of the true state of the case, reviewing this book, perhaps, but at any rate showing the true character of the Sunday; and then if the periodicals will have none of it, we can set up a printing-press for ourselves, as Horace Walpole did, on Strawberry Hill. You hunt up the book.

H. Very well, if you like. It will be of service to yourself, and do nobody any harm, though I question whether it does much good.

I. O, things in general do not do much good, but you have to do them just the same.

So it came to pass in process of time that I presented myself with a formidable roll of manuscript. Halicarnassus made woful eyes at it, but there was no escape. "If it is inevitable," he pleaded, however, "let us take advantage of all possible mitigating circumstances. Get your work, and we will go down in the orchard and have it out there."

I. You already enjoy to the full the advantage designated by the Abbot Trublet a hundred years ago, namely, that "it is advantage to every particular person not to have too much sense."

It was a little sharp I admit, but Halicarnassus is very apt to suggest to me to take my work, and we will do thus and so; but I do not *wish* to take my work and be read or talked to. Work means sewing, and sewing spoils everything. It is a bad habit, hard to form and hard to break. It is demoralizing; never to be resorted to except as a relief or a necessity, or, like involuntary servitude, as a punishment for crime. There are states of mind for which sewing is soothing. It attracts just enough of your attention and vitality to draw off the surplus electricity and give you a chance to come down from your excitement, get wholesomely tired and able to sleep. Also when it is a question between rags and sewing, I suppose one should choose the sewing. But for persons who are not obliged to sew, to spend day after day in pulling a string through a piece of cloth seems a lamentable waste of time. And lamentable too is it that this busy idleness should be lauded as a virtue. In a world where there is so much real work to be done, necessary work, eternal work, all who can free themselves from the petty necessities ought to do so both for the sake of the world's work and the world's poor. There are always people enough glad to do all the sewing we can give them, to whom the money which it brings means common comfort, perhaps sustenance, perhaps a sense of self-respect and self-help. I fear a great deal of what we call industry is unnecessary narrowing to small issues. A soul's life is pricked out with the point of a needle, when it ought instead to be always ripening by and for the great busy-ness of eternity: and all the while it is doing this it flatters itself that it is doing duty and being exemplary.

No, if sewing must be done, let us go into our chambers and shut the doors, and forbid all profane approach, and forget that there is a great, glorious world outside, and sew as long as we can keep our temper, but let us not sully the splendor of summer afternoons with needle and thread.

This is a doctrine that will suit men, whatever women think about it! I know one man who likes it, at least to the degree that he is firmly convinced it conduces more to his happiness to have one enjoy life according to one's tastes, than to work and lose one's temper. If a man has no button on his wristband, he can do without it; if the coffee is bad, he can drink water, and be just as well off in half an hour. There is talk sometimes of health and spirits depending on wholesome food; but why is it not just as disastrous for me to destroy my health and temper in cooking you good food as it is for you to impair yours by eating bad? For you know I could not endure existence over a cooking-stove; and life would be no boon to you without me, would it, Halicarnassus? He is whittling a whistle out of a willow twig, and does not seem to hear me. A little louder, "Would it, Halicarnassus?" "Eh? no. O, no!" But he need not have hallooed his sentiment as if he had been driving oxen. As I was saying, slight annoyances may be put aside, but an unhappy face is an ever-present sorrow. Work that one does against one's nature will be fiercely avenged. Tastes,— what were they given us for but enjoyment and guidance? The thing which one likes to do, that is the thing which one can do best, and which he will do the most good in doing. The existence of the liking is the sign of the power. There is no calling in life, be it embraced with ever so much delight, that will preclude the necessity of attention and care and sacrifice; but when these come in the natural way, the natural attendants of hearty work, they nerve and strengthen. How unwise to engage, from some mistaken notion of duty, or simply because everybody else does, in an uncongenial calling, where the friction tends to weary not only, but to baffle and dispirit. Why make life harder than it need be, or was meant to be? I hate that religion or that philosophy which pretends to look complacently upon troubles as if they were something to be quietly borne and not stoutly resisted. These light afflictions are but for a moment, said Paul; but he climbed out of a window and dropped down in a basket to escape them, and not till he had made every effort to put them aside did he stand up and endure them. Then it was manliness. To have done it earlier would have been weakness. It is trouble, it is discomfort, it is unhappiness, that brings in sin and crime. It is never so easy to be good as when you are happy. It is never so easy to be cross as when you are crossed. The good God has provided, in the nature of things, all the trial which the human constitution needs. Men may strenuously endeavor to make every pathway as smooth as possible, without fearing that the soul will become a Sybarite. All trouble that is wantonly or carelessly or needlessly made for us by friend or foe is an injury. The heart can stand wear and tear only within certain limits. Beyond those there is harm of some kind to temper, health, or spirits, and no amount of Christian resignation can prevent it; for the Christianity that is necessary to bring resignation might have been used aggressively against some wrong. When the cupidity or negligence of a railroad company costs a limb, you may be resigned to the will of God, but you can never be sound again; and a lost happiness, a lost hopefulness, a lost mirthfulness, is as fatal to character and to the best life as a bodily disaster.

"It seems to me," says Halicarnassus, dubiously, "that there is another side which you — "

I. If there is, let it alone. One side is enough at a time. Now read the Essay.

H. An' 't please your Majesty, is it a review of Gilfillan?

I. Well, yes, of Gilfillan and matters in general. That is, Gilfillan serves as a pretext for the whole thing, though I can't say it has much to do with him.

H. The saints defend us! (turning over the manuscript.) It has much to do with something. Thirty pages, and foolscap!

I. Not a line too much.

(There is this to be said in defence of my friend, that in his first estate he does not take kindly to these matters. But I am fond of theology, and he is fond of me, so it happens that, from whatever quarter we set sail, we generally find ourselves bearing down upon theology, — though the big ship often flies signals of distress, of which the little pilot-boat takes no heed.)

I. But I can tell you, that after I had looked through the book, I was wellnigh discouraged —

H. Discouraged to the tune of thirty pages of foolscap!

I. To find that so many people had written on this subject. I supposed the error was simply because attention had never been called to the truth. On the contrary, the truth has been held up for centuries, and here we are groping in error still. What good can one little squeak do, when the thunders have been rolling for hundreds of years, and rolling in vain?

H. Heaven defend our ears from thunder, if this is what you call a squeak!

I. Shall I tell you what it was that put heart into me again?

H. I am powerless in your hands.

I. You know how the earthworms make each his little hole in the soil, and pile each his little pile of pulverized earth. And you know it is said these earthworms mellow the soil, and so fit it for cultivation. And I thought, that is the way with us all. We are earthworms, mellowing the hard pan of prejudice, that the truth may presently spring up and be fruitful. One earthworm cannot do much, but he can at least mellow his little sphere.

H. Make his little pile, commercially speaking.

I. And by and by we, or our successors, who have been delving so long, shall look up and find the whole earth softened, and the truth all green and vigorous everywhere.

We had now reached the orchard, and having disposed ourselves suitably, Halicarnassus attacked the manuscript, though not without casting grudging eyes at me, who divided the shining hours between watching an ant-hill and reading for the seventeenth time the charming chatter of " Little Prudy."

Here is the paper, to be read or skipped as one chooses; but I hope you will read it, for it is excellent, — though I say it who should not. Excellent of course I mean for substance of doctrine, and otherwise as good as I could make it.

GILFILLAN'S SABBATH.*

FROM the time of their deliverance out of Egypt to their captivity in Babylon, the Jews were continually lapsing into idolatry; and from the time of St. Paul to the present, the Christian world seems ever tending to lapse into Judaism. It is apparently a most difficult task to believe that the Messiah has come, or that, having come, he has introduced any change in our economy.

The book whose title we have placed at the head of this paper has been widely distributed by a special effort of the " New York Sabbath Committee." A copy is furnished gratuitously to every pastor connected with the General Assembly of the Presbyterian Church, and with the Baptist and Orthodox churches. We have taken the trouble to examine the volume carefully, in

* The Sabbath viewed in the Light of Reason, Revelation, and History, with Sketches of its Literature. By the Rev. JAMES GILFILLAN, Stirling, Scotland. Published by the American Tract Society, 150 Nassau Street, New York, and the New York Sabbath Committee, 5 Bible House, Astor Place.

order to ascertain what it is that merits so extensive and important a circulation. We find a treatise whose aim is to put the world back exactly where it was eighteen hundred years ago : to take us from under the law of Christ and put us under the law of Moses. In execution, it is prolix to weariness, singularly devoid of sprightliness, grace, and vigor of style and originality of treatment; rambling and rhetorical where it should be concise and logical, involved in its argument, often obscure and always dull. On the other hand, it bears marks of unwearied industry. It has gathered from all quarters facts, doctrines, and opinions bearing on its theme, whether they are friendly or hostile to its own theory. It is — we cannot say animated, so lively a term being quite inadmissible, but it is evidently actuated by an honest desire to do God service. It seems to be conscientious, and means to be fair. Happily for the author's self-complacency, he is endowed with an inability to see the bearings of things, and plods along with equal serenity, whether the argument makes for or against him. He utters great truths which are fatal to his theory, in the innocent belief that they confirm it. He is not especially bitter, seldom attributing to his opponents anything worse than a blindness born of prejudice, or describing their hypothesis in any harsher terms than " an expedient foolish as well as allied to the irreverent and profane." From a candor and consideration so unwonted, what may we not expect?

The intellectual calibre of the man may perhaps be best learned from the statement, that he calls the interpretation which makes the six days of creation denote periods of long duration, " in reality a libel on the simplest and most perfect style of historical writing," and finds an " unanswerable objection " to the "dogma which would convert the days of creation into millenary cycles, and confound, to borrow an expression from Bishop Horsley, 'the writing of a history with the composition of riddles.' "

We do not design formally to review the book; to follow the tortuous paths of its logic, its rhetoric, and its history. For such an enterprise we should need to borrow the pages of an encyclopædia. But believing truth to be the best refutation of error, we shall present, as concisely as possible, what we consider to be the nature and purpose of the Jewish Sabbath and the Christian Sunday, referring to the views of Mr. Gilfillan only where they obviously impinge upon our own.

We premise first, that we shall found our argument on the Bible. From the opinions of wise men, both in the earlier and later ages, from the hints of nature, and from our own preconceived notions of what ought to be, we may get what help we can, but the court of last resort is the Scriptures of the Old and New Testament. If the

Sabbath is enjoined upon us in the Bible, we accept it; if it is not, we shall use our own judgment in accepting or rejecting it.

In order to arrive at a right understanding and a full comprehension of the Bible, we need to know and always to bear in mind that the Bible has a body and a spirit, and that the body is like our own, of the earth earthy, and limited by time and space, while its Spirit is Divine and illimitable. In spirit, it is the will of God revealed to man. In body, it is history, poetry, prophecy, narrative, epistles, chiefly relating and addressed to a single nation. To this nation it was a direct revelation. To us it is an oblique revelation. To both all-sufficient for the life that now is and for that which is to come, — if we use it and do not simply abuse it.

For example: when God said to Abram, "Get thee out of thy country, and from thy kindred, and from thy father's house, unto a land that I will show thee; and I will make of thee a great nation, and I will bless thee," he spoke to Abram alone, and not to us Americans of the nineteenth century. When Christ said to the eleven Apostles, "Go ye into all the world and preach the Gospel to every creature," he spoke to the eleven Apostles and not to us. But believing with the Apostle Paul, on his authority combined with that of our own reason, that all these things are written for our admonition upon whom the ends of the world are come, we think it our part to ascertain what it is that God means to teach us by what he did and said to the Jews. While we judge, therefore, that he did not enjoin upon every man to leave his country and his kindred and go to a foreign land, since that would be manifestly useless, impossible, and absurd, we do infer that he requires every man to separate himself from all wickedness, and to constitute himself and his family a church of God. While we do not believe it is every man's duty to go to China or Turkey or Persia as a missionary, we do believe, from Christ's command, that it is his duty to spread the good tidings wherever and whenever he can find opportunity. God founded the Jewish nation that he might commit to them his oracles. Until Christ came, that revelation was sufficient for salvation. Christ established a new covenant, inaugurated a new era. Narrowness, separation, was the essence of Judaism. Universality, permeation, is the essence of Christianity. The force of Judaism was centripetal; that of Christianity is centrifugal. "Get thee out of thy country, and I will make of thee a great nation," was the key-note of the old Dispensation. "Go ye into all the world and preach the Gospel to every creature" was the key-note of the new. Yet Judaism was as essential as Christianity, was essential indeed to Christianity, *was* Christianity. Judaism was the seed of which Christianity was the flower. Judaism was intensely local that Christianity might by and by be world-wide. Judaism went first through the deserts of the world preparing the way for Christianity; and if at this day we are not subject to the same discipline, and amenable to the same laws as the Jews were, it is only because we have so profited by their lessons as to be prepared to enter an advanced class. Thus we hold the Old and the New Testament in equal reverence. Each is a revelation from God. But only the latter is binding on us, — and that only in such parts as concern us, — because only the latter was addressed to us. Neither the Old Testament nor the New is binding on us in those precepts which concern only the society to which they were addressed. Many things it is our duty to do which were enjoined upon the Jews; as, for instance, to befriend the orphan and the widow; but this is not our duty because the Jews were exhorted to justice and benevolence, but because the obligation is written on our hearts and confirmed by the teachings of Christ. We have no need to resort to the Old Testament to learn our duty. It is far more clearly revealed in the New. The Old Testament is a sacred book, but it is not ours. It is a Divine revelation, but not to us. Moses belonged to the Jews, but we have Christ. Moses earnestly besought God to show him His glory, and received for answer, "Thou shalt see my back parts, but my face shall not be seen." Jesus

Christ, the brightness of God's glory, and the express image of His person, we have heard, we have seen with our eyes, we have looked upon, and our hands have handled. Shall we go back from the sunshine into the twilight? Shall we resort to the precepts and laws of the Old Testament, framed for a people hardly snatched from idolatry, a people gross, sensual, ignorant, and stiff-necked, a people who had scarcely any spiritual sense, or any idea of future existence, or of inherent right and wrong, — we who live upon an earth warmed, softened, and spiritualized by eighteen centuries of Christian sunshine?

Yet just here rages the controversy regarding the Sabbath. Christians have universally relinquished Judaism to the extent of giving up circumcision, sacrifice, priesthood, and sanctuary, but there are many who retain the Sabbath on the ground that it is enjoined in the Fourth Commandment, and therefore of more force than the law to wear girdles of fine-twined linen. Thousands of injunctions concerning work and worship are labelled "ceremonial law," and very unceremoniously hustled aside, while the "ten commandments" are named "moral law," and reckoned still binding. But who made this distinction? Where in the Bible do we find the Mosaic laws thus classified and disposed of? We affirm that it is done solely on human authority; that the Bible countenances no such arrangement; that, on the contrary, the whole Mosaic law, decalogue and all, was, by the coming of Christ, disannulled. We are no more under the law of the ten commandments than we are under the law of ablutions and fringes. Christ and his Apostles taught as clearly as it is possible to teach that the Mosaic law was superseded. They drew no dividing line between moral and ceremonial law, but dismissed the whole law as a thing of the past.

What then! are we at liberty to commit murder and adultery, to steal and covet and worship false gods? Yes, if these things are the law written on our hearts, if these things are enjoined in the Gospel, — if these things are the fulfilling of the law. For, let it be remembered, the old law was superseded, not by a worse, but by a better hope; not because it was too strenuous, but because it was not strenuous enough; not in that it was to be violated, but in that it had been fulfilled. One people among the peoples had been turned from the worship of false gods. Into their hard hearts had been drilled a belief in the existence of one God, his concern in the affairs of men, his sovereignty, his justice, his mercy, his righteousness. They were taught that oppression and unchastity and idolatry were sins and crimes. The Mosaic law drew for the world the outline of a holy life. Then the world was ripe for further knowledge. Christ took the fair sketch and filled it in with tints of heavenly beauty.

The words of the law passed away, that the spirit of the law might have free course. "Thou shalt not kill," said the law. "Whosoever is angry with his brother, without a cause, shall be in danger of the same judgment," said the spirit. "Thou shalt not commit adultery," said the law. "Whosoever looketh on a woman to lust after her hath committed adultery with her already in his heart," said the spirit of the law. The people were astonished to hear such words, and for these eighteen hundred years they have not sufficiently recovered from their astonishment to believe them. To this day, Christian men have the veil upon their hearts, and the Ten Commandments read in the churches every Sabbath day.

It is difficult and it is humiliating to cite proofs of these statements. It is humiliating, that, with the face of Christ shining upon us now these eighteen centuries, we should still be fumbling over the decalogue. It is humiliating, that persons living in this latest age of the Christian era should need just as strong argument, and just as earnest remonstrance, to keep them from turning again to the weak and beggarly elements, whereunto they desire again to be in bondage, as did persons of the first age. It is difficult to cite proof, for the whole New Testament is proof. The going out of the law of Moses, and the coming in of the law of Christ, is the burden of the Gospel. Christ announced it and his Apostles reiterated it. Again and again, with impassioned earnestness, with vehement logic, with figure and illustration, by precept and example, they labored to impress this truth upon their time, for all times. With steadfast hands, they tore away the scaffolding of the law, and displayed to mankind the beautiful edifice, which all the while had been slowly rising behind the once necessary and symmetrical, but now unnecessary, and therefore cumbrous and disfiguring framework. Law was to give place to love.

At the outset of his ministry Christ, knowing what he was to do, forestalled the objections which would be brought against him, and declared that he was not come to destroy the law or the prophets, but to fulfil. " One jot or one tittle shall in no wise pass from the law till all be fulfilled." "The law and the prophets," he said to the Pharisees, "were until John : since that time the kingdom of God is preached." Yet, to guard against misapprehension, he affirmed the next moment that it is easier for heaven and earth to pass than one tittle of the law to fail. How the law was to be fulfilled he explicitly told. When the lawyer asked him which was the great commandment, he replied, " Thou shalt love the Lord thy God with all thy heart, and with all thy soul, and with all thy mind. This is the first and great commandment. And the second is like unto it. Thou shalt love thy neighbor as thyself. *On these two commandments hang all the law and the prophets.*" Paul says that "Christ is the *end of the law* for righteousness to every one that believeth." "He that loveth another hath fulfilled the law. For this, Thou shalt not kill, Thou shalt not steal, Thou shalt not bear false witness, Thou shalt not covet, and if there be any other commandment it is briefly comprehended in this saying, namely, Thou shalt love thy neighbor as thyself. Love worketh no ill to his neighbor: therefore love is the fulfilling of the law." Is it the "ceremonial law" of which Paul speaks? Again he says, illustrating his position from the case of a woman freed from her husband by his death, "Now we are delivered from the law, *that being dead wherein we were held;* that we should serve in newness of spirit, and not in the oldness of the letter. What shall we say then? Is the law sin?" That is, is it sinful? Is it a bad law which must be broken? "God forbid. Nay, I had not known sin but by the law; for I had not known lust except the law had said, Thou shalt not covet." (Is it "the ceremonial" or the "moral" law that says Thou shalt not covet?) No, declares Paul, the law is not sinful, "the law is holy" as far as it goes, but there are certain things which "the law could not do, in that it was weak through the flesh," wherefore God sent his own Son, and the law of the spirit of life in Christ Jesus hath made us forever free from the law of sin and death. "There is verily a disannulling of the commandment going before, for the weakness and unprofitableness thereof. For the law made nothing perfect, but the bringing in of a better hope did." "For the priesthood being changed, there is made of necessity a change also of the law." "If ye be led by the Spirit, ye are not under the law." "The fruit of the Spirit is love, joy, peace, long-suffering, gentleness, goodness, faith, meekness, temperance: against such there is no law." "For I, through the law, am dead to the law, that I might"—not live in sin to my heart's content, but—"that I might live unto God." "Tell me," he cries to the stiff-necked Galatian Jews who found it so hard to give up their traditions and their pride of Abraham,—"tell me, ye that desire to be under the law, do ye not hear the law? For it is written, that Abraham had two sons; the one by a bond-maid, the other by a free woman. .... Which things are an allegory: for these are the two covenants; the one from the Mount Sinai, which gendereth to bondage, which is Agar, ... and answereth to Jerusalem which now is, and is in bondage with her children. But Jerusalem which is above is free, which is the mother of us all. .... So then, brethren, we are not children of the bond-woman, but of the free. Stand fast, therefore, in the liberty wherewith Christ has made us free, and be not entangled again with the yoke of bondage..... For, brethren, ye have been called unto liberty; only use not liberty for an occasion to the flesh, but by love serve one another. For all the law is fulfilled in one word, even in this, Thou shalt love thy neighbor as thyself..... Bear ye one another's burdens, and so fulfil the law of Christ." "If the first covenant had been faultless, then should no place have been sought for the second. For, finding fault with them, he saith, Behold, the days come, saith the Lord, when I will make a new covenant with the house of Israel..... For this is the covenant that I will make..... I will put my laws into their mind, and write them [not on tables of stone, but] in their hearts..... In that he saith, A new covenant, he hath made the first old. Now that which decayeth and waxeth old is ready to vanish away."

Can language be more perspicuous?

But it was exceedingly difficult to convince the Jews that Christ really had broken down the middle wall of partition between Jew and Gentile, and abolished even the law of commandments. Nor need we be surprised that they should look with the utmost reluctance upon the abolition of their law, and with the utmost disfavor upon any which should be brought forward. The law was to the Jews their badge of honor, the token of their place in the vanguard of the world. They charged Stephen with designing to change the customs which Moses delivered them. They accused Paul of teaching the Jews to forsake Moses, and not to walk after the customs. But while Paul was careful to walk orderly and keep the law, not objecting even to vows and purifications, he and the other apostles steadfastly maintained that the Gentiles should be required to observe no such thing. When Peter separated himself from the Gentiles, through fear of the Jews, Paul withstood him to the face because he was to be blamed. "Why compellest thou the Gentiles to live as do the Jews? .... Knowing that a man is not justified by the works of the law, but by the faith of Jesus Christ. .... Wherefore, then, serveth the law? [Of what use is the law?] It was added because of transgressions, *till the end should come to whom the promise was made*. .... Wherefore the law was our schoolmaster to bring us unto Christ, that we might be justified by faith. But after that faith is come, we are no longer under a schoolmaster." When Paul and Barnabas were teaching in Antioch, certain men came down from Judæa and preached to the new converts, 'Except ye be circumcised after the manner of Moses, ye cannot be saved.' After much dissension and disputation, a delegation was sent to Jerusalem where also certain partially converted Pharisees maintained that it was needful to circumcise and to command the Gentiles to keep the law of Moses.

Therefore a council of the apostles and elders was convened to consider the matter. And when there had been much disputing, Peter rose up and said unto them, 'Men and brethren, ye know how that a good while ago God made choice among us, that the Gentiles, by my mouth, should hear the word of the Gospel, and believe. And God, which knoweth the hearts, bare them witness, giving them the Holy Ghost, even as he did unto us: and put no difference between us and them, purifying their hearts by faith. Now, therefore, *why tempt ye God to put a yoke upon the neck of the disciples, which neither our fathers nor we were able to bear?*' Then Paul and Barnabas confirmed Peter's words by relating the wonders God had wrought among the Gentiles. Afterwards James gave his sentence, and the result of council was framed into an encyclical letter: "The apostles, and elders, and brethren send greeting unto the brethren which are of the Gentiles in Antioch and Syria and Cilicia. Forasmuch as we have heard that certain which went out from us have troubled you with words, subverting your souls, saying, Ye must be circumcised and keep the law; to whom we gave no such commandment. .... It seemed good to the Holy Ghost, and to us, to lay upon you no greater burden than these necessary things: That ye abstain from meat offered to idols, and from blood, and from things strangled, and from fornication; from which, if ye keep yourselves, ye shall do well. Fare ye well."

As the greater includes the less, the abrogation of the Mosaic law, is the abrogation of the Sabbatic law so far as the latter depends for its force upon its incorporation with the former. If it were instituted prior to and distinct from the Mosaic law, or if it were exempted from the disannulling of the latter, we may still be under a Sabbath law. We have only to call upon those who maintain the existence of such a law to produce it. Until they do this, we affirm that it cannot be done. To say, with Mr. Gilfillan, that Abraham and Noah could not have been the good men they were without it may answer every purpose in the pulpit, but has no foundation in logic. There is no such law, no semblance of such law, and no reference to such law in the Bible, until the Israelites were assembled in the wilderness of Sin. Then we have a circumstantial account of a mandate issued to them, together with the reasons for such issue, which mandate about a fortnight afterwards was framed into a law and incorporated into a code. The story is simple and natural. The Lord was about to rain bread from heaven, and, for the express purpose " that I may prove them, whether they will walk in my law or no," they were to gather a certain quantity on five days, to double it on the sixth, and to gather none at all on the seventh. The experiment was entirely successful. Some obeyed the precept and some disobeyed. Some gathered too much on the five days, and some attempted to gather on the seventh, exciting the indignant question, " How long refuse ye to keep my commandments and my laws?" The people, childlike and unquestioning, obeyed and disobeyed according to their several dispositions. The rulers, further advanced in mental training, received an explanation from Moses. " To-morrow is the rest of the Holy Sabbath unto the Lord." Soon afterwards it was generalized into a law, " Remember the Sabbath-day to keep it holy." Mr. Gilfillan advances this narrative, to show that there had been a "preceding institution of the Sabbath." We adduce it as the account of the original institution of the Sabbath. Mr. Gilfillan reads it, and infers from it that " if we would not impute to a sacred writer literary inability or intentional deception, we have no alternative but to believe that the Sabbath was instituted at the creation." We read it, and accept neither alternative.

The only text cited in proof of a pre-existent law is Genesis ii. 2, 3, which gives no law to man, and makes no allusion either to law or man. It is the statement of a fact concerning God, which we but faintly comprehend; it states no fact concerning man. God's Sabbath existed then, but He did not then give it to man. What that Sabbath was we do not know. We do not even know what was meant by the term *day*, some supposing it to be the present day of twenty-four hours, and others (begging Mr. Gilfillan's pardon) equally eminent in Christian knowledge, candor, and clear-sightedness supposing it to stretch over vast ages, and to measure in its going the unseen, slow processes of geologic change. And as the work-days of God are to us uncomprehended, and for the present incomprehensible, so must the Sabbath of His solitude be. The loving Creator bends low to our human speech, and we learn what we may of His character and His ways; but with it all, the wisest among us, as well as the little child, can but slightly know the nature of His work, His rest, His blessing. The Bible comes to us out of the great deep of a mysterious past. It leaves us on the shore of a mysterious future; and though its promises, precepts, and examples are so plain that the wayfaring man, though a fool, need not err therein, yet the shadows of its infinite source linger still upon its opening pages, and the glories of the waiting heavens fling a bewildering radiance upon its closing lines.

It is interesting to compare the two versions of the ten commandments given, one in the twentieth chapter of Exodus, the other in the fifth chapter of Deuteronomy. The first gives as a reason of the fourth commandment, " For in six days the Lord made heaven and earth, the sea and all that in them is, and rested the seventh day ; wherefore the Lord blessed the Sabbath-day, and hallowed it." The second version makes no reference to the creation, but says, " And remember that thou wast a servant in the land of Egypt, and that the Lord thy God brought thee out thence through a mighty hand and by a stretched-out arm: therefore the Lord thy God commanded thee to keep the Sabbath-day."

Here are two entirely distinct reasons given for the same command. It may be said that the one does not exclude the other; that both may have been given on the mountain, though only one is mentioned at a time; but Moses, after reciting the commandments to the people according to the second version, immediately adds, " These words the Lord spake unto all your assembly in the mount, out of the midst of the fire, of the cloud, and of the thick darkness, with a great voice: *and he added no more:* and he wrote them in two tables of stone, and delivered them unto me."

The preface to the two versions is identical. " I am the Lord thy God which have brought thee out of the land of Egypt, out of the house of bondage." The captivity in Egypt was the great calamity of the Hebrews: the deliverance from that captivity the great event in their history. One day in seven consecrated to rest would be an appropriate memento of their redemption from the unceasing toil of slavery. Why it is, that, in spite of the preponderance of evidence in favor of the second version, we have almost universally discarded it and adopted the first, it is difficult to conjecture, unless it be that even the most thoughtless among us knows at once that he never was a servant in Egypt, and therefore the absurdity of applying the commandment to an American, or to any one but a Jew, becomes at once palpable.

We are dealing with facts, not inferences nor opinions. It is a fact that we have in the Bible an account of a Sabbath-day set apart in the wilderness of Sin, and a Sabbath law promulgated from Sinai, and we have no account of either before this time. This is enough. We are not concerned with what may have happened, but only with what Moses has recorded as having actually happened. But Nehemiah gives stronger proof than this negative testimony. When the children of Israel kept their solemn fast, the Levites stood upon the stairs and publicly recounted the goodness of God to them : " Thou camest down also upon Mount Sinai, and spakest with them from heaven, and gavest them right judgments, and true laws, good statutes and commandments ; and *madest known unto them thy holy Sabbath.*" If the Sabbath had been a world-old institution, could God have made it known to them on Sinai ? But Mr. Gilfillan says : " To insist that such language establishes the origination of the Sabbath at the time to which it refers requires us no less to believe, that all the other statutes mentioned in connection with that institution were then also enacted. According to this doctrine, sacrifices, the decalogue, and circumcision must have then in the first instance been appointed. .... Circumcision, like the Sabbath, is mentioned as given at the commencement of the Levitical dispensation: 'Moses *gave* unto you circumcision; not because it is of Moses, but of the fathers.'" The fact that these glaring fallacies have escaped the eyes of the Sabbath Committee must be our sole excuse for pointing them out. Without such positive proof we should assume that no living man, save Mr. Gilfillan, could fail to see that no statute is mentioned in connection with the Sabbath. The Sabbath is singled out from all, and it alone is said to have been *made known* upon Mount Sinai. A law may be commanded again and again, a judgment may be many times repeated; but an institution with which we have been familiar from our infancy cannot rightly be said to be made known to us in our manhood. "Circumcision, like the Sabbath, is mentioned as given," says Mr. Gilfillan. "Circumcision, unlike the Sabbath," he should have said. This is a sufficient answer. It may not be amiss, however, to show Mr. Gilfillan and his coadjutors that it does not at all follow, because good statutes and commandments were given for the first time from Mount Sinai, that none were ever given before. He misuses a particular for a universal. "Thou gavest them (some) right judgments and true laws," said the Levites. Therefore, "Thou gavest them (all) right judgments and true laws," says Mr. Gilfillan. Although circumcision and sacrifices had been long employed, Mr. Gilfillan will hardly deny that many, perhaps the great bulk of precepts, given upon Mount Sinai, were given for the first time ; so that even on that ground the Sabbath may have been among them, while from the popular use of " make known," it must have been. That the act of giving is generally limited to the time mentioned in connection with it is evident from the very text instanced to prove the contrary. " Moses gave unto you circumcision," said Christ, apparently using the word *Moses* in a general sense for the law, but seeing the possibility of misapprehension, he immediately corrects himself, " not because it is of Moses, but of the fathers." Without that correction he might be supposed to say that circumcision was of Moses. As the Sabbath is mentioned without any such qualifying clause, we do suppose that it was of Moses and not of the fathers.

Finding, then, that the New Testament abrogates the whole code of laws in which alone any Sabbath law is recorded, we infer that the Sabbath law is abrogated. Confirmation of this is furnished, if confirmation be needed, by the unbroken silence of the New Testament regarding Sabbathbreaking. Throughout the Old Testament, though its precepts grow less and less positive and more and more spiritual, approaching the time of Christ, there are ever-recurring warnings, promises, and exhortations concerning the Sabbath. In the New Testament it is enjoined upon neither Jew nor Gentile. Every reference made to the Sabbath is made in rebuke of those who demand its observance or complain of its violation. Every allusion either lessens its stringency or wholly destroys its force. Nor are we left to mere inference or negative testimony. Christ issued commands which could not be obeyed without disregarding not merely Pharisaic traditions, but Mosaic laws, regarding the Sabbath. He commanded the impotent man on the Sabbath-day to take up his bed and walk; and the Jews had the law on their side when they objected, "It is not lawful for thee to carry thy bed," since the command, "Thou shalt not do any work," had been explained by God's own words through Jeremiah, "Take heed to yourselves, and bear no burden on the Sabbath-day." Paul expressly transfers the whole matter out of the sphere of Divine command into the sphere of private judgment. "Who art thou that judgest another man's servant? To his own master he standeth or falleth. One man esteemeth one day above another; another esteemeth every day alike. Let every man be fully persuaded in his own mind. He that regardeth the day, regardeth it unto the Lord, and he that regardeth not the day, unto the Lord he doth not regard it." Christ, he said, hath blotted out "the handwriting of ordinances that was against us, which was contrary to us, and took it out of the way, nailing it to his cross. . . . . Let no man therefore judge you in meat, or in drink, or in respect of an holy-day, or of the new moon, or of the Sabbath-days, which are a shadow of things to come; but the body is of Christ."

The Christian world has universally recognized the abrogation of the Sabbath. Nowhere does it confer upon the seventh day any distinction above the other days. In this it is right.

But it has widely and strenuously sought to transfer to the first day of the week the duties and obligations of the seventh day; to extend to all Christians forever what was allotted only to the Jews for a limited period. It is not content to rest on the proper ground of human judgment, but with presumptuous hand it brings forward a "Thus saith the Lord." Nay, it does worse than this. It not only transfers the commandment, but it tampers with it. The law says, "Thou shalt not do any work, thou, nor thy son, nor thy daughter, thy man-servant, nor thy maid-servant, nor thy cattle." Its modern substitute says, "Thou mayst do some work, in fact a good deal, especially thy maid-servant. Thy cattle may work enough to carry thee to church, either to preach or to hear a sermon, though thou art quite able to walk, or couldst have made the journey the evening before. But thou shalt in no wise wander in the fields, or drive across the country unless thou have a meeting-house in view. And for the most part thou shalt go to church all day, and devote what time is left to Sunday school and evening meeting."

So the Christian world picks to pieces the Fourth Commandment, separates such part as it is convenient to observe from the parts it is convenient to disregard, adds thereto whatever seems good in its eyes, and sets up this nondescript animal with a loud cry, "These be thy gods, O Israel!"

In this it is wrong, — teaching for doctrine the commandments of men. But though the men who issue these commandments be numerous, learned, and powerful, we can only say, "When for the time ye ought to be teachers, ye have need that one teach you again, which be the first principles of the oracles of God!" Yea, though an angel from heaven preach any other gospel than that which Christ and the Apostles preached, let him be accursed. We call no man master, for Christ is our Master. Let those then who would graft the Jewish Sabbath upon our Christian system produce their Divine authority for doing so. We have chapter and verse for the enforcement of the Sabbath upon the Hebrews. We have chapter and verse for the abrogation of the Sabbath. Let us have chapter and verse for the establishment of the Christian Sabbath. Until this is done, we confidently affirm that it cannot be done.

The few instances, in the New Testament, in which the first day of the week is mentioned, make against, rather than for, its Sabbatic claim. When the Sabbath-day was in force, it was called always the Sabbath-day, not the Seventh day. If the first day were meant to be the heir of all the glories, the duties, and the mementos of the seventh, would it not also have inherited the name? Is it probable that so great a change would have been made, with no change of name or addition of title?

Shall we then close our churches, open our workshops, and reduce our Sunday to the level of Monday? Most assuredly not.

First, though the laws made for Hebrews alone are not binding on Americans, yet these things are written for our admonition. The more we learn of God and of His world the more surely we see that His commands are not mere arbitrary mandates, but wise provisions for human needs. Many directions, whose bearings are hidden from the common sight, science and experience recognize as wise social or sanitary regulations. When, therefore, God commanded the Jews to refrain from labor one day in seven, we do not regard it as an indifferent matter. We do not say it might as well have been one day in three, or one day in eight, had God so chosen, nor do we think that God considered a day of idleness and uselessness the best way of commemorating his creative sovereignty. We regard it rather as a significant hint, that the human being is so organized as to need, besides his regularly recurring sleep, one seventh part of time for rest. We consider the time thus devoted to rest as not thrown away, but most wisely employed. This view is confirmed by our own personal experience and observation, and by those of many wise and good men. We believe the time will come when it will be universally adopted, — when the world will see that its work is sooner and better done by six days of labor and one of rest, than by unintermitting toil. This truth, however, if it be a truth, belongs to the domain of science. It is only hinted at, not laid down, in revelation. On strictly reasonable grounds, we infer it to be the duty of every man, a duty founded in his nature and recognized by God, to rest from labor one seventh part of the time, and so to arrange his affairs that those dependent upon or ministering to him shall be able to command an equal rest. And as this can be most effectually done when all act in harmony, and as the first day of the week has been for ages, and is now most nearly redeemed from labor and consecrated to rest, it is proper to adopt this as the rest-day, thus at once consulting one's own convenience and paying one's deference to the world's wisdom. If this rest is allowed to be for the general good, it is a fit subject of legislation, to the extent of protecting men in their right of rest. And though we may not and do not, by legislation, force upon any man any religious observance of the day, we may by legislation prevent him from hindering others in their religious observances.

But this, though a just and healthy view as far as it goes, is a low and material one. Man's highest rest is not in inactivity. The world is weary through sin, and her children, over-worked, sometimes need too much on Sunday the mere rest of inactivity. Many more need the day for closer and more tender intercourse with wife and child than the working-days can give. They need it for calmness and reflection, for friendly interchange of thought and feeling, for the upspringing of love, that, repressed too much, decays; for a fuller development of all the gentleness and amenities of life, for a little curve and verdure to soften the harshness of a too severe destiny. But especially and universally we need the opportunity of the day for direct and avowed social worship. Honest work is as good in its way as worship, but it is not worship. Love works mightily for its object, but none the less it craves direct expression. Knightly feats will never supersede the hunger for sweet phrase. Words alone are nothing, but works alone can never give heart's-ease. There is not one stone upon another of the Temple wherein the Most High once delighted to dwell; nevertheless, the Apostle exhorted his converts not to forsake the assembling of themselves together. There is neither priest nor sacrifice; but as children of a common family, we need to go up with the multitude and pay our offerings of broken, and contrite, and therefore happy hearts. We need to recognize the kinship of man, and kindle in our souls the fire of sympathy that comes only from contact. Rich and poor, we should meet together in the great congregations, and, forgetting all minor distinctions, bow our knees unto the Father of our Lord Jesus Christ, of whom the whole family in heaven and earth is named.

We are not bound to this weekly worship because the Apostles commanded it to their congregations, nor because the disciples were wont to assemble on the first day of the week, though these are considerations which should influence us; but because our inmost natures demand it. The Apostles directed weekly contributions and a weekly participation in the Lord's Supper, and sanctioned, at least, a social life which held all things common; none of which things we do. But because our hearts burn within us to preach righteousness in the great congregation, to declare the faithfulness and salvation of God, to celebrate his lovingkindness and his truth, we go up to the house of God, with the voice of joy and praise, with a multitude that keep holy-day.

But more than this: If the Sabbath of the Jews

was instituted not only for the purpose of giving them needed rest, but of commemorating the creation, how much greater a cause have we to commemorate! Redemption outshines creation. God spake, and the world was made; He died before it could be redeemed. Jesus Christ was conceived of the Holy Ghost, born of the Virgin Mary, suffered under Pontius Pilate, was crucified, dead, and buried. The third day, as it began to dawn toward the first day of the week, he came up from the grave, scattered the darkness and despair, and for all and for ever brought life and immortality to light. Did God sanctify the seventh day because that in it he rested from all the work which he created and made? Let us, for love, not duty, sanctify this infinitely more blessed day, this first day of the week, on which was sealed the truth of our redemption from death and sin. So long as the stable earth blossoms under the tread of human feet, let human hearts celebrate this glorious day which saw the Lord arise. It is no Sabbath of restriction and penalty, but the Redeemer's gift, sacred and over-full with joy of birthday and thanksgiving. The bud of every anniversary flowers in the bright hope of this weekly festival. It is a day for congratulation and jubilee, for songs of praise and adoration,—a day of triumph and of victory. Day of days, day of days, that saw the Lord arise! Never enough to be exulted over and rejoiced in. Let thy mountains and hills break forth into singing, O Earth, that thrilled once to the tread of the Redeemer's feet, and let all the trees of the field clap their hands. Rejoice, O man, forever exalted in lending thy form to the Son of God, rejoice on this His resurrection-morn. Go up into His courts with psalms and hymns and spiritual songs. Let the whole earth be garlanded with gladness and the breath of her life ascend, a sweet incense to the Holy One, the Blessed, the Beloved, our Friend, our Redeemer.

Is this a day to wrangle about? Is this a day to be prescribed with *ought*, and *must*, and *shall?* Strange we do not see that such support is fatal! Men may be exhorted to rest on that day, as they may be exhorted to cleanliness and prudence; but its worth as a day of sacredness and worship is in its spontaneity. Neither Christ nor his Apostles ever commanded to keep the Sabbath-day. They strove to rescue the life from the dominion of sin, to lift it into the light; and when the heart is right, when the face is turned toward God, and the mind is fixed on God, and love is the universal law, will there be any trouble about Sunday?

Is it said that we have not yet arrived at that point? that men are not yet spiritual enough to dispense with external restrictions? Perhaps so; but the Maker of men would be likely to know when they are ready to ascend from one plane to another, and if it seemed to him that, after four thousand years of precept and practice, they had become sufficiently rooted and grounded in the ideas of Divine sovereignty and human duty, of obedience, chastity, justice, and what may be called the outside virtues, to be ready to be rooted and grounded in love, is it worth while for us to say, "Not so, Lord"? There is so much violence in the earth, that we can hardly help questioning, sometimes, whether it would not have been wiser in God to have delayed his work of redemption, to have kept us under the stress of external law a few centuries longer, till the fierceness of our manners should become a little more softened, and our hard hearts mellowed to receive the truth. But if God does not know times and seasons, no one does; and the question is, not what it would have been well for him to do, but what he did do. If he saw fit to abolish the law of ordinances, and trust to the law of love, the part of faith and modesty is to do the best we can without the one, not to attempt to reinstate it, and thus insult the other. It is presumption, not humility, it is rebellion, not loyalty, that would set up what God has put down.

But, it is asked, if Sunday rest is granted to be for man's physical good, and if Sunday worship is allowed to be not only a source of spiritual benefit, but the natural outgrowth of a high spiritual condition, why attempt to pull down the strongest props of the Sabbath? If the noblest life will give just such a Sabbath as the Sabbath preachers desire, why not have the Sabbath preached? If the prevalent belief be not strictly scriptural, yet if it tends to useful ends, why disturb it? We answer, Because truth is truth, — too sacred and steadfast a thing to be warped to any man's uses; because the wrath of God is revealed from heaven against all ungodliness and unrighteousness of men, who hold the truth in unrighteousness; because to fortify the truth by a "thus saith the Lord," when the Lord has not spoken, is to change the truth of God into a lie. So doing we take a false position, and foolish as false. Our strength is made weakness, and our weakness wickedness. Men have an instinct of the falsehood, and, not discerning the truth, cast away both together and profane their own souls. Every sermon that is preached, and every tract that is issued directly inculcating as a Bible law the observance of the Sabbath-day, is not only useless, but mischievous. It calls attention away from sin, which God hates, to a rite which He has discarded. Instead of exhorting people to keep the Sabbath-day holy, we should exhort them to keep their own hearts holy. Sabbath-keeping as Sabbath-keeping is dangerous. It tends to formalism, not to Christianity. What saith the Apostle Paul? It is the one exception to the annulling referred to before. "The law is not made for a righteous man, but for the lawless and disobedient, for the ungodly and for sinners, for unholy and profane, for murderers of fathers and murderers of mothers, for man-slayers." Remember this, you who enforce the law. When you class yourselves with man-slayers and murderers, when you betake yourself to the law, you count the blood of the covenant an unholy thing, and crucify the Son of God afresh. Those who will not give themselves up to the Gospel are indeed under the law, but for condemnation, not for salvation. For what the law could not do before Christ came, it can never do. To adopt Judaism is to reject Christ. And what is it to reject Christ?

A Sabbath imposed from without is an easier thing to preach and to practice than a Sabbath springing from the soul, its ornament and delight. The one is obvious, exact, tangible. It gathers religious duty into a visible shape and a limited time, and does not interfere with the other six days. It lies on the surface of life, and does not meddle with its depths. It gives rise to no doubts, and demands no nice distinctions. The morning and the evening are the first day, and there is an end of the matter.

But to keep the soul's Sabbath is a work of quite another quality. It is indefinite, exacting, unending. It goes down into the deep places, and concerns the thoughts and intents of the heart. It is not satisfied with one day's prayer and praise, but it lays hold on every day, and considers nothing human foreign to itself. Its Divine radiance shines down through all the week, and every day is flooded with the heavenly light. Preach the gospel of pure hearts, not of new moons and Sabbath-days. Preach the gospel of a holy life, and let every man judge for himself what best helps him to lead a holy life. Cease the attempt to establish what God has overthrown, and show the people that without faith it is impossible to please Him. Show them that it is lying lips, impure thoughts, dishonest gains, unpaid debts, unkind words, materialism, and sensuality, and selfishness, that are an abomination to the Lord, not Sunday walks. Instead of imposing Sabbath-keeping upon the ungodly, show the ungodly that no Sabbath is possible to them. There is no such thing as keeping the Sabbath unless the heart keeps it; and when the heart keeps holy-day all days are holy.

I. Well?

H. Well it is then.

I. Thank you. Do you think it sounds lordly enough?

H. Lordly?

I. Why yes. It must have a certain magisterial weight to secure confidence, — a sort of high-and-mighty-ness. I should not want it to sound like me.

H. Like whom, then?

I. O, no one in particular. Like ministers. Like theological authorities. Has it in the least the air of Professor Park or Scott's Bible? Do you suppose the world can be —

H. Wheedled.

I. Well, wheedled, into thinking it came from Andover or Princeton, if it should be printed in any of the reviews? I have made a most unsparing use of " we."

H. After mature reflection, with a glass of high magnifying power, an experienced and skilful student of style might perhaps detect certain minute points or pellicles which would lead him to suspect that Professor Park did not write it. But it is not the fault of the " we." That is a great stroke. It comes in now and then with immense force. I don't hesitate to say you have added a hundred per cent to your substance of doctrine by that shrewd little arrangement.

I. And it did not seem so very long did it, when you had once fairly grappled with it?

H. Not so long as if there had been a dozen pages more. But have you not rather laid yourself open to the charge of slighting the Old Testament? I suppose you do not mean to discourage an acquaintance with it.

I. Surely not. It is the best book we have next to the New Testament, — profitable for doctrine, for reproof, for correction, for instruction in righteousness.

Why, it is just like the Mammoths and the Plesiosaurians and the Megatheriums. We study them with intense interest. The knowledge enlarges our minds: we learn something of the laws of life, and are more deeply impressed with the power and wisdom and goodness of God. But when we wish to find how to manage our sheep and cows we go to the Massachusetts Ploughman and the New England Farmer. It is harnessing the mastodons to our hay-carts that makes the trouble. It was yoking the Plesiosaurians to our ploughs that fastened American Slavery upon Moses. The Christian conscience of the country would not suffer it to remain there; but it did so at the expense of its logic. So far as a precept goes, I am just as much commanded to pin my servant's ear to the door with an awl as I am to keep the Sabbath-day. Rightly understood, the rules which God gave regarding Hebrew slavery show His goodness just as clearly as the Fourth Commandment. Both were given in love and care for human welfare, not with a selfish regard for his own will and pleasure, or with an unjust disregard of the rights or pleasure of any. Wrongly understood, both may be wrested over to the side of injustice.

H. Yes, and we are too apt to look upon the Jewish Sabbath as something hard, rigid, and unpleasant, whereas it was a mark of thoughtful tenderness on God's part. He imposed no onerous duty. The sole thing he insisted on was rest for man and beast. Mindful too of the lowly, he provides " that thy man-servant and thy maid-servant may rest as well as thou." In fact, I suspect the Jewish Sabbath was much more a holiday than is generally supposed.

I. It turns on what was the meaning to the Jews of the word "holy."

H. They were forbidden to work, but I do not find anywhere that they were forbidden to play upon the holy day. Nehemiah helps us to an understanding of the word. When he was reconstructing Israel he read the law to the people —

I. Yes, and that was not all; for he read it distinctly, he takes care to tell us, and gave the sense, and caused them to understand the reading. That is something worth while.

H. And then he told them, " This day is holy unto the Lord your God." How were they to spend a holy day ? " Go your way, eat the fat, and drink the sweet, and send portions unto them for whom nothing is prepared : *for this day is holy unto our Lord :* neither be ye sorry ; for the joy of the Lord is your strength."

I. Why, it was a sort of Thanksgiving Day.

H. The people made it so, certainly, for they all "went their way to eat, and to drink, and to send portions, and *to make great mirth*, because they had understood the words that were declared unto them."

I. There! now you see what comes of having people understand the Bible instead of merely reading it. If we understood what we read, we should be as mirthful as they. But how Jonathan Edwards would have quarrelled with Nehemiah for such monstrous laxity. Do you remember one of his seven hundred or so good resolutions was, "Never to utter anything that is sportive, or matter of laughter, on the Lord's Day"?

H. I dare say Edwards and Nehemiah have talked the matter over since and come to a better understanding. But it is significant that all the examples of Sabbath-breaking in the Bible — at least I remember no others — are of work done on the Sabbath. There is no example of its violation by any kind of amusement.

I. There is not much in the Bible about playing, any way.

H. No. There is a passage in Jeremiah where the Lord says, "but hallow the Sabbath-day, to do no work therein"; as if the abstaining from work was hallowing it.

I. I think we fall into the same mistake about the Puritan Sunday that we do about the Jewish Sabbath. I do not believe it was nearly as tiresome, nor the Puritans themselves nearly as morose, as they are often supposed to be. I have seen a good deal of that part of it that has descended to us, and I never found it tiresome. It has only pleasant associations for me.

H. Doubtless its character would depend a good deal on individuals. It would bear harder on some than on others, and would be a severer thing in some families than in others.

I notice you have spoken as if the New Testament were not always binding on us.

I. Its principles are always binding on us, but it belongs to ourselves to adjust our practice to those principles. We all do this. It is only when we say we do it that objections are raised. Many commands of Christ Christians accept, others they reject, and others they profess to obey only in part. They hold as a reserved right the application of his principles. Christ bade, "Love thy neighbor as thyself." We obey him after a fashion. He bade also, "Swear not at all," which we heed not at all. He says again, "Provide neither scrip for your journey, neither two coats, neither shoes." We do or do not, according to our convenience. All I say is, if one man uses his judgment to disregard one precept, he has no right to forbid another man to use his judgment in disregarding another. Still less has he a right to object to our saying that we ought to use our judgment in determining what part of Christ's teachings were meant for us. What is true of Christ's teachings is, of course, true of his Apostles' teachings. They applied the Gospel to the society of Rome and Corinth and Galatia under the emperors. We have to apply it to America under presidents. To know what they, divinely inspired, did is a great help in deciding what we ought to do, but it does not at all dispense with our own judgment. And if Saint Paul were now living, no doubt he would be the very first to condemn this blind adherence to the letter of his epistles, and the blind violation of their spirit, which has wrought so much disaster to the best interests of man. But as with the teachings of Christ so with those of the Apostles and of other sacred writers, however strenuously we insist on adherence to the letter, in our practice we consult only tradition, our own will, or prejudice, or judgment. Certain passages we take literally, and certain others figuratively or spiritually, with no guide but our own judgment, and often not even that; we simply go with our denomination. Certain passages we take with qualifications and certain others without. But if a person, in the use of his judgment or following his denomination, makes a different classification from ours, him we oppose, and it shall go hard but we call names, — "rationalist" or "neologist."

H. Yes. I remember a good illustration. One of our ablest Orthodox writers, a few days ago, in reviewing Dr. Bushnell's last book, charges that his reduction of the Biblical doctrine of the Devil to a mythical personification of evil, and of the account of the fall to a poetic representation, admits a principle of interpretation fatal alike to the historical and the moral weight of the Scriptures. He quite overlooks the fact that Dr. Bushnell does not admit the destroying monster. It was there before. In fact, the Devil gets into the garden only by a figure. In the original narrative he is not once mentioned. It is a serpent, and nothing else; a beast of the field. If we can figure the serpent into the Devil, why can we not figure the Devil into evil? There is not nearly so broad a gulf between the last two as between the first two.

I. You know Saint John speaks of " that old serpent, called the Devil."

H. I don't know that he means this old serpent, though he probably does, but he calls him also the great dragon, and the whole is the description of a great wonder that appeared in heaven. It is all a figure or vision, and seems rather to indicate that the account in Genesis may also be an allegory. Certainly the flaming sword of the first book of the Bible sounds as mythic as the scarlet woman of the last; and surely, too, the farther back we go into the night of time, the more we look for allegory. It is no more literal to say " the serpent said unto the woman" than " this is my body," and it is just as natural for human flesh to be changed into bread as for a snake to use human speech. It is a merely arbitrary rule that commands a mythical interpretation in one place and forbids it in another, on the ground of the fatality of mythical interpretation.

But come, here is another point. How do you

account for the fact, that so many criminals trace back the beginnings of their evil course to Sabbath-breaking?

I. I should think I was a candidate for ordination, and you the Examining Council.

H. Heaven forbid!

I. Why should Heaven forbid?

H. O, never mind! Go on with your Sabbath-breaking. Don't get too many irons in the fire.

I. Don't you believe in Councils?

H. In their existence, yes. If there is no Sabbath, why is its violation injurious, *à la Milesian?*

I. Don't you believe in their expediency?

H. Partially. Are the criminals then self-deceived?

I. Which part of them do you believe in?

H. Of the criminals? In the whole man, mind, body, and estate.

I. And which part of the Councils?

H. (With a groan.) I believe in the ministers coming together and interchanging friendly greeting, and eating a good dinner if it is offered them, and ordaining their man —

I. Thou —

H. Don't interrupt. If you will —

I. If I cannot interrupt I will not listen at all.

H. What were you about to remark?

I. I was about to remark, and will now remark, that in thy injunction anent the good dinner thou savorest not the things that be of God, but those that be of men. We Congregationalists pride ourselves in following hard after the Apostles in our church organization and administration, but it seems to me the modern ordination dinner is anything but Apostolic. The ordinations of the New Testament were with fasting as well as praying and laying on of hands.

H. I don't suppose they were all day about it; but that is a point you must settle with the ministers, while I get on to the negative side, and do not approve of their putting the candidate through a course of catechism preliminary to his ordination.

I. But they must find out what a man believes. They could not give him their sanction without knowing something about him.

H. He can write on a sheet of paper a better account of himself than three hours of clerical questioning will elicit from him. Or a statement of belief might be prepared for such occasions, embracing those points whereon it is considered requisite that Orthodox clergymen should agree. If he can sign it, they will ordain him at once; if he cannot, he will know it beforehand, and not apply for ordination. Or his Seminary diploma may be taken as evidence. A vast amount of time would be saved, and not a little rambling talk that amounts to nothing, and does not tend to increase respect for council or candidate in the minds of intelligent persons. At the councils which I have attended both questions and answers have been often unsatisfactory. The members of the council walk in a vain show. There is little real examination. Objections are put and answered, investigations supposed to be made into creeds; if the candidate, loses himself in the maze now and then, the good-natured questioner gives him a leading question and brings him out tenderly. But if you are going to lead him out, why put him in? The trial is supposed to be in seeing whether he can get out of himself. Not unfrequently questions are of such a nature that they might puzzle a wiser and older brain than any divinity student can be expected to have. As to the objections, there is little learned by the answering of infidel objections put by believers, or Universalist objections put by Orthodox. They are not the things he will be likely to meet in the world, nor will any such contests strengthen him for real encounters. As a general thing, there is no faith to be put in one man's representation of another man's belief. It is the easiest thing in the world to overthrow the argument of your foe when it is presented by your friend, to win battles in your chimney-corner. If you really wish to see what a man can do in the way of polemics, bring up your Universalists and your Unitarians and your Roman Catholics in the flesh and set them on him.

I. Of course a young man fresh from school could not stand such an onslaught as that, however able he is or may become. Besides, it is not practicable. It would be just an interminable wrangle.

H. I do not suppose the young man could stand the onslaught. But if he cannot do it, it is mischievous to make him believe that he has done it. Let us have a fair fight or peace, but no sham fight. The times are too warlike for such flummery. If there is to be a public examination of the candidate, it should be such as we would not be ashamed of before the most bitter opponent of revealed religion or of our denomination. If examinations must continue as they are, they should be held with closed doors. Every person who is accustomed to use his own mind or his eyes and ears, instead of other people's, should be rigorously excluded. If the powers that be ordained of councils are to hold sway over us, they must not admit us behind the curtain too freely. What is that sticking out from under your hat?

I. Nothing. (Moving the hat a little farther along on the grass.)

H. I am glad to hear it. I thought it looked like a manuscript.

I. O no. It is only an ox-eye daisy.

H. I could swear it had black stamens.

I. Not at all. It was the reflection of your eyes.

H. That is a comforting assurance. I only hope you will stand by it. Am I told that mine are ox-eyes?

I. If they were they would be a thing of beauty as well as what they already are to me, a joy forever. You know the venerable ox-eyed Juno. By the way, Derby's Homer puts it "stag-eyed," which is not half so nice, somehow.

H. Derby's Homer is Homer with the poetry left out. Is there anything else before this council? If not, we had better adjourn before you bring out your axe.

I. What axe?

H. The axe you have to grind to pay for all your blandishments.

I. Why yes, don't think of breaking up yet! It is my turn now. I have not answered your question about the Sabbath-breakers.

H. Fire away then.

I. The gentleman wishes to know why, if there be no such thing as Sabbath-breaking, so many criminals consider Sabbath-breaking their first step towards ruin. Permit me to say, with all respect to the honorable gentleman, that any one, who had as much knowledge of the laws of the human mind as might be looked for in the brains of a mouse which had nibbled three nights at a dictionary, would not need to ask such a question. If you train a child to believe that the Divine word commands him to wear black shoe-strings, and that the Divine displeasure, and all sorts of moral and worldly evil, will follow the adoption of red; if you drill it into him, from his childhood to his youth, support your doctrine by conclusive prooftexts, such as "Look not upon the wine when it is red," "I am black but comely," "Wherefore art thou red in thine apparel?" you may expect to hear him, as he is about to expire on the gallows, trace back his career of crime, step by step, to the fatal day when, allured by fashion and evil companions, he cast aside the moral shoe-strings in which he had been reared, and indulged first for an hour secretly, then for a day, and then openly and unblushingly, month after month, in the abomination of red cord and tassels. And the one case will be just as conclusive as the other. Shame and blame on you who have hedged him around with barriers which God never set.

H. I trust that is a rhetorical, not a logical "you."

I. It is a sort of general apostrophe to the enemy. But look at the Quakers.

H. Friends you mean. "Quakers" is a nickname, and uncourteous.

I. The King of the Quakers told me, he would just as soon be called a Quaker as a Friend. Puritan is a nickname, and we glory in it. Methodist is a nickname. Christian is most likely a nickname. Quaker I like best, therefore, as I was saying, look at the Quakers. They hold all days in equal honor. Is it a cause of immorality? Do they fill the jails and build the gallows? Look at the Germans.

H. Most people would advise you to look the other way.

I. There is no need. Germany is not indeed an example of a warm-hearted Christian nation. But not only is there an adequate cause for her scepticism and indifference, entirely apart from her opinions concerning Sunday, but her most active and spiritual Christians share these opinions, showing that it is not her Sunday views which produce the deadening effects. I have never heard, that those who are must desirous of a reformation wish to introduce the English Sabbath into the Fatherland.

H. I was talking with Agincourt the other day. He was somewhat stirred by the Sunday habits of the Germans whom he saw in California. But he was compelled to admit that they were honest, sober, and as I inferred generally well-behaved.

I. Yes, and do you not remember Charles Loring Brace, in " Home-Life in Germany," says the appearance of Hamburg at night is a wonderful contrast to the hideous rioting and drunkenness of Glasgow and Edinburgh. And how beautiful is the family life that he saw, — the mutual forbearance of all, — the simple, cordial ways, the free respect for the old father, the care for the amusements and plays, the sunny, confiding life through the whole family. And how polite are all classes, and how capable of enjoyment. O, we Pharisees plume ourselves on our righteousness, but in some of the best lessons of life we might go to school to these Germans.

H. About the best thing which I remember in that book was what one of their clergymen, I think it was, told Mr. Brace; that, as one good result of German indifference, there was no resting in forms as in England. *There were plenty of Sadducees in Protestant Germany, but very few Pharisees.* Mr. Brace himself could see that Rationalism had done away to a great extent with intellectual narrowness in theology. No one dared to come out with a crude opinion. He knew if it could not stand the boldest attacks, it must go down, whatever of authority was behind it. The consequence was, real liberality combined with real piety, breadth of view as well as depth of feeling.

I. You see, one of our Pharisaisms is to call every way of celebrating Sunday except our own immoral. Then of course, it is easy enough to convict a whole nation of immorality or even a whole continent. But there are plenty of sins to ravage on the soul, without setting up some of our own invention. When I see and hear of the boating and driving, and what is called the Sabbath-breaking, it gives me pain, for I feel sure that it is done against conscience, and will inflict harm upon the persons who indulge in it. But if I could know that a young man was a Christian, a lover and follower of Christ, I should not feel any more disturbed to know that he was taking a drive on a Sunday evening, than that he was eating his breakfast Sunday morning. Only give Christ the first place in the heart, not by word or profession, but in fact, and then let every man do what he is fully persuaded in his own mind will most conduce to the well-being of himself and of society. The true social rule is, to do nothing which will tend to deprive other people of their rest-day, by making them work, or deprive them of their worship-day, by disturbing them with noise. On this ground I should object to all public concerts, to the opening of reading-rooms and museums, to elaborate Sunday dinners, and especially dinner-parties, to Sunday newspapers, and horse-cars or steam-cars —

H. To churches and Sunday schools.

I. What?

H. You cannot have church-services and Sunday schools without a good deal of work from minister, choir, sexton, teachers.

I. There does seem to be a little hitch here; but the churches must be open, logic or no logic. If I had thought of it myself, I could have managed it, I dare say, but I never can think when anything is sprung upon me. Come now, help me out of this, you ordaining Council, you.

H. You have only to bring in another principle,

which is constantly at work, that of making a small outlay for a large income; of using the inconvenience of the few for the convenience of the many. The closest adherent of the Jewish Sabbath admits this. He finds no fault with his minister for working harder on that day than on any other of the seven. He considers that the good accruing to the congregation balances the evil accruing to the minister.

I. But the minister ought to take another day for his rest-day.

H. Certainly. Many of them do. So it should be with all. If the opening of a reading-room is discovered to be serviceable to the morality, and for general benefit of a community, some arrangement should be made to give the person who is employed in it on that day opportunity to take another day for rest. If the running of the horse-cars on Sunday is decided to be of more good to the community than of harm to the company, the harm can be reduced to its minimum by employing extra hands for the extra day, or by having the different drivers take turns in Sunday labor.

I. Have you seen that there is a good deal of excitement in Philadelphia about running the horse-cars on Sunday?

H. I have seen that some of the clergymen and other citizens have taken very active measures against it, in the way I believe of petition and public meetings for protest. I have also seen something else going on in Philadelphia. There were statements in the Atlantic Monthly months ago, some of which were afterwards copied into the Boston Congregationalist. I believe I have the slip in my pocket now if I have not lost it. Yes, here it is. Now listen to this: "One widow taking out shirts at the arsenal, earned two dollars and forty cents in two weeks, but was denied permission to take them in when done, though urgently needing her pay, being told that she would be making too much money. . . . . A third, whose husband was then in the army, found the price of infantry pantaloons reduced from forty-two to twenty-seven cents, — reduced by the government itself, — but she made eight pair a week, took care of five children, and was always on the verge of starvation. She declared that, if it were not for her children, she would gladly lie down and die. A fourth worked for contractors on overalls, at five cents a pair! Having the aid of a sewing-machine, she made six pair daily, but was the object of insult and abuse from her employer. . . . . An aged woman worked on tents, making in each tent forty-six button-holes, sewing on forty-six buttons, then buttoning them together, then making twenty eyelet holes, — all for sixteen cents. After working the whole day without tasting food, she took in her work just five minutes after the hour for receiving and paying for the week's labor. . . . . She asked them to pay her for what she had just delivered, but was refused. She told them she was without a cent, and that if forced to wait till another pay-day, she must starve. The reply was, 'Starve and be d—d! That is none of my business. We have our rules, and shall not break them for any —.' A tailor gave to another sewing-woman a lot of pantaloons to make up. The cloth being rotten, the stitches of one pair tore out, but by exercising great care she succeeded in getting the others made up. When she took them in, he accused her of having ruined them, and refused to pay her anything. She threatened suit, whereupon he told her to 'sue and be d—d,' and finally offered a shilling a pair, which her necessities forced her to accept."

"One public praying man paid less than any other contractor, and frequently allowed his hands to go unpaid for two or three weeks together. Another would give only a dollar for making thirteen shirts and drawers, of which a woman could finish but three in a day. . . . . What but fallen women must some of the subjects of such atrocious treatment become! It was ascertained from a letter sent by one of this class, that she had given way under the pressure of starvation. She said: 'I was once an innocent girl, the daughter of a clergyman. Left an orphan at an early age, I tried hard to make a living, but unable to endure the hard labor, and live upon the poor pay I received,

I fell into sin. Tell your public that thousands like me have been driven by want to crime.' Yet the men who thus drove virtuous women to despair were amassing large fortunes. Their names appeared in the newspapers as liberal contributors to every public charity that was started,—to sanitary fairs, to women's-aid societies, to the sick and wounded soldiers, to everything that would be likely to bring their names into print. They figured as respectable and spirited citizens. Of all men they were supremely loyal. . . . . Some of them were church-members, famous as class-leaders and exhorters, powerful in prayer, especially when made in public."

These things have been published for months; but if there has been any denial of their truth or any attempt on the part of the Church to clear itself of this scandal before the world, I have not seen it. But if I were an unbeliever in Christianity, I think I should be much more likely to be won over to it by seeing the clergymen and churchmen of Philadelphia ejecting from their communion the men who grind the faces of the poor and disclaiming all complicity with the devils of extortion and greed, than I should by seeing them run a muck against the horse-cars. Monday is far more wickedly profaned by oppression than Sunday by a six-penny ride. One is moved also to inquire whether the Christian population of Philadelphia has ever taken any steps towards putting a stop to the running of private carriages on Sunday. Or is there to be class legislation in the city of Brotherly Love ? Are rich people to be allowed to drive in their own coaches while poor people are not to be allowed the use of hired cars?

I. Take care! The papers say a man was expelled from one of these Philadelphia meetings for charging some of the clergy with the inconsistency of riding to and from church in their private carriages, the driver being left out doors through service.

H. Served him right. It was all the answer they could make. When you know a man is more than your match, the demands of our enlightened and Christian civilization require that you say your own say and then turn your opponent out doors. We have not only high clerical but political precedent for such a procedure.

I. But you would not have transportation going on through Sunday as on other days?

H. No. I would have the business of the world come to a stop as far as possible, and the more perfect the pause the better; but an absolute stop is not possible. The business relations of life cannot safely or wisely be meddled with by those who know nothing about them.

I. But do not let people be eaten up alive by their business relations. "The world is too much with us." I am rather suspicious of "business relations." They cover a multitude of sins.

H. You would fare ill without them. Let Sunday work be spun down to the very finest thread that will keep Saturday and Monday together, but let no one insist on a rupture that shall make more work on Monday in uniting the broken ends than would have been caused by no change at all. I would have the current of life sweep into another channel as far as may be. The lawyer should not look at his briefs, nor the merchant at his accounts, nor the scientific man at his science, nor the writer at his book. The school-teacher and pupil should not go into Sunday school, and the cook should have no dinner to get. I would send the student into the field, and the farmer to his books, not, however, forsaking the assembling of themselves together. So business should loose its grasp of a man's soul, and give him a chance to look up and see God. Anything like fastening upon Sunday the ordinary routine of week-day toil I should consider with the utmost grief as an irreparable calamity. I do not think it can ever be done, but even the attempt would be disastrous.

I. Now I have something to say on that point very appropriate, if you would but listen to me. Here is a little paper—

H. O, the axe-head is peeping out, is it?

I. Well, you can see for yourself that we are led directly up to it by our subject. I am not wantonly trifling with your domestic happiness.

H. Is it something funny?

I. Not exactly funny, — why of course not! but of the first importance.

H. Then I won't listen to it. (Swinging off up the orchard.)

I. Why! Hali—— (gathering up my rejected addresses and following him).

H. First, because it is not funny, and second, because it is important. I will none of it.

I. Perhaps to-morrow then.

H. Or week after next.

I. Week after next never comes.

H. It might do a worse thing.

I. If you would only be reasonable and promise to read it to-morrow, I would let you off to-day.

H. To-morrow is quite out of the question. I have pressing engagements for to-morrow. Notice has been served on me, that the meal-chest is empty, and to-morrow I go to mill.

I. It will not take you all day just to go to mill. Four hours at furthest.

H. And four more very likely to wait for the grist. I go in for the eight hour movement, and will not work over time.

I. So do I go in for it, as you will see; and I hereby invite myself to go to mill with you, — "Thank you, I shall be very happy to accept the invitation," — and while we are waiting, you can improve the shining hours by reading this profound and truly admirably essay.

So the next day the wagon was brought out, — none of your airy, fairy hints of wagons, with nothing really certain about them except the wheels; but a good solid wagon with a palpable body, sides a foot and a half high, made in panels, painted green outside and drab within, wheels with spokes in them and not spindles, a back seat and a front seat, movable and removable at pleasure, a buffalo-robe to sit on, and an honest, unambitious nag to draw you, — that is what I call a wagon. On the present occasion the front seat was taken out, and the back-seat pushed forward for the better bestowing of the freight. With a lively consciousness that possession is nine points of the law, I pre-empted this seat as soon as the horse was harnessed, and so anticipated any objections that might be raised to my part of the journey grounded on the character or bulk of the load. The wagon is backed up to the gate, and the tail-board let down. The load is brought out on the shoulders of a stalwart Atlas, — bushel-bags of tow cloth, puffed out with shelled corn on its winding way to become Johnny-cakes, brown-bread cakes, and Indian puddings, or, with rye, which is equally sure to suffer a fire-change into drop-cakes, muffins, and other things rich and strange, — gathered up at one end and bound with a strong cord, — just such sacks, for aught I know, as Joseph's brethren carried down into Egypt, and with plenty of room in every sack's mouth for a silver cup and corn-money; — but never in my experience was cup or corn-money found there. These bags Atlas dumps down on the wagon-floor, causing the ancient vehicle to groan and tremble through all its frame, and raising little puffs of flour-dust in the air, remnants of many a vanished grist. Then come baskets of corn on the cob, to which I offer constitutional objections; but Halicarnassus maintains that it is the cream of classic elegance, — the very style of Oriental splendor in which Dido entertained Æneas, —

"Cereremque canistris
Expediunt,"—

a theory which I vehemently demolish, having no manner of doubt that her "Cereremque canistris" was frosted fruit-cake in silver baskets, as becomes a queen; and while the dispute is yet hot between us the final touches are given, the tail-board is screwed up, Rosinante stretches her old bones, the harness rattles, the wheels revolve, and we lumber down the lane dew-besprent in the early morning. How bright the sky, how cool the air, how fresh the smells! The rough gates sagging slowly back, grating harsh thunder, seem to be the ever-during gates on golden hinges turning. Sedately we wind through the open pasture, lingering long among the broad tracts of sweet fern, past the black, sullen pool in the hollow, — sullen to me, but most winsome to the panting cows, when the sun waxes hot and they saunter down to stand knee-deep in the muddy coolness and while away the noontide with lashing their tails. And the stagnant pond will by and by bloom out with a brilliant beauty which no garden of Istamboul can surpass. Up from its black bed will leap an army of lilies, fair as the sun, clear as the moon, all spotless of the slime from which they sprung, and breathing only sweetest odors. And on past the berberry hedge, with its sharp-set acid leaves dear to child-tongues, and beautiful now with clusters of graceful, drooping yellow flowers, to be still more beautiful when the deepening summer and the glowing autumn shall festoon them with crimson fruit. Berberry,—the children will look askance at the word,—but a *bar*berry-bush they know full well; and joining hands in a circle they dance wildly around, singing at the top of their voices,—

> "As we go round the barberry-bush,
> The barberry, barberry, barberry-bush,
> As we go round the barberry-bush
> So early every morning.
> This is the way we wash our clothes,
> We wash, we wash, we wash our clothes,
> This is the way we wash our clothes
> So early every morning."

And all the time you are dancing around in the circle you must imitate the motion of washing, washing, washing clothes, or ironing, ironing, ironing clothes, or combing, combing, combing hair, or whatever else you take it into your head to do so early every morning, and woe to him who first loses breath. What fun it was! And now we turn an acute angle, and passing through another gate are in the swamp, the sunniest, most un-dismal swamp that ever settled on its lees. The sweet, dry, aromatic pasture smells have given place to the sweet, damp, thick odors of the spongy bog. The roadside at first is pink-studded with the regular, ornate sheep-laurel. The low blueberry and huckleberry bushes give promise of future feasts; and now the road narrows, and is shut in between two walls, which, indeed, are quite covered up and lost in the clasp of wild grape-vines, and clematis, and roses just opening to the sun. A narrow road, but the swamp begrudges us even that, and presses up closer and closer, and the trees reach out and join hands over our heads, and we ride through a green tunnel, rose-bedecked, — a green bough bolder than the rest, now and then dashing the dew slap! in our faces, and splendid rhodoras swinging their censers afar, unseen. Long delaying, we come at last upon the high road, and "vage" through the village, — not swiftly, I know, but that is no excuse for the saucy urchin, lounging with his mates under the churchyard fence, calling and drawling, "Mister! your wheels turn round!"— the rambling, straggling village over which broods the quiet of a perpetual Sabbath. On under the shadows of the great elms and out of the village again upon the broad causeway built across the meadows, and fringed with willows, winding around the vine-clad rocks and into the woods again, — a charming road to walk in alone, till Satan was unloosed in these later days, and peopled its dear solitude with dread phantoms. I remember the last time I ventured there, I had just left the village out of sight, and passing round a bend came upon some cows grazing among the bushes, and a man, half hidden, leaning against a pair of bars. I was a good deal afraid of the man and not at all afraid of the cows, so I pretended to be very much afraid of the cows and utterly trustful towards the man. "These cows won't hurt me, will they?" I called out, with what was designed to be a most winning confidence, to my bandit, shying around the leader of the drove, a soft-eyed creature that would not have harmed a fly. I think the wretch saw through the flimsy subterfuge, for surely the Evil One sparkled in his wicked eyes as he called back sonorously, "No, I guess not; that one next you is apt to hook, but I guess she won't as long's I'm round." A little farther on a cavalcade of teamsters came up with their great square loads of English hay, and I felt safe. There is something intrinsically honest about teamsters. They seem to be a sort of country police. Whenever they rumble by in the night they give a sense of security. You know there are honest men stirring.

Is your barn catching fire? Is a burglar tampering with your locks? A teamster comes up and gives the alarm, and the fire is put out and the burglar cuts across lots. For we get but a second-rate order of burglar in the country. There is nothing to attract a connoisseur. He must be but a bungler in his business who will prowl around o' nights for the mere chance of stealing a little dirty paper currency, mostly counterfeit. I remonstrated once with a woman for sleeping with her doors unfastened. "If any burglar has any thought of making us a visit," she cried, emphatically, with uplifted hands, "all I ask is that he will come and take one look at the silver, just one. He will never come again, for it is all sham." I was counting up once, with another friend, the number of outside doors in his rambling old house. To the best of my knowledge and belief we made out fourteen. "I hope you fasten them all at night," said one. "O, we generally fasten some of them," was the careless reply, — "three or four, and by that time we get tired of it and let the rest go." Which is very bad for the burglar. Of course no respectable member of the profession would care to open a front door and walk in like a Christian.

After the teamsters had gone by, and before I was well out of the wilderness, two men appeared in sight, real Italian brigands, with stilettos dancing in their eyes. Up they came to me as soon as they saw me, and one of them held out his hand. "Would you be pleased to accept the gift of a young robin that I found on the ground out here," and indeed he had a pitiful little bird well feathered, but half educated. I took it from his brown Florentine hand, thanked him with voluble, and I trusted disarming gratitude, and walked on as fast as possible till I had reached a settled country again, when I placed my little foundling tenderly on the grass, believing that Nature could take care of her minors better than I. I am convinced he was no robin at all, but a partridge or a quail, for he hopped off directly in the best of spirits, and so did I, and that was his end and the end of that walking.

And now with many a crook and turn the mill is gained, the bags and baskets are hauled out and deposited in the mill; we watch the process of grinding so long as it amuses us, see the slow whirlpool of corn slowly sinking, and the little rivulet of meal trickling into the waiting trough, and learn that it is not only the mills of the gods, but the mills of men also, that

"grind slowly,
But they grind exceeding small";

and then we stroll out and down the mill-stream, and where an overhanging tree gives pleasant shade, and green turf a pleasant seat, and tumbling rocks in the mill brook a pleasant sound of gurgling waters, and all the place is full of peace, we dispose our luncheon on the grass, and the huge black ants gallop in and get their share of the gingerbread; but there is no harm done, and we eat our meat with gladness and singleness of heart, and scatter the fragments to the fishes, and then out comes the inevitable manuscript, to which my friend meekly betakes himself; and as for me, I climb upon a mossy rock jutting out over the water, and go sailing round the world.

This is the manuscript. You can call it a new chapter if you like, or you can call this interlude a chapter. Strictly speaking, I suppose there ought to be a break-off where we go to mill. But arrange it any way you choose; and if you think it is an easy matter to make a book, and have all the machinery running smoothly, I should like to have you try it. The main body of it is manageable enough: it is the joints and hinges that cost.

THE KINGDOM COMING.

IF one looks to the individual for proof of the power of Christianity, he will generally look in vain. Creeds differ; but of persons from the same rank in life, one is, on the whole, apparently about as good as another. If we are virtuous where we are not tempted, liberal in matters concerning which we are indifferent, reticent when we have nothing to say, — in one word, pleasant when we are pleased, — it is all that our best friends have any reason to expect of us. What religion does for a man may be great, and even radical, from his near point of view; but from the world's position it is scarcely visible, and is often wholly lost in the more palpable influences of temperament and circumstance. But when we look at society, we can see that some silent agency is at work, slowly, but surely, attuning our life to finer issues than the Golden Ages knew. The hidden leaven of Christianity is working its noiseless way through the whole lump. Christendom is on a higher plane than Pagandom, and is still ascending. In the stress of daily life, we are sometimes tempted to lose heart, and cry, " Who shall show us any good for all this toil and watch and struggle ? " but in calmer moments, looking back over the Difficult Hills, we cannot fail to see that we have gained ground. The sacredness of humanity is gradually overtopping the prerogatives of class. More and more clearly man asserts himself, the end of every good, the standard by which every change is to be judged. With many an ebb, the tide of all healthful and helpful force is flooding our associated life ; and the brotherhood of the race attests itself by many infallible signs.

But they are not always nor only found where they are sought. Workmanship does not show to the best advantage in workshops. The din and whirl of machinery confuse us. We need to see the wonderful engine in actual operation, the beautiful ornament fitly placed, before we can decide finally upon its character. The churches have been the workshops of Christianity. There it has been received, fused, hammered, polished, fashioned for all human needs ; but nothing less than the whole world is the true theatre of its activity. Not what it has done for the Church, but what it has done, is doing, and purposes to do for humanity, is the measure of its merit. Not upon the mitre of the priest, but upon the bells of the horses, is the millennial day to see inscribed " Holiness unto the Lord ! "

Since, then, the kingdom of God cometh not with observation, we need not look for fearful sights and great signs in the heavens. They are but false prophets who cry, " Lo, here ! " or " Lo, there ! " when the still, small voice is whispering all the while, " The kingdom of God is within you." Yes, within this framework of society, in the midst of this busy, trivial daily life, which seems so full of small cares and selfish seeking, the Divine Spirit lives and works, and will yet raise it to the heights of heavenly fellowship. It breathes in the thousand methods devised by ingenuity to lighten the burdens of labor, by benevolence to soothe away the bitterness of sorrow, by taste to beautify the homes of poverty. The little photograph leaves that flutter down into every household in the land are a great cloud of witnesses showing us that science is but the handmaid of God, whose service is to bear to all the blessings once reserved for a class. In the old time it was only the few who could fix for future years the beloved features of a friend. Now every fond mother may transcribe from birthday to birthday the face of her darling, to note its beautiful changes, and every lowliest bride preserve for her children's children the bloom of her budding youth.

The religious world has hardly learned to look for its millennium in the horse-cars. Nevertheless, its signs are there, not to be mistaken. The poor sewing-woman feels their presence, if she does not trace them to their source. The humble invalid knows them, the domestic drudge, the ailing, puny child, the swart and stalwart workman, who ride their one or ten miles as swiftly and smoothly as a millionnaire, and are set down at shop or home, or among the freshness and fragrance and song of the beautiful country. The horse-car is the poor man's private carriage, as carefully fashioned for his convenience, as tidy and comfortable and comely, as if it cost him hundreds of dollars, instead of the daily sixpence. With a lifted finger he commands his coachman, who waits promptly on his wish. Without care, he is cared for. Without capital, he controls capital. Free society does more for him than the richest despot does for the enslaved people whom the instinct of self-preservation forces him to cajole, and does it, too, without any infringement upon his manhood. We call it energy, enterprise, modern conveniences. It *is* the millennium.

But these matters are under full headway. Science and self-interest have taken them in hand, and there is no danger that they will not be carried out to their farthest beneficial limits. There is another measure just struggling into uncertain life, — a measure that appeals less directly to self-advantage, but which is yet so fraught with good or evil, according as it is carefully studied, clearly understood, and wisely managed, or suffered to fail through inattention, or to lead an irregular, riotous life for a few years and then to be abated as a nuisance, that we cannot safely pass it by. I refer to the movement making itself felt in various ways, but aiming always to give more leisure to the working classes. In one phase, it is seeking to reduce the hours of daily labor; in another, it is trying to close the shops on Saturday afternoons. In both, it is a step so radically in the right direction, that we can but give thanks for the opportunity, while we tremble lest it may not be firmly and wisely laid hold of. In planning for human weal, one is met on every side by the want of leisure. Every day and every hour comes so burdened with its material necessities, that the wants of heart and mind and spirit can find no adequate gratification. The work goes on satisfactorily; wealth accumulates; farms are well tilled; mechanism becomes more and more exquisite; but drunkenness, profligacy, stupidity, insanity, and crime undermine the man, for whom all these things are and were created, and to whom they ought to bring wisdom and power and peace. Thus our boasted improvements become our folly. All labor-saving machinery that does not save labor in the sense of giving leisure, that merely increases the quantity or improves the quality of that which is produced, but does not redound to the improvement of the producer, rather contributes to his degradation, has somewhere a fatal flaw. Mind may legitimately fashion matter into a machine; but when it would reduce mind also to the same level, it steps beyond its province. When it fails to continue through the sphere of mind the impulse it communicates to matter, — when its benefit stops with fabric, falling short of the man who stands over it, — it lags behind its duty, and is so far unsuccessful.

The movement for diminishing the number of laboring hours has already been brought before the notice of the Massachusetts Legislature, and has been made the subject of careful and extensive inquiry. It is to be hoped that nothing will be left undone to secure a just and righteous decision. In the intelligence and virtue of its workingmen lies the hope of the Republic. If the proposed change shall tend to promote that intelligence and virtue, it will be the part of true patriotism to effect it. Whether this particular means be or be not the wisest for the end in view, the path of a higher life unquestionably lies in this direction. The accomplishment of the greatest results with the least outlay of time and toil is the problem in physical science. With the leisure and strength thus redeemed from lower needs, to build up manhood is the problem of moral science.

The Saturday half-holiday is less an affair of law and legislature, depends more upon private men and women, but is of scarcely less importance. It is not to be disguised that there are difficulties and dangers attending the plan. It is as yet probably regarded only as an experiment, though certain classes of mercantile men have been trying it for years, with what satisfaction their persistence in it indicates. Undoubtedly there are many young men who misspend their holiday, and many more who do not know what to do with it, and who will finally fall into mischief through sheer idleness. The hours drag so heavily that they half conclude they would about as soon be at work as at liberty with nothing to do. Possibly there are more who abuse their holiday than use it advantageously. But just as far as this evil extends, so far it shows, not the harm of leisure, but the sore straits we have been brought to for lack of it. There is no sadder result of the disuse of a faculty than the decadence of that faculty. Time is the essential gift of God to man, — essential not merely to providing for his physical wants, but to forming his character, to developing his powers, to cultivating his taste, to elevating his life. Is it, then, that he has devoted so disproportionate a share of this time to one of its uses, and that not the noblest, that he has lost the desire and the ability to devote any of it to its higher uses? Have young men given themselves to buying and selling till they have no interest in Nature, in books, in art, in manly sport and exercise? Then surely it behooves us at once to change all this. No man can have a well-balanced mind, a good judgment, who is interested in nothing but his business. If, when released from that for a half-day each week, he is listless, aimless, discontented, it is a sure sign that undue devotion to it has injured his powers, and is making havoc of his finer organization.

It is to be feared that many of our young men do not know what recreation means. They confound it with riot. Fierce driving, hard drinking, violence, and vice they understand; but with quiet, refining, soothing, and strengthening diversions they have small acquaintance. This is very largely the fault of the community in which they live. Do Christian families in our large cities feel the obligations which they are under towards the young men who come among them? I believe that a very large part of the immorality, the irreligion, the scepticism and crime into which young men fall is due to their being so coldly and cruelly let alone by Christian families. A boy comes up from the country, where every one knows him and greets him, into the solitude of the great city. He has left home behind him, and finds no new home to receive him. When he is released from his work in shop or counting-room, nothing more inviting awaits him than the silent room in the dreary boarding-house. He misses suddenly, and at a most sensitive age, the graces and spontaneous kindnesses of home, the thousand little teasings and pettings, the common interests and tendernesses, that he never thought of till he lost them. He is surrounded by men and boys all bent on their several ways. He must have amusement. It is as necessary to him as daily food. What wonder, then, if he accepts the first that offers? And if Satan, as usual, is beforehand with his invitations, what shall hinder him from following Satan? The saloon, warmed and lighted, and enlivened with music or merry talk, is more attractive than the dingy, solitary room; and if his feet do slip now and then, who is the worse for it? He will never write it home, and there is nobody in the city who will discover it; provided he is prompt at his business, no one will meddle with his leisure hours. And if full-grown men are found to need the restraining influences of wife and child and neighbor, and to plunge into brutality whenever they form a community by themselves, what can prevent boys, when cast adrift, from drifting into sin? Genius is supreme, but genius is the heritage of but few; while passion and appetite, love of society and amusement, need of watchfulness, and susceptibility to temptation, belong to all. "I don't like wine," said a young man, "I hate the taste of it; but what am I to do? A lot of fellows carousing is n't the best company in the world; but I can't stay moping in my room alone all the time. There's my violin. Well, I took it out once or twice, but it was no go. When I could go into the parlor after supper, and mother sewing and Bess to sing, it was worth while; but there is no fun in fiddling to yourself by wholesale. Besides, I suppose it bores the rest to have a fellow sawing away." And this was a fine, healthy young man, all ready to be made a warm friend, a patriotic citizen, a pure and happy man, and just as ready to become a reckless, dissipated, sorrow-bringing failure. And alas! where were the hands that should have helped him? Alas! alas! what are the hands that will *not* be backward to lay hold on him?

If any holiday is to be made useful, if young men are to be saved from ruin, saved to their mothers and sisters and wives, saved to themselves, to their country, and to God, Christian people must bestir themselves. Young Men's Christian Associations may be ever so efficient, but they cannot do everything. The work that is to be done cannot be wrought by associations alone, nor by young men, nor by any men. It needs fathers and mothers and sons and daughters and firesides. The only way to keep boys from the haunts of vice is to open to them the abodes of virtue. Give them access to loving families, to happy homes. Nothing can supply this want. No attendance at any church is to be for a moment compared to attendance at the sacred shrine of an affectionate family. But when, a little while ago, a young man who had been for years a clerk in a large city, was asked in how many families he was acquainted, he replied quickly, "Not one." Yet he was a member of an Orthodox Congregational Church, which, I take it, is to be as good as anybody can be in this world, and a regular attendant upon religious services in one of the most influential Orthodox churches in the city. Sunday after Sunday he was in his seat, yet neither pastor nor people — not one of all that great congregation — ever took him by the hand and constrained him to sit by their hearthstones, ever welcomed him to the warmth and gladness and gentle endearments of their homes. What is the communion of saints? If that young man had brought a letter of introduction from some distinguished person, would they have thus let him go in and out among them unnoticed and uncared for? But to church-members, surely, a certificate of church-membership ought to be as weighty as a letter of introduction. A Christian church should be so managed that it should be impossible for any attendant upon its services to escape observation; and it should be so trained to its social duties that every person who takes shelter in its sanctuary should at least have the opportunity to find shelter in its homes. I think it would be well, even, that those who are present at a single church service should be courteously noticed and encouraged to repeat the visit. If the church is indeed God's house, let the servants of the Master dispense His hospitalities in such a manner as befits His divine character, remembering that the world judges of Him through them. Let fathers and mothers be on the watch to speak kindly words to such homeless wanderers as may roam within the circle of their influence. If a stranger is introduced into the family pew, let him be no longer a stranger, but a guest. Let him not remain during the service and pass out at its close without some brotherly or fatherly recognition, without some assurance by word or look or little attention that his presence there gave pleasure. This is a beginning of home feeling.

It would be a fit thing, if every country pastor should give to every boy who leaves his parish a letter of introduction to some clergyman in the city whither he is going, so that there should be no interregnum, — no time when the boy should be utterly unfriended, loosed from restraint, and a prey to unclean and hateful things. But this is not done, and we should not wait for it. The Prince of Evil never stands upon etiquette. He is instant in season and out of season; and those who would circumvent him must be equally prompt and vigilant. The Church should weave its meshes of watchful care and love and friendship so close that nobody can slip through unseen.

A duty rests upon all merchants and tradesmen, upon all, indeed, who employ clerks or apprentices, which is not discharged when their quarterly payments are made. A man is in some respects the father of the young men whom he employs, and he should do them fatherly service. It is not possible to enter into relations with any human being without at the same time incurring responsibility concerning him. How much might be done for young men, if merchants would feel a domestic as well as a mercantile interest in them! It may not be advisable to renew the old custom of making clerks and apprentices members of the master's family; but surely they can be made occasional guests without any sacrifice that shall seem too great to the followers of Him who laid down the glory which He had with the Father before the world was, only that He might save sinners. Is it a dangerous thing to introduce strangers into a young family? But is the character that is not good enough for the drawing-room quite harmless in the counting-room? If merchants, master mechanics, and employers generally would set a premium upon integrity and good manners, those qualities would not long be found wanting. Incalculable is the influence which these civilizing surroundings would have upon a susceptible boy. Only let them come in early. Do not wait till sin has thrown out its more showy lures, and then attempt to tear him away from them already half polluted; but while his soul is yet unstained, while, lonely, inexperienced, self-distrustful, he is ready to be moulded by the first skilful touch, let it come from the wise hands of honorable and responsible men whose position gives weight to their opinions and from the gentle hands of motherly women. Provide, — even if it be at the cost of a little pains, a little sacrifice of the quiet and seclusion of home, — provide for his youth its fitting and innocent delights, that sinful pleasures may have no charm for him. The good which the merchant does to his clerks will redound to the good of his own children. There is probably as much intelligence and virtue and youthful promise among his clerks as among his sons and daughters. The influence of man upon woman, also, is just as healthful as that of woman upon man; for both are in the order of Nature. The brothers and sisters will dance to their mother's playing all the more gleefully for a stranger or two in the set; and Mary will enter with fresher zest into the game of cards, because courteous Mr. Gordon is her partner instead of her teasing brother. And it is not whist nor dancing that harms young people. It is outlawry. Whist does not lead to gambling. Dancing does not lead to dissipation. It is playing cards "on the sly" that leads to gambling. It is having to get out of the way of ministers, and church-members, and all religious people, when there is to be dancing, that leads to dissipation. It is loneliness, want of interest and diversion, any unjust and unnatural restriction that leads to all manner of wild and boisterous and vicious amusements, which prey upon the soul. If to a young man, on his first coming to the city, there open only two or three houses, where he can now and then find welcome, — where are two or three excellent women who exercise a gentle jurisdiction over him, who will notice if his eye be heavy or his cheek pale, who will administer, upon occasion, a little sweet motherly chiding, mend a rent in his gloves, advise in the choice of a necktie, and call upon him occasionally for trifling service or attendance, — where he can find a few hot-headed, perhaps, but well-fathered and well-mothered boys, who have the same headstrong will, the same fierce likes and dislikes, the same temptations and weaknesses as himself, but who are saved from disaster by gentle but firm authority, and constant yet scarcely perceptible influence, — a few bright girls, who will sing and dance and talk with him, and probably pique and tantalize him, — how greatly are the chances multiplied against his ever turning aside into the debasing saloon! He naturally likes purity better than impurity. The interests of a man at whose table he sits, whose children are his companions, whose wife is his friend and confidante, will be far nearer to him than those of one whom he rarely sees and little knows. Something of the home atmosphere will cling to office-walls, and soften the sharp outlines and sweeten the unfragrant air of perpetual traffic and self-seeking. Pure society will be a constant inducement to keep himself pure. Reading, studying, riding, singing, driving, boating, ball-playing with well-bred and high-hearted young friends will give plentiful outlet to his animal spirits, plentiful gratification to his social wants, plentiful food for his mental hunger; and while he is thus enjoying the pleasures which are but the lawful dues of his spring-time, he will be all the while becoming more and more worthy of love and respect, more and more fitted to bear, in his turn, the burdens of Church and State. And if, in spite of it all, his feet are still swift to do evil, it will be a satisfaction to those who thus have striven for his welfare to know that his blood is not on them nor on their children.

There are other things to be taken into account. The leisure of Saturday afternoon must, it would seem, conduce greatly to quiet Sundays. When young men are confined six long days behind the counter, it is but natural that on the seventh they should give themselves to merry-making. For, let it be remembered, sport is as natural, yes, and as necessary, to youth as worship; and in the order of human development, it comes first. It is very hard to say to a boy: "You have been writing, and weighing, and measuring all the week. Now the sun is shining, the birds are singing, the flowers blooming, the river sparkling, and boat and horse await your hand, but you must turn away from them all and go to church. You have been boxed up for six days, and now you must be boxed up again. There is no fresh air, there are no summer sounds for you; but only noise and dust and pavements all the days of your life." It happens, at any rate, that there is no use in saying this; for young blood overleaps it all, and city suburbs resound on Sunday with the clatter of hoofs and the rattle of wheels; and no one need be surprised, who has any acquaintance with human nature on the one side, or any conception of the irksomeness of continued confinement on the other. It would, indeed, be a strange, and, I think, a sad thing, if young people *were* willing to let suns rise, and stars set, and all the beautiful changes of Nature go on, without an irresistible, instinctive prompting to fly from the grave monotony of the city, and live and breathe in her freshness and her loveliness. If a young man must choose between play of muscle, the free air of the hills, and sitting in an ill-ventilated church, he will often choose the former; and if he cannot enjoy these things without going in opposition to the best sense of the community, if they cannot be compassed without a certain consciousness of wrongdoing, they will lead to recklessness and lawlessness; for compassed they will be.

But let the young men have Saturday afternoon for their boating and bowling and various other pastimes, and they will be far more disposed to hear what the minister has to say on Sunday,—

far more disposed, let us hope, to join in prayer and praise. One very obvious and practical consideration is, that many of them, probably the larger part, can spend on a single holiday all the holiday money they have to spend; so there will be nothing for it but to stay at home on Sunday by force of the *res angustæ domi*. And is it too much to believe, that, the half-day having given them that physical exercise, amusement, and change which they need, Sunday will find them the more ready to receive and appropriate spiritual nourishment? I have said that sport is as natural and necessary as worship. But, on the other hand, worship is as natural as sport. Very few, I think, are the persons, young or old, in all of whose thoughts it may be said God is not. And if this natural, spontaneous turning to God were not interfered with by our pernicious modes of training and management, we should not become so fearfully alienated from Him. Play and work and worship would be animated by one spirit. Many surely there are who would be *more likely* to devote a part of their Sunday to the direct worship of God, and to a more intimate knowledge of His works and words, who would be more likely to come under the influence of the Bible and the pulpit, from having had opportunity first to free their lungs from the foul air, and their limbs from the lifelessness, which a long confinement to business had caused. At least let us not tempt any to make Sunday a day of fun and frolic, by giving them no other day for their fun and frolic. Provide things honest in the sight of all men.

Women can do much towards bringing about this holiday, and towards keeping it intact when it is once secured. Let every woman make a point of doing no shopping on Saturday afternoons. A very little forethought will prevent any inconvenience from the deprivation. If a tradesman chooses to keep his shop open on Saturdays, when others of the same kind are shut, let every woman take care not only not to enter it on that day, but not to enter it on any day. And in order that the holiday may begin as promptly as the working-day, women should not put off their purchases till the last minute before closing. If the shops are to be shut at two o'clock, let no one enter them after one o'clock, except in case of emergency. If the clerks have to take down goods from their shelves, overhaul box and drawer, and unroll and unfold and derange till the time for closing arrives, an hour or an hour and a half of their holiday must be consumed in the work of putting the store to rights. Let this last hour of the working-week be spent in arrangement, not in derangement. Be ashamed to ask a clerk to disturb a shelf which has just been set in Sunday order. Let the young men be ready, so that, when the clock strikes the hour, release may come.

H. Did I ever tell you about my talk awhile ago with Mr. Ambrose?

I. No. What Mr. Ambrose?

H. O yes I did, and you got the idea of this essay from it.

I. What assurance! I never heard a word about it. I did not know you had seen him.

H. Well, I have, and he gave me a chapter of his experience and experiments on this very point. He employs six or eight men on his farm. When his head man went there last spring, Mr. Ambrose told him that he wanted the Sabbath respected, and only such work done on that day as could not be done on Saturday or Monday. Afterwards, reflecting on this matter of observing the Sabbath, he became convinced that, as an employer, requiring six working-days in the week of his men and boys, he was to a great degree responsible for whatever wrong was done in the way of spending the Sabbath in recreation. The first thing he did was to write an article for some country paper, arguing that the fractions of a day now at the laborer's command were wholly insufficient. After taking time to mature the plan in his own mind and give it a practical shape, he told his boys that for the future, such weeks as contain national holidays excepted, he should give them each Saturday afternoon, on condition that they would attend meeting on the Sabbath. They agreed to this gladly enough. Benny, the oldest, spoke up and said, "I go to meeting now all day and the evening too." He omitted to mention that as sure as he did go he slept through the services, and Mr. Ambrose felt that it did not become him to cast a stone at poor Benny, holding that he himself had done too much thus far to close his eyes.

I. Did he say how the experiment fared?

II. So well that he means to try it with the men.

I. Now that is good news. One such case is worth more than a dozen theories, because it shows that the thing is practical. It can be done. And it ought to be done. There is charming Rose Crichton fretting in her new home because Fred has to be at the store so much. It is the trial of her life, her one daily cause of vexation and useless longing. "It is a shame, and a disgrace, and an utter mistake," says Rose, who is apt to fall into the Pauline style when she is very much in earnest. "Just see how it is with Fred," she writes, and I brought the letter along on purpose to read it to you "in this connection," as the ministers say, "and I can't find out that it is really much better with any gentlemen, except that salaried ones are less their own masters. But those who own business are so foolish that they won't give themselves much more time. Fred has to be at the store at half past seven, — then he has an hour at noon to come home a mile for dinner, and can't leave till half past six at night. There is never a holiday, — even on the regular holidays,

Christmas, Thanksgiving, and so forth, he can't get more than half a holiday, and the whole rest and recreation of the year has to be crowded into three weeks in August. Ah, but Sunday is a blessed day! I never fully appreciated it before we were married. We go to church and Sunday school in the morning, and in the afternoon, if it is pleasant, Fred takes a long walk, and I go with him when I can. Don't you think it is right? I am quite clear on that point. You see he can never take me anywhere in the week days. I think every store should be closed by five o'clock, and then, as soon as people get used to that, by four; and then there should be a half-holiday once in a week or two for men in every kind of business." There you have Rose's opinion, "all for love and nothing for reward."

H. You can hardly expect the traffic of the world to turn on a girl's wish to have her Fred come home to an early supper.

I. Now, Halicarnassus, excuse me, but that is a stupid speech for you to make. Sometimes you are thoughtful and sensible and reasonable, and it is really pleasant to talk with you. And again you seem somehow to shut up all your sense in a shell, and turn into a fossil, and one cannot make the least headway with you.

Instead of being shamed by this reproof, Halicarnassus only fanned himself languidly with his hat, and hummed some silly old song or other.

> "If I had a donkey
> And he would n't go,
> Do you think I'd wallop him?
> O no, no, no!"

Sometimes there is no getting on with him. He takes a position from mere whim, and holds it. The most faithful and searching rebuke produces no visible effect. He looks upon it as a good joke. All your earnestness is so much phenomenon, helping him to analyze your character, but bearing not the least on the question. I feared he was ossifying into such a mood at the present time. But I went on.

I. You may depend upon it, if the traffic of the world considered more the nature of girls and boys too, there would be less sin in the world. And I should like to know if it is not better for traffic to wait upon souls than it is for souls to wait upon traffic? Business is for man's uses; man is not made for business.

II. Yes, I have seen a good many men who did not seem made for business.

I. Fred Crichton has good principles and a good wife. So the harm done him is chiefly in the way of cheapening, not corrupting life. It is made less productive, less satisfying, than it ought to be. But many a man who has not firm principles or a good wife suffers a sore injury. Worldly people are not expected to act from other than worldly motives, but the Church professes to stand on higher ground. Now if the religious community would at once and resolutely decree that all in her employ should have time for rest, how long would it be before the irreligious community would follow suit?

H. Don't bring whist into theology.

I. Whist yourself! No, we are too greedy. We will not miss a chance for making money. We cannot work on Sunday. The law forbids it. So we can afford to be religious then, but as for wasting good working time in religion, it is not to be thought of.

H. By "religion" I suppose you now mean recreation, holiday amusements.

I. Yes, sir, I do, notwithstanding your sneer. If from love to God and love to man, or, more simply, because he thinks he ought, an employer gives his men a half-holiday every week, or an hour or two of leisure every day, I call it religion, and religion of the very best kind. And I believe in it far more than in the piety that keeps every one at hard labor all the week and arrogates to itself superior virtue because it would keep them at hard labor on Sunday if it could.

H. Yet the numerous holidays of Europe do not seem to have had a good effect on the people.

I. A carnival every now and then is a different thing from a regularly recurring day, or hour of rest, — so different that you cannot reason from the one to the other. The regular rest falls at once into the general plan, has its portion allotted to it duly like any day. An hour at the close of every work-day for fifty days is a boon where fifty hours of idleness taken together might be a bane. Besides, I suspect there is a greater *intensity* of work in our country than in any other.

H. I was looking at one of the base-ball matches on Boston Common one day, and I overheard a portly old gentleman at my elbow say to another, " Two thousand people here; that is four thousand dollars thrown away." That was a conscientious old codger, no doubt.

I. " Thrown away! " The most wasteful habit we have is squandering time, and happiness, and health for money, which in the greatest quantity is no equivalent.

H. They who feel no need of amusement themselves are apt to suppose that no one else needs it.

I. Never a soul was made that did not need amusement. Only some can make it for themselves and others need to have it provided.

H. I did not say those who have no need, but those who feel no need. Stick a pin there.

I. Well, that is a proper distinction. Why, I can count up ever so many people, excellent persons, fathers and mothers in Israel, who do not know in the least what ails them, but really they are languishing for want of concert, and opera, and theatre, and dancing —

H. Here, here! What heresies are you pouring forth? I will have you read out of meeting!

I. Heresy or orthodoxy, it is truth. Their lives lack ideality. They are painfully empty. They need something fine and grand to take them above the plane of mere labor.

H. Something finer and grander than religion!

I. Religion is not a definite department, — a ponderable substance, something visible, and tangible, and to be disposed of. Religion is more like air. You may furnish a house with every comfort and every elegance, and if it has no air it will be only a tomb. If you fill it with air and nothing else, you will die of starvation. To make air a substitute for food or warmth or shelter, or to make these a substitute for air, is fatal. So if you furnish your life with employment, recreation, leisure, but close it against religion, you fail at a vital point, and if you undertake to exclude employment or recreation or leisure, and put religion in its stead, you are in equally imminent danger. Religion, like air, takes up no room. What it finds vacant it leaves vacant. But it permeates everything. You want your life just as full as if there were no such thing as religion, and when it is thus full you want a steady current of religion to flow in upon it and flood it and sink into it, so that everything should be as it were tainted with religion.

H. A felicitous expression!

I. Well, everything should savor of religion, if that is any better. Love to God and love to man should, — not be harped upon, — but should be the living soul, the hidden principle, of life.

H. You picture the mind as a room, which is too mechanical. It is more like a field.

I. And religion ripens the seeds which have been planted in it? yes. But never mind the figures. What I want to get at is, that religion does not occupy any place, and cannot be made a substitute for anything that does occupy place. It may save you in the last extremity, but it saves from despair, not from death. So of course you cannot take out anything which the soul really needs, and expect to fill up the void with religion. But that is just what many attempt to do. And what is the result? The young people, denied refining and ennobling pleasures guided by experience, fall into coarse and degrading ones. That is one very common result. Another, almost universal, is that the life of religious communities becomes thin and meagre. We take a good deal of satisfaction in deploring the hollowness and frivolity of fashionable circles, and doubtless they are often hollow and frivolous, but if you compare the conversation that takes place at the sewing-circle, or the tea-party, or the Fair of the Orthodox or the Baptist or the Methodist Society and that which takes place at the dinner-party or the evening party of the gay leader of fashion, you will hardly find any more spirituality, any more lofty and generous views, more breadth or depth or quickness of insight, any more traces of inward experience in the one than in the other. There seems to be little more real acquaintance with the Divine Being, or conception of the Divine character, in the one than in the other. If you think, my hearers, that by going to sleep you will hush me up any sooner, I fear you are doomed to disappointment. It clears my mind wonderfully to empty it. I do not know what I think myself till I talk it over. (Halicarnassus nodded, but whether it were a nod of wakeful assent or sleepy indifference was not quite certain.) A fine woman is a fine woman wherever you find her; but I have found fine women as often in gay society, in opera-going, and theatre-going, and party-giving society as in any other. The moral perpendicular seems to be as often attained out of church as in it. If I know that a man is a member of the Church, I am confident he is not a drunkard, nor a thief, nor an adulterer; but I am by no means sure that he is not unjust, extortioner, and very much like the publicans. Church teaching, or pulpit teaching, or whatever you may call it, — you know what I mean, or would know if you were awake, — does not, as far as I can see, produce any more sweetness of disposition, or charity of judgment, or love to one's neighbor, or any more divorce from the pleasures of the world and of sense, from envy and backbiting, than the teachings of the stage and the ball-room. It is not in the least more heavenly-minded to be discussing your minister's wife, than Hackett or Charlotte Cushman. I do not feel any more devotional when I turn with the audience to face Miss Jones as she is trilling out her solo, in her best clothes Sunday morning, than I do or did when listening to Patti singing her songs in her best clothes Monday evening.

II. O, Patti was a sweet little singing-bird. I hope they will not spoil her and marry her and bury her over there. Is it the opera you are speaking of and the theatre? No harm in the thing itself, of course. It is the attendant evils that make it an evil.

I. My friend, no emergency forces you to speak; but if you do speak, pray do not say a thing which has been said a hundred times before, and had no substance to begin with.

H. Libenter tuis præceptis obsequar, si te prius idem facientem videro.

(Let not the unlearned reader be terrified by this show of erudition. It is only Latin Lessons, and too ill-mannered for our mother tongue.)

I. But whenever I repeat an old truth, it is to give it new force. When you do it, it is from poverty of resources. Observe, now, the standing argument against these things is not themselves, but their attendant evils. But you and I have been to theatre many times. Did we ever drink there, or gamble, or fall into bad company?

H. You were in good company, without cavil.

I. That was a rhetorical question, and you need not have troubled yourself to answer it; but why shall we fear that others will not fare as well as we? If the evils that cling to the outskirts of an institution are a reason for the abolition of the institution, theatres are not the only things that must go by the board. Precisely the same kind of vice that attaches to the theatre attaches to the camp-meeting; but I have never heard that our Methodist brethren propose to give up their camp-meetings in consequence. What they do is, by vigilant efforts, by an efficient police, to check the evil as far as possible; but they have their camp-meetings every year, in spite of the drunkenness and immorality of their camp-followers. Who can show cause why theatres may not be conducted on the same principle? Let them be supported by Christian people, and become a school of Christian manners and morals. Nobody objects to the dialogues spoken in the schools. Let a theatre be the same thing on a larger scale.

H. The experiment has been often tried without success.

I. It is high time, then, to try it with success.

H. You will find also that some of the best persons on the stage are the most opposed to having their friends adopt the actor's profession. They believe it to be hurtful to health and to character. Is it right to encourage a profession which, in the judgment of those who know most about it, is fatal to those who adopt it?

I. That I cannot tell. If what you say is true, it must just stand on the *per contra* side. But it is inconsistent in us to bring up such an objection in any other spirit than that of benevolence, for we encourage similarly hurtful exhibitions. Our seminaries and high schools have their public examinations. The public rushes in and fills the schoolroom. The teachers, though they are often young women, are forced to conduct their classes through a recitation in the presence of the promiscuous assembly. There is just as much publicity about it as there is about acting in a theatre, with the additional cruelty, that the teachers do not like their part, and act it from compulsion only, while the actress does like hers, and acts it from choice.

H. Yet very often —

I. Please not keep thrusting in when I am talking. You don't give me a chance to say anything. (I am sure he laughed under his hat, but I am proof against ridicule. He has plenty of opportunity to promulgate his views, but just now I have the floor.) In these same thronged public halls young girls not out of their teens go through their recitations, face the great audience alone to read a composition, straining their girlish voices to unnatural and unmusical loudness —

H. Queen Victoria —

I. There you are at it again! I suppose you are going to say that Queen Victoria reads her speech to the Parliament. But she is public property, and nothing to the purpose. The point is, that we object to the world's putting women on the stage, and yet we put our young girls on the stage without scruple; and not only to recite and to read composition, but to play plays; and not only plays, but poor plays. I have been at school-exhibitions, some in church and some in school-house, and have seen young girls take part in dialogues that were coarse and pert, dialogues whose direct tendency was to make these girls forward, flippant, unladylike, and disagreeable.

H. Amen!

I. I knew that you would agree with me, and, what is more, I know that you have been agreeing with me, only more so, all along, in spite of your futile attempts at objections. But I do not mean to go on a crusade for theatres. I do not care about them particularly, though I do maintain it would be an advantage to more than one community I wot of if it could go to a good play once a week or so, and thereby enlarge its sphere of knowledge, get its thoughts turned away from itself, so as to have something to talk about besides its own affairs; for the constant contemplation of self is fatal to the whole man. Selfishness gets into religion, and is just as poisonous there as anywhere else. To hear some of our good Christian brethren speak in meeting, one would suppose the main object of life is to save your soul; now I suspect if people would let their souls alone and pay their debts, and keep their promises, and try to make everybody happy, — children and horses and dogs and cats, — and not be suspicious and envious, and not offend the tastes or the feelings of their associates, and keep their communication with Heaven always open, it would be better every way. In this great world, this great universe, this great eternity, it does not seem to be very dignified, nor very ennobling, to be all the while coddling your own one little soul. We ought to be filled with God, not with ourselves.

H. Our souls may not be as big as the universe, but they are a pretty important object to us. But I was thinking of the tenacity with which society clings to the theatre, in spite of all religious opposition; and seeing this, it is singular that we do not recognize the power of dramatic representation, and take possession of it in the name of the Lord.

I. It is so much easier to condemn outright and by wholesale than it is to discriminate.

H. Easier in the process, but bitter hard in the result.

I. It seems to me, Halicarnassus, that there is something in everything —

H. Yes, dear, I think so myself.

I. But I mean that there is some truth in every great, spreading falsehood, — a core of virtue in every vice; at least, it is something like that. I cannot seem to get at it precisely, but if you study closely and wisely the follies and vices of society, you will find out its real wisdom and goodness.

H. What you mean is, I suppose, that our sins as well as our holinesses are in the line of our nature, and it is only by looking at both that you can find what nature is.

I. Yes, I rather think that is it; and having found that, we are to cut off only the sin, not the nature itself. Now you speak of taking possession of the theatre. I would take possession of everything which is confessed to be in itself, or to be capable of becoming sinless, and which is seen to be agreeable, and would bring it into the service of man. For it is a question between liberty and license, between rational pleasure and irrational excess, between a natural life and unnatural death. Nature, nature is what we need to know.

H. And we should know it by theorizing less, and dogmatizing less, and observing more.

I. And by looking at other communities, and other nations, and other ages instead of confining our observations to our one little spot in time and space, and assuming that we are the people and wisdom shall die with us. Think now how fair a thing our society might be if we would cull the choicest flowers of every age and nation to adorn it, — retain all that is strong in New England life and combine with it all that is sweet in foreign life. If we could be as graceful as we are energetic! If we could know how to play as well as how to work!

H. We do not know how to work until we know how to play.

I. Not truly, for they are one in aim and both alike religious.

H. Do you suppose you will accomplish anything from all your lucubrations?

I. Oh! No. That is, if you bring it down to a plain statement of fact, — no.

Coleridge used to answer his opponents by courteously admitting their objections, and then going on with his magnificent harangues as if nothing had been said. That is the way of the world. And sometimes it seems as if one might as well let everything go and just go with it. But that is impossible. And, besides, for all this logical despair, in my feeling there is a great assurance of hope, a confidence of expectation. I know the fixity of things is terrible, yet I *feel* if you speak it is done. Especially in summer. No summer opens but I feel it has something beautiful for me in its gift. Some strange happiness, some marvellous good fortune is about to befall. The tenth Avatar descends.

H. What form does it take?

I. No form at all. Do not ask me now any of your miserable mathematical questions. It is only that something is going to happen.

H. That is enough. I am convinced.

I. I know that nothing ever does happen, but all the same I am filled with a vague expectation, — the foretaste of coming bliss. Do not laugh. Heaven opens in the summer-time. Her sunshine is the shadow of the angels. Every power feels the thrill of its coming development. Every need hears through the still air the far, faint music of its answering wealth. The wildest dream finds dear fulfilment. Nothing is too high to be hoped for, too sweet to be believed.

O, let me tell you the ideal life which Summer paints on her lilies and roses —

And we talked on through the pulsing hours of what you perhaps would not care to hear, nor I to report, till the miller's horn rung sonorous through the woods, — preconcerted signal of his completed work; in obedience to which we gathered our goods and chattels and returned homeward, no less slowly, a little more silent, no more sad, under the lengthening shadows of the afternoon.

KING JAMES THE FIRST.

 WAS determined no longer to resort to a course of humiliating strategy, not to say trickery. So the next time I had something to say, I waited till there came a rainy day. Then stealthily watching the movements of my victim, I saw him enter his lair for the purpose, as he informed me, of tracing a quotation to Aristophanes or Heliogabalus, or some of those old masters. He was very sure it was there, but it had hitherto eluded him. He should find it now if it took him all day, since it was rainy, and he had nothing in particular on hand. Fatal admission! Did he see the eyes of the wild beast in me flash exultation? "*Quem Deus vult perdere*," and so forth; but I held my peace till he should have become thoroughly absorbed in his pursuit, and off his guard. Then I advanced. So-ho! There lay my fine gentleman and scholar, stretched on his lounge fast asleep. Research indeed! The fact is, I am becoming sceptical as to the quantity and quality of masculine scholarship. The popular belief,

which I have hitherto shared, is, that men who have been through college, with all its antecedents and consequents, can

> "speak Greek
> As naturally as pigs squeak;
> That Latin is no more difficile
> Than to a blackbird 't is to whistle";

but I find that men who have graduated with all the honors fight shy of Greek, and have no inordinate passion for Latin, preferring their own tongue wherein they were born as decidedly as we unlearned rabble. Even Atalanta in Calydon, the work of that wondrous man, if indeed he be a man, who not only reads Greek, but writes it, and not only writes it, but writes verses in it, — even Atalanta, I find, is not very easily imposed upon an intelligent community. "Any new books lately?" says my friend the Secretary.

"Yes," I answered, blandly, "'Atalanta in Calydon' has just come in."

"*Who?*"

"'Atalanta in Calydon,' a Greek tragedy."

"Don't want it."

"It is not written in Greek. It is only modelled upon the Greek, I suppose. It gives Greek life and thought. It is really very —"

"Don't want it."

My friend, the Judge, is recovering from an illness. I meet his wife in an unfrequented street, and proffer Atalanta, sugar-coated with various toothsome authors. She declares (with a misgiving which she cannot conceal from me) that the Judge will be delighted. I promise to send the books betimes next morning; but an early bird hops up on the door-step, and chirps out, "Papa says he is much obliged for the books, but he does n't care for the Greek."

Happy they who are content to know nothing. To hum and hover in the sunshine over broad fields of learning, gathering only honey-dew from the cups of the sweetest flowers, — it is hardly worth the name of study, but it is wondrous pleasant. If Queen Caroline finds entertainment before breakfast in Butler's Analogy, by all means let her eat the fat and drink the sweet of it to her heart's content. If people like to calculate eclipses, it is an innocent amusement; let none gainsay or resist them. It would be very mortifying if none of us knew anything about it, and we had to go to England for our Almanacs. But as for turning Bishop Butler, or sines and cosines, into moral duty, after one has left school, and bruising one's spirit over them, I never could see that it was desirable. Augite and andesite, diorite and dolerite, give an uncertain sound. Glauber salts are but indifferent welcome, even when decked out with the honorary titles of $Na\ O\ SO_3 + 10\ HO$. The stars shine scarcely more serene for knowing their altitude and azimuth; but when Geology, from her primeval rocks, gropes back into the

twilight of the dawn, or reaches down into the
underworld to set the whole earth aglow; when
Chemistry leaves her alphabet to swathe the sun
in robes of fire, to feed him with endless streams
of meteors, and give him a universe to work his
magic in; when Astronomy lays down her mathematics and takes up her pencil of light, to paint
the belts of Jupiter and the rings of Saturn, piles
up her mountains and scoops out her valleys in
the moon, peoples space with suns and suns with
souls, and, sweeping world around world and gathering circle upon circle, binds them fast in one
radiant zone of life around the central orb, till

> " Every sphere can, swinging, hear
> The ripples of our atmosphere,
> The growing circles of our prayer;
> Circling beyond all time, all place,
> And breaking with its finite grace
> Upon dim shores of God's illimitable space,"

their charm commences. You see how it is; as
it was in the beginning, is now, and ever shall be,
fools rush in where angels fear to tread. Where
science leaves the solid ground of fact, and spreads
her wings for fancy-flights, where knowledge melts
away into poetry, and induction becomes conjecture, all hail, science, knowledge, induction! Go
on, wise men. Watch out the night with your
stars, singe your eyebrows with the fiery breath
of the genii you have caught, but not tamed, in
your prison-jars, hammer up the rocks steadfastly
chip by chip, till you have broken the spirit of

their secret. We, sitting by the ingle-side on winter evenings, or resting under the cool shadows of the summer-time, enter into your reward. All your weary work makes pleasant paths for us. We are not in love with your processes, but we have a warm glow of greeting for your results.

You are doubtless disgusted, Messrs. Magi, and perhaps not without reason. I am ready to confess that, if you look at it as learning, it is, like my friend's silver, all sham, but if you look at it as life, it is, like my friend herself, all sincerity. And after all, is not life better than learning? When you will tell what good your science does you, if it does not make you happy, of what advantage it is to you to unlock the treasures of antiquity, if to you those treasures are mere rubbish, what boots it with incessant care strictly to meditate a thankless muse, then it will be time enough to reconsider. Meanwhile I do but copy yourselves. You do not, as a general thing, take all knowledge to be your province, and if you do, you enter into possession of but a very small part of it. You select from the Universe your specialty, and I select from your selection mine. You skim the cream of thought, and I the *crême de la crême*, and we are both suited, with only this difference, that you have the name of savant and I the name of smatterer. All well so long as we wear our honors smilingly, — though it is pleasant now and then to strut in stolen plumes. And Webster's Dictionary is such a royal road to fame! Thither flock from every quarter the choice phrases of dead and living tongues, and whosoever will may garnish his speech with store of polyglotic mysteries, which shall speak to the uninitiated of boundless wealth in reserve. And surely, to elicit the admiration, the envy, and the wrath of the ignoble crowd who do not own the great Unabridged, and who cannot therefore understand your foreign lingo, is a pleasure not to be lightly esteemed or foregone.

But all I meant to say, — though you will never believe it, seeing I have said so much, — was, that, not pretending to know anything, and never having been in a situation from which it would be expected that I should know anything, I am not obliged to keep up appearances, and can afford to like Atalanta. It does not in the least trouble me that I do not always know what Althæa, and Chorus, and Meleager are talking about. The rhyme, the rhythm, the melodious jingle, do not depend upon logical sequences. Why be distressed to understand everything? Why rave against a beautiful, fruitful darkness star-sown with splendor? That is one thing to like the book for, — because it is not to be understood; because it is far, and strange, and ideal; because you can read at it forever.

Some psychical influence conveyed my mood to the soul of my Sleeping Beauty. Wandering in his distant dream-land, he became evidently conscious that trouble was brewing at home, threatening his supremacy. An appalling sight meets his opening eyes. It is I and my manuscript. There is no escape through the rain, and then that fatal confession of leisure! His doom settles down upon him.

"Here I am," I cry, smiling sweetly, "like Christian with his precious roll."

"And here *I* am," he growls and scowls, "like Christian with his grievous burden."

I make no parley, but advance at once into the middle of things by unfolding my manuscript.

"What is it all about?" he at length asks.

"It is a historical piece."

He stares at me. "My dear, this is madness! Sheer midsummer madness! You know nothing about history."

I. Don't I? History is philosophy, teaching by example, and always repeats itself. Christopher Columbus, a native of Genoa —

H. You know a few bald facts that have been sifted out and set before you; but for anything like independent investigation —

I. This, perhaps, is more in the nature of biography. It is a kind of personal history.

H. What person?

I. I have called it King James the First.

H. Have you found any sources of information that escaped the eyes of Macaulay and —

I. Yes, Halicarnassus, I have. I think I know a good deal more about this matter than Macaulay.

H. Go on. Read. Least said, soonest mended.

KING JAMES THE FIRST.

A merry monarch two years and four months old —

H. O, that is it, is it? History in petticoats.

I. Don't interrupt. Now I shall have to begin all over again. The beauty of the paper depends upon its unity and continuity. You know that I always listen to your remarks with resignation if not with pleasure, as it is my duty to do. But I particularly dislike to be interrupted.

KING JAMES THE FIRST.

A merry monarch two years and four months old.

If we could have stood by when the world was a-making, — could have sniffed the escaping gases, as they volatilized through the air, — could have seen and heard the swash of the waves, when the whole world was, so to speak, in hot water, — could have watched the fiery tumult gradually soothing itself into shapely, stately palms and ferns, cold-blooded Pterodactyles, and gigantic, but gentle Megatheriums, till it was refined, at length, into sunshine and lilies and Robin Redbreasts, — we fancy we should have been intensely interested. But a human soul is a more mysterious thing than this round world. Its principles firmer than the hills, its passions more tumultuous than the sea, its purity resplendent as the light, its power too swift and subtile for human analysis, — what wonder in heaven above or earth beneath can rival this mystic, mighty mechanism? Yet it is formed almost under our eyes. The voice of God, "Let there be light," we do not hear; the stir of matter thrilled into mind we do not see; but the after-march goes on before our gaze. We have only to look, and, lo! the mountains are slowly rising, the valleys scoop their levels, the sea heaves against its barriers, and the chaotic soul evolves itself from its nebulous, quivering light, from its plastic softness, into a world of repose, of use, of symmetry, and stability. This mysterious soul, when it first passed within our vision, was only not hidden within its mass of fleshly life, a seed of spirituality deep-sunk in a pulp of earthliness. Passing away from us in ripened perfection, we behold a being but little lower than the angels, heir of God and joint heir with Christ, crowned with glory and honor and immortality.

Come up, then, Jamie, my King, into the presence of the great congregation! There are poets here, and philosophers, wise men of the East who can speak of trees, from the cedar-tree that is in Lebanon, even unto the hyssop that springeth out of the wall: also of beasts, and of fowl, and of creeping things, and of fishes. But fear them not, little Jamie! you are of more value, even to science, than many fishes. Wise as these Magi are, yesterday they were such as you, and such they must become again or ever they shall enter the kingdom of heaven. Come up, little Jamie, into the hall of audience! Blue eyes and broad brow, sunny curls, red lips, and dainty, sharp teeth, stout little arm, strong little hand, sturdy little figure, and most still and steadfast gaze: truly it is the face and form of a king, — sweetness in power, unconsciousness in royalty.

"Jamie, you are a little beauty! You are too handsome to live!"

"No!" says Jamie, vehemently, for the fiftieth time, stamping the royal foot and scowling the royal brows. "Gamma say *not* too ha'some!"

"But you are a young Apollo."

"No my 'Pollo!"

"What are you, then?"

"I goo e baw," which is Jametic for good little boy.

This microcosm, like the macrocosm, may be divided into many departments. As the world is viewed geographically, geologically, historically, astronomically, so in this one little Jamie we have many Jamies. There is the Jamie philological, Jamie theological, Jamie psychological, Jamie emotional, Jamie social; in fact, I can hardly think of any natural, moral, or mathematical science, on which a careful study of Jamie will not throw some light. Would you frame a theory of metaphysics? Consult Reid, and Locke, and Hamilton warily, for they are men, subject to like mistakes as we are; but observe Jamie with utmost confidence and the closest care, for he is the book of God, and will teach only truth, if your eye is single to perceive truth. Theologically, Jamie has points superior to both Andover and Princeton; he is never in danger of teaching for doctrine the commandments of men; nor have passion and prejudice in him any power to conceal, but, on the contrary, they illuminate truth. For the laws of language, mark how the noble tree of human speech springs in his soul from mustard-seed into fair and fruitful symmetry. In good sooth, one marvels that there should be so much error in the world with children born and growing up all over it. If Jamie were, like Jean Paul, the Only, I should expect philosophers to journey from remotest regions to sit at his feet and learn the ways of God to man. Every one who presumed to teach his fellows should be called upon to produce his diploma as a graduate of Jamie, or forfeit all confidence in his sagacity. But, with a baby in every other house, how is it that we continually fall out by the way? It must be that children are not advantageously used. We pet them, and drug them, and spoil them; we trick them out in silks and fine array; we cross and thwart and irritate them; we lay unholy hands upon them, but are seldom content to stand aside and see the salvation of the Lord.

Tug, tug, tug, one little foot wearisomely ranging itself beside the other, and two hands helping both: that is Jamie coming up stairs. Patter, patter, patter: that is Jamie trotting through the entry. He never walks. Rattle, clatter, shake: Jamie is opening the door. Now he marches in. Flushed with exertion, and exultant over his brilliant escapade from the odious surveillance below, he presents himself peering on tiptoe just over the arm of the big chair, and announces his errand, —

"Come t' see Baddy."

"Baddy does n't want you."

"Baddy *do*."

Then, in no wise daunted by his cool welcome, he works his way up into the big chair with much and indiscriminate pulling: if it is a sleeve, if it is a curtain, if it is a table-cloth whereon repose many pens, much ink and paper, and knickknacks without number, nothing heeds he, but clutches desperately at anything which will help him mount, and so he comes grunting in, all tumbled and twisted, crowds down beside me, and screws himself round to face the table, poking his knees and feet into me with serene unconcern. Then, with a pleased smile lighting up his whole face, he devotes himself to literature. A small, brass-lined cavity in the frame of the writing-desk serves him for an inkstand. Into that he dips an old, worn-out pen with consequential air, and assiduously traces nothing on bits of paper. Of course I am reduced to a masterly inactivity, with him wriggling against my right arm, let alone the danger hanging over all my goods and chattels from this lawless little Vandal prowling among them. Shall I send him away? Yes, if I am an insensate clod, clean given over to stupidity and selfishness; if I count substance nothing, and shadow all things; if I am content to dwell with frivolities forever, and have for eternal mysteries nothing but neglect. For suppose I break in upon his short-lived delight, thrust him out grieved and disappointed, with his brave brow clouded, a mist in his blue eyes, and — that heart-rending sight — his dear little under-lip and chin all quivering and puckering. Well, I go back and write an epic poem. The printers mangle it; the critics fall foul of it; it is lost in going through the post-office; it brings me ten letters, asking an autograph, on six of which I have to pay postage. There is vanity and vexation of spirit, besides eighteen cents out of pocket, and the children crying for bread. I let him stay. A little, innocent life, fearfully dependent on others for light, shines out with joyful radiance, wherein I rejoice. To-morrow he will have the measles, and the mumps, and the croup, and the whooping-cough, and scarlatina; and then come the alphabet, and Latin grammar, and politics, and his own boys getting into trouble: but to-day, when his happiness is in my hands, I may secure it, and never can any one wrest from him the sunshine I may pour into his happy little heart. O, the time comes so soon, and comes so often, that Love can only look with bitter sorrow upon the sorrow which it has no power to mitigate!

Language is unceremoniously resolved into its original elements by Jamie. He is constitutionally opposed to inflection, which, as he must be devoid of prejudice, may be considered indisputable proof of the native superiority of the English to other languages. He is careful to include in his sentences all the important words, but he has small respect for particles, and the disposition of his words waits entirely upon his moods. *My* usually does duty for *I*. "Want that Uncle Frank gave me hossey," with a finger pointing to the mantel-piece, is just as flexible to his use as "Want the hossey that Uncle Frank gave me." "Where Baddy *can* be?" he murmurs softly to himself, while peering behind doors and sofas in playing hide-and-seek. Hens are cud-dah, a flagrant example of Onomatopœia. The cradle is a cay-go; corn-balls are ball-corn; snow-bird, bird-snow; and all his rosy nails are toe-nails. He has been drilled into meet response to "How d' ye do?" but demonstrates the mechanical character of his reply by responding to any question that has the *you* and *how* sounds in it, as, "What do you think of that?" "How did you do it?" "How came you by this?" "Pit-*tee* well."

But his performances are not all mechanical. He has a stock of poetry and orations, of which he delivers himself at bedtime with a degree of resignation, — that being the only hour in which he can be reduced to sufficient quietude for recitation; nor is that because he loves quiet more, but bed less. It is a very grievous misfortune, an unreasonable and arbitrary requisition, that breaks in upon his busy life, interrupts him in the midst of driving to mill on an inverted chair, hauling wood in a ditto footstool, and other important matters, and sweeps him off to darkness and silence. So, with night-gown on, and the odious bed imminent, he puts off the evil day by compounding with the authorities and giving a public entertainment, in consideration of a quarter of an hour's delay. He takes large liberties with the text of his poems, but his rhetorical variations are of a nature that shows it is no vain repetition, but that he enters into the spirit of the poem. In one of his songs a person

"Asked a sweet robin, one morning in May,
That sung in the apple-tree over the way,"

what it was he was singing.

"Don't you know? he replied, you cannot guess wrong;
Don't you know I am singing my cold-water song?"

This Jamie intensifies thus, —

"Do' know my sing my co'-wotta song, hm?"

When he reaches the place where

"Jack fell down
Boke cown,"

he invariably leaves Gill to take care of herself, and closes with the pathetic moral reflection, "'At *too* bad!" Little Jack Horner, having put in his thumb and picked out a plum, is made to declare definitely and redundantly, —

"My *ga-ate* big boy, jus' so big!"

He persists in praying, —

"'F I should die 'fore I wake up."

Borne off to bed at last, in spite of every pretext for delay, tired Nature droops in the "fringed curtains" of his eyes, and gapes protractedly through his wide-dividing lips.

"I seepy," he cries, fighting off sleep with the bravery of a major-general, — observing phenomena, *in articulo somni*, with the accuracy and enthusiasm of a naturalist, and reasoning from them with the skill of a born logician.

A second prolonged and hearty gape, and

"I two seepies," he cries, adding mathematics to his other accomplishments.

And that is the last of Jamie, till the early morning brings him trudging up stairs, all curled and shining, to "hear Baddy say 'Boo!'"

Total depravity, in Jamie's presence, is a doctrine hard to be understood. Honestly speaking, he does not appear to have any more depravity than is good for him,—just enough to make him piquant, to give him a relish. He is healthy and hearty all day long. He eats no luncheon and takes no nap, is desperately hungry thrice a day and sleeps all night, going to bed at dark after a solitary supper of bread and butter, more especially bread; and he is good and happy. Laying aside the revelations of the Bible and of Doctors of Divinity, I should say that his nature is honest, simple, healthful, pure, and good. He shows no love for wrong, no inclination towards evil rather than good. He is affectionate, just generous, and truthful. He just lives on his sincere, fun-loving, playful, yet earnest life, from day to day, a pure and perfect example, to my eye, of what God meant children to be. I cannot see how he should be very different from what he is, even if he were in heaven, or if Adam had never sinned. There is so fearful an amount of, and so decided a bent towards, wickedness in the world, that it seems as if nothing less than an inborn aptitude for wickedness can account for it; yet, in spite of all theories and probabilities, here is Jamie, right under my own eye, developing a far stronger tendency to love, kindness, sympathy, and all the innocent and benevolent qualities, than to their opposites. The wrong that he does seems to be more from fun and frolic, from sheer exuberance of animal spirits and intensity of mirthfulness, than anything else. He seems to be utterly devoid of malice, cruelty, revenge, or any evil motive. Even selfishness, which I take to be the fruitful mother of evil, is·held in abeyance, is subordinate to other and nobler qualities. Candy is dearer to him than he knows how to express; yet he scrupulously lays a piece on the mantel for an absent friend; and though he has it in full view, and climbs up to it, and in the extremity of his longing has been known, I think, to chip off the least little bit with his sharp mouse-teeth, yet he endures to the end and delivers up the candy with an eagerness hardly surpassed by that with which he originally received it. Can self-denial go further?

It seems to me that the reason of Jamie's gentleness and cheerfulness and goodness is, that he is comfortable and happy. The animal is in fine condition, and the spirit is therefore well served; consequently, both go on together with little friction. And I cannot but suspect that a great deal of human depravity comes from human misery. The destruction of the poor is his poverty. Little sickly, fretful, crying babies, heirs of worn nerves, fierce tempers, sad hearts, sordid tastes, half-tended or over-tended, fed on poison by the hand of love, nay, sucking poison from the breasts of love, trained to insubordination, abused by kindness, abused by cruelty, — that is the human nature from which largely we generalize, and no wonder the inference is total depravity. But human nature, distorted, defiled, degraded by centuries of misdealing, is scarcely human *nature*. Let us discover it before we define it. Let us remove accretions of longstanding moral and physical disease, before we pronounce sentence against the human *nature*. Let it become an established and universally recognized principle, as fixed and unquestionable as the right and wrong of theft and murder, that it is a sin against God, a crime against the state, an outrage upon the helpless victim of their ignorance or wickedness, for an unhealthy man or woman to become the parent of a child, and I think our creeds would presently undergo modification. Disease seems to me a more fertile source of evil than depravity; at least it is a more tangible source. We must have a race of healthy children, before we know what are the true characteristics of the human race. A child suffering from scrofula gives but a feeble, even a false representation of the grace, beauty, and sweetness of childhood. Pain, sickness, lassitude, deformity, a suffering life, a lingering death, are among the woful fruits of this dire disease, and it is acknowledged to be hereditary. Is not, then, every person afflicted with hereditary disease debarred as by a fiat of the Almighty from becoming a parent? Every principle of honor forbids it. The popular stolidity and blindness on these subjects are astonishing. A young woman whose sisters have all died of consumption, and who herself exhibits unmistakable consumptive tendencies, is married, lives to bear three children in quick succession, and dies of consumption. Her friends mourn her and the sad separation from her bereaved little ones, but console themselves with the reflection that these little ones have prolonged her life. But for her marriage, she would have died years before. Of the three children born of this remedial marriage, two die in early girlhood of consumption. One left, a puny infant, languishes into a puny maturity. Even as a remedy, what is this worth? To die in her youth, to leave her suffering body in the dust and go quickly to God, with no responsibility beyond herself, or to pine through six years, enduring thrice, besides all her inherited debility, the pain and peril, the weariness and terror of child-bearing, to be at last torn violently and prematurely away from these beloved little ones, — which is the disease, and which the remedy? And when we look further on at the helpless little innocents, doomed to be the recipients of disease, early deprived of a mother's care, for which there is no substitute, dragging a load of weakness and pain, and forced down into the Valley of the Shadow of Death before years shall have blunted the point of its terrors, or religion robbed them of their sting, — it is only not atrocious because so unwittingly wrought.

And bodily health is only one of the possessions which every child has a right to claim from its parents. Not merely health, but dispositions, traits, lie within human control far beyond the extent of common recognition. We say that character is formed at fourteen or sixteen, and that training should begin in infancy; but sometimes it seems to me, that, when the child is born, the work is done. All the rest is supplementary and subordinate. Subsequent effort has, indeed, much effect, but it cannot change quality. It may modify, but it cannot make anew. After neglect or ignorance may blight fair promise, but no after wisdom can bring bloom for blight. There are many by-laws whose workings we do not understand; but the great, general law is so plain, that wayfaring folk, though fools, need not err therein. Ever one sees the unbridled passions of the father or mother raging in the child. Gentleness is born of gentleness, insanity of insanity, truth of truth. Careful and prayerful training may mitigate the innate evil; but how much better that the young life should have sprung to light from seas of love and purity and peace! Through God's mercy, the harsh temper, the miserly craving, the fretful discontent may be repressed and soothed; but it is always up hill work, and never in this world wholly successful. Why be utterly careless in forming, to make conscious life a toilsome and thankless task of reforming? Since there is a time, and there comes no second, when the human being is under human control, — since the tiny infant, once born, is a separate individual, is for all its remaining existence an independent human being, why not bring power to bear where form is amenable to power? Only let all the influences of that sovereign time be heavenly, — and whatever may be true of total depravity, Christ has made such a thing possible, — and there remains no longer the bitter toil of thwarting, but only the pleasant work of cultivating Nature.

It is idle, and worse than idle, to call in question the providence of God for disaster caused solely by the improvidence of man. The origin of evil may be hidden in the unfathomable obscurity of a distant, undreamed-of past, beyond the scope of mortal vision; but by far the greater part of the evil that we see — which is the only evil for which we are responsible — is the result of palpable violation of Divine laws. Humanity here is as powerful as Divinity. The age of miracles is past. God does not interfere to contravene His own laws. His part in man's creation He long ago defined, and delegates all the rest to the souls that He has made. Man is as able as God to check the destructive tide. And it is mere shuffling and shirking and beating the wind, for a people to pray God to mitigate the ill which they continually and unhesitatingly perpetuate and multiply.

The great mistake made by the believers in total depravity is in counting the blood of the covenant of little worth. We admit that in Adam all die; but we are slow to believe that in Christ all can be made alive. We abuse the doctrine. We make it a sort of scapegoat for shortcoming. But Christ has made Adamic depravity of no account. He came not alone to pardon sin, but to save people from sinning. Father-love, mother-love, and Christ-love are so mighty that together they can defy Satan, and, in his despite, the soul shall be born into the kingdom of heaven without first passing through the kingdom of hell. And in this way only, I think, will the kingdoms of this world become the kingdoms of our Lord and of his Christ.

"Now, Jamie, having set the world right, — you and I, for which the world will be deeply grateful, — let us see what you are about, for you have been suspiciously still lately. What doing, Jamie?"

"Hay-puh!" says Jamie, very red, eager, and absorbed, with no intermission of labor.

"Making hasty pudding!" O yes! I know what that means. Only taking all the chips and shavings out of the wood-box in the closet and carrying them half across the room by the eminently safe conveyance of his two fat hands, and emptying them into my box of paper, and stirring all together with a curling-stick. That is nothing. "Keep on, Jamie, and amuse yourself; but let us hear your geography lesson."

"Where are you going one of these days?"

"Min-nee-so-toh."

"Where is Minnesota?"

Jamie gives a jerk with his arm to the west. He evidently thinks Minnesota is just beyond the hill.

"Where is papa going to buy his horses?"

"Ill-noy."

"And where does Aunt Sarah live?"

"Cog-go."

"What river are you going to sail up to get to Minnesota?"

"Miss-iss-ipp-ee."

"That's a *good* little boy! He knows ever so much; and here is a peppermint. Open his mouth and shut his eyes, and pop! it goes."

There is, however, a pretty picture on the other side, that Jamie thrusts his iconoclastic fists through quite unconcernedly; and that is the dignity of human nature. The human being can be trained into a dignified person: that no one denies. Looking at some honored and honorable man bearing himself loftily through every crisis, and wearing his grandeur with an imperial grace, one may be pardoned for the mistake, but it is none the less a mistake, of reckoning the acquirement of an individual as the endowment of the race. Behold human nature unclothed upon with the arts and graces of the schools, if you would discover, not its possibilities, but its attributes. The helplessness of infancy appeals to all that is chivalric and Christian in our hearts; but to dignity it is pre-eminently a stranger. A charming and popular writer — on the whole, I am not sure that it was not my own self — once affirmed that a baby is a beast, and gave great offence thereby; yet it seems to me that no unprejudiced person can observe an infant of tender weeks sprawling and squirming in the bath-tub, and not confess that it looks more like a little pink frog than anything else. And here is Jamie, not only weeks, but months and years old, setting his young affections on candy and dinner, and eating in general, with an appalling intensity. It is humiliating to see how easily he is moved by an appeal to his appetite. I blush for my race, remembering the sparkle of his eyes over a dainty dish, and the intensity of his devotion to it, — the enthusiasm with which his feet spring, and his voice rings through the house, to announce the fact, "Dinnah mo' weh-wy! dinnah mo' weh-wy!" To the naked eye, he appears to think as much of eating as a cat or a chicken or a dog. Reasons and rights he is slow to comprehend; but his conscience is always open to conviction, and his will pliable to a higher law, when a stick of candy is in the case. His bread-and-butter is to him what science was to Newton; and he has been known to reply abstractedly to a question put to him in the height of his enjoyment, " Don' talk t' me now!" This is not dignity, surely. Is it total depravity? What is it that makes his feet so swift to do mischief? He sweeps the floor with the table-brush, comes stumbling over the carpet almost chin-deep in a pair of muddy rubber boots, catches up the bird's seed-cup and darts away, spilling it at every step; and the louder I call, the faster he runs, half frightened, half roguish, till an unmistakable sharpness pierces him, makes him throw down cup and seed together, and fling himself full length on the floor, his little heart all broken. Indeed, he can bear anything but displeasure. He tumbles down twenty times a day, over the crickets, off the chairs, under the table, head first, head last, bump, bump, bump, and never a tear sheds he, though his stern self-control is sometimes quite pitiful to see. But a little slap on his cheek, which is his standing punishment, — not a blow, but a tiny tap that must derive all its efficacy from its moral force, — oh, it stabs him to the heart! He has no power to bear up against it, and goes away by himself, and cries, bitterly, sonorously, and towards the last, I suspect, rather ostentatiously. Then he spoils it all by coming out radiant, and boasting that he has "make tear," as if that were an unparalleled feat. If you attempt to chide him, he puts up his plump hand with a repelling gesture, turns away his head in disgust, and ejaculates vehemently, "Don' talk t' me!" After all, however, I do not perceive that he is any more sensitive to reproof than an intelligent and petted dog.

His logical faculty develops itself somewhat capriciously, but is very prompt. He seldom fails to give you a reason, though it is often of the Kilve weathercock type.

"Don' talk t' me! I little Min-nee-so-toh boy!" — as if that were an amnesty proclamation. You invite him to stay with you, and let Papa go to Minnesota without him. He shakes his head dubiously, and protests, with solemn earnestness, "Mus' go Min-nee-so-toh ca'y my fork," which, to the world-incrusted mind, seems but an inadequate pretext. I want him to write me a letter when he is gone away; but after a thoughtful pause, he decides that he cannot, "'cause I got no pen." If he is not in a mood to repeat the verse you ask for, he finds full excuse in the unblushing declaration, "I bashful." He casts shadows on the wall with his wreathing, awkward little fingers, and is perfectly satisfied that they are rabbits, though the mature eye discerns no resemblance to any member of the vertebrate family. He gazes curiously to see me laugh at something I am reading, — "What 'at? my want to see," — and climbs up to survey the page with wistful eyes; but it is "a' a muddle" to him. He greets me exultantly after absence, because I have "come home pay coot with Jamie"; and there is another secret out: that it is of no use to be sentimental with a child. He loves you in proportion as you are available. His papa and mamma fondly imagine they are dearer to him than any one else, and it would be cruel to disturb that belief; but it would be the height of folly to count yourself amiable because Jamie plants himself firmly against the door, and pleads piteously, "Don' go in e parly wite!" He wants you to "pay coot" with him,—that is all. If your breakfast shawl is lying on a chair, it would not be sagacious to attribute an affectionate unselfishness to him in begging leave to "go give Baddy shawl t' keep Baddy back warm." It is only his greediness to enter forbidden ground. Sentiment and sensibility have small lodgement in his soul.

But when Jamie is duly forewarned, he is forearmed. Legally admitted into the parlor to see visitors he sits on the sofa by his mother's side, silent, upright, prim, his little legs stuck straight out before him in two stiff lines, presenting a full front view of his soles. By the way, I wonder how long grown persons would sit still, if they were obliged to assume this position. But Jamie maintains himself heroically, his active soul subdued to silence, till Nature avenges herself, not merely with a palpable, but a portentous yawn.

"You may force me to this unnatural quiet," she seems to say; "but if you expect to prevent me from testifying that I think it intolerably stupid, you have reckoned without your host."

And here Jamie comes out strongly in favor of democracy, universal suffrage, political equality, the Union and the Constitution, the Declaration of Independence, and the rights of man. Uncontaminated by conventional rules, he recognizes the human being apart from worldly state. He is as silent and abashed in the presence of the day-laborer, coarsely clad and rough of speech and manners as in that of the accomplished man of the world, or the daintiest silken-robed lady. With simple gravity, and never a thought of wrong, he begs the poet, "Pease, Missa Poet, tie up my shoe." He stands in awe before the dignity of the human soul; but dress, and rank, and reputation receive no homage from him. He is reverent, but not to false gods. The world finds room for kingdoms and empires and oligarchies; but undoubtedly man is born a democrat.

Is there only one Jamie here? Can one little urchin about as high as the table so fill a house with mirth and mischief, so daguerreotype himself in every corner, possess, while claiming nothing, so large a share of the household interest? For he somehow bubbles up everywhere. Not a mischance or a misplacement but can pretty surely be brought home to him. Is a glass broken? Jamie broke it. Is a door open that ought to be shut? Jamie opened it. Or shut that ought to be open? Jamie shut it. Is there a mighty crash in the entry? It is Jamie dropping the crowbar through the side-lights. The "Atlantic" has been missing all the morning.

"Jamie," — a last, random resort, after fruitless search, — "where is the 'Atlantic Monthly'?"

"In daw."

"In the drawer? No, it is not in the drawer. You don't know anything about it."

Not quite so fast. Jamie knows the "Atlantic Monthly" as well as you; and if you will open the drawer for him, he will rapidly scatter its contents till he comes to the missing "Monthly," safe under the shawls where he deposited it.

If you are hanging your room with ground-pine, he lays hold of every stray twig, and tucks it into every crack he can reach. Will you have some corn out of the barrel? It is Jamie for balancing himself on the edge, and reaching down into the depths after it, till little more than his heels are visible. If in a sudden exuberance, you make a "cheese," — not culinary, but *whirligig*, — round go his little bobtail petticoats in fatuous imitation. You walk the floor awhile, lost in day dreaming, to find this little monkey trotting behind you with droll gravity, his hands clasped behind his head like yours; and he breaks in upon your most serious meditations with, "Baddy get down on floor, want wide on Baddy back," as coolly as if he were asking you to pass the salt. All that he says, all that he does, has its peculiar charm. Not that he is in the least a remarkable child.

> "I trust we have within our realme
> Five (thousand) as good as hee."

Otherwise what will befall this sketch?

I do not expect anything will ever come of him. In a few years he will be just like everybody else; but now he is the *peculiar* gift of Heaven. Men and women walk and talk all day long, and nobody minds them; while this little ignoramus seldom opens his lips but you think nothing was ever so winsomely spoken. I suspect it is only his complete simplicity and sincerity. What he says and what he does are the direct, unmistakable effusions of his nature. All comes straight from the secret place where his soul abideth. Even his subterfuges are open as the day. You know you are looking upon virgin nature. Just as it flashed from its source, you see the unadulterated spirit. If grown-up persons would or could be as frank as he, — if they had no more misgivings, concealments, self-distrust, self-thought than he, — they would doubtless be as interesting. Every separate human being is a separate phenomenon and mystery; and if he could only be unthinkingly himself, as Jamie is, that self would be as much more captivating as it is become great and fine by growth and experience. But we — fashion, habit, society, training, all the culture of life, mix a sort of paste, and we gradually become coated with it, and it hardens upon us; so it comes to pass, by and by, that we see our associates no longer, but only the casing in which they walk about; and as one is a good deal like another, we are not deeply fascinated. Sometimes a Thor's hammer breaks this flinty rock in pieces. Sometimes a fervid sun melts it, and you are let in to where the vigilant soul keeps watch and ward. Sometimes, alas! the hardening process seems to have struck in, and you find nothing but petrifaction all the way through.

Perhaps, after all, it is just as well; for, if our neighbors won upon us unawares as Jamie does, when should we ever find time to do anything? On the whole, it is a great deal better as it is, until the world has learned to love its neighbor as itself. For the present, it would not be safe to go abroad with the soul exposed. You fetch me a blow with your bludgeon, and I mind it not at all through my coat of mail; but if it had fallen on my heart, it would have wounded me to death. Nay, if you did but know where the sutures are, how you would stab and stab, dear fellow-man and brother, not to say Christian! No, we are not to be trusted with each other yet, — I with you, nor you with me; so we will keep our armor on awhile, please Heaven.

And as I think of Jamie frisking through the happy, merry days, I see how sad, unnatural, and wicked a thing it is, that mothers must so often miss the sunshine that ought to come to them through their little ones. We speak of losing children, when they die; but many a mother loses her children, though they play upon her threshold every day. She loses them, because she has no leisure to loiter, and live in them. She is so occupied in providing for their wants, that she has no time to sun herself in their grace. She snatches from them sweetness enough to keep herself alive, but she does not ripen in their warmth for all the world. And the hours go by, and the days go by, evening and morning, seed-time and harvest, and the little frocks are outgrown, and the little socks outworn, and the little baby — O, there is no little baby any more, but a boy with the crust formed already on his soul.

I marvel what becomes of these small people in heaven. They cannot stay as they are, for then heaven would be a poorer place than earth, where all but idiots increase in wisdom and stature. And if they keep growing, — why, it seems but a sorry exchange, to give up your tender, tiny, clinging infant, that is still almost a part of your own life, and receive in return a full-grown angel a great deal wiser and stronger than you. Perhaps it is only a just punishment for our guilty ignorance and selfishness in treating the little things so harshly, that they die away from us in sheer self-defence. And how good is the All-Father thus to declare for His little ones, when the strife waxes too hot, and the odds too heavy against them! We can maltreat them, but only to a certain limit. Beyond that, the lovely, stern angel of Death steps in, and bears them softly away to perpetual peace. I read our vital statistics, — so many thousands under five years of age dying each year; and I rejoice in every one. If their chances were fair for purity and happiness, the earth is too beautiful to slip so quickly from their hold; but with sin and suffering, twin beasts of prey, lying in wait to devour, oh! thrice and four times happy they who escape swiftly from the struggle in which they are all too sure to fail. So many, at least, are safe within the fold.

And thus, too, it seems providential, that the sin of pagan nations should take the form of infanticide. It is Satanic work, but God overrules it for good. Evil defeats itself, and hatred crowds the list of love. From stifled cities, overfull, from heathen lands, steeped centuries long in vice and crime, from East and West and North and South, over all the world, the innocent souls go up, — little lily-buds, springing white and pure from earthly slime to bloom in heavenly splendor.

Jamie, Jamie, do you see birdie has put his head under his wing and gone to sleep? What does that mean? It means "Good night, Jamie." Now come, let us have "Cr-e-e-p, cr-e-e-p, cr-e-e-p!" And two fingers go slowly, measuring Jamie from toe to neck, and Jamie cringes and squirms and finally screams outright, and almost flings himself upon the floor; but, as soon as his spasm is over, begs again, " Say, ' K-e-e-p, k-e-e-p, k-e-e-p!' " and would keep it going longer than I have time to wait.

In this very passion for reiteration may be found a sufficient answer to those uneasy persons who are perpetually attempting to bring new singing-books into our churches, on pretext that people are tired of the old tunes. You never hear from Jamie's pure taste any clamor for new songs or stories. Whenever he climbs up to your lap to be amused he is sure to ask for the story of " Kitty in Ga'et Window," though he knows it as Boston people know oratorio music, and detects and condemns the slightest departure from the text. And when you have gone through the drama, with all its motions and mewings, he wants nothing so much as " Kitty in Ga'et Window 'gen." Let us keep the old tunes. It is but a factitious need that would change them.

Gentle and friendly reader, I pray your pardon for this childish record. Some things I say of set purpose for your good, and the more you do not like them, the more I know they are the very things you need; and I shall continue to deal them out to you from time to time, as you are able to bear them. But this broken, rambling child-talk — with " a few practical reflections, arising naturally from my subject," as the preachers say — was penned only for your pleasure — and mine; and if you do not like it, I shall be very sorry, and wish I had never written it. For we might have gone away by ourselves and enjoyed it all alone; could we not, Jamie, you and I together? O no, no! Never again! Never, never again! for the mountains that rise and the prairies that roll between us. Ah well, Jamie, I shall not cry about it. If you had stayed here, it would have been but a little while before you would have grown up into a big boy, and then a young fellow, and then a man, and been of no account. So what does it signify? Good night, little Jamie! good night, darling! Do I hear a sleepy echo, as of old, wavering out of the West, " *Goo-i-dah-ing* "?

H. I suppose that " gentle and friendly reader " does not mean me. I am saluted with bayonet and blunderbuss rather than such sweet supplicatory phrase.

I. Yes, I am obliged to cárry matters with a high hand towards you. But is not this nice? You have enjoyed it I know. Do not deny it. On the whole, what do you think of me as a historian?

H. Ah! — well, yes, I have enjoyed it so far as general character is concerned. I think it quite the best piece of style I have ever seen from you.

I. Charming! Only there is no style about it.

H. But you —

I. O, now do not go and spoil it all. It is so seldom you pay me a compliment, do let me have the good of it for once.

H. I can't tell a lie, Pa, you know I can't tell a lie.

I. Don't tell a lie, then; just stop where you are.

H. O well. Anything to please you. What have you done with my book?

I. What were you going to say if I had not hindered you?

H. I was going to say my name is Norval on the Grampian hills!

I. Nonsense! Tell me.

H. Well, then, it strikes me you have, as usual, lugged in some theology —

I. No, I have not lugged in anything, — theology or physiology. Everything that is there came of its own accord. I tell you theology is in everything, and you cannot keep it out.

H. At any rate it is there, and you are responsible for it, however it got there. You intimate that the theory of the Doctors of Divinity and the statements of the Bible in regard to human depravity are not sustained by the facts in Jamie's case; yet he is expressly not exceptional, only that he is well and well-conditioned. But in the popular estimate, to reject human depravity is to reject Orthodoxy.

I. But I —

H. Wait a minute, I am not quite through. And to reject Orthodoxy is to range on the side of Rationalism against Evangelical religion —

I. Let me just ask you one question. Are you speaking your own thoughts or making believe for some imaginary objector?

H. Truth is truth. Never mind sources. For your argument, is it not something of a broken reed? You might pick up the cub of a grizzly bear of the same relative age with Jamie and hold forth over it: "Laying aside the revelations of the Natural History books, and of the professors of that science, I should say that its nature is honest, simple, healthful, pure, and good. It is affectionate, clumsy, playful, and lives wholly on milk. It shows no carnivorous propensity, no inclination to prefer blood and bones to mush and molasses. It just lives on its fun-loving, playful yet earnest life from day to day, a pure and perfect example to my eye of what God meant a kitten or a lamb to be. I cannot see how it could be very different from what it is, if it were intended to be a poodle-dog in heaven. In spite of all theories and probabilities, here is this little grizzly under my own eye developing a far stronger tendency to love, kindness, sympathy, and all the innocent and benevolent qualities than to their opposites." And yet I fancy I see you trusting yourself within reach of the paws and jaws of grizzly when he has had time to become a little more "developed" in this nature whose youngness is so cunningly safe and piquantly good.

The flaw is, that you have left out of your argument the great influence which infancy has in masking character. Almost any ill beast is pleasant in its immaturity. I have seen little pigs than whom I could scarce conceive of "cunninger" pets, yet all the while on their swift, unswerving way to unmitigated hog-hood. Here endeth the first lesson.

I. You have finished your sermon?

H. For the present.

I. I think it is as poor a sermon as ever I heard.

H. Free your mind, brother, as they say in class-meeting.

I. It is very good, in fact it is quite picturesque in point of style, but for substance of doctrine it is just nothing at all. I can demolish it so easily that I really do not know where to begin.

H. O, pitch right in anywhere.

I. No, I shall go to work systematically. You say that I say that the doctrine of total depravity is not sustained by the facts in Jamie's case. I do not say that exactly, but rather by the appearance of Jamie's case; by what seem to me to be the facts. But never mind that. Does the doctrine of depravity depend upon the development of a two-year-old boy? I simply affirm, leaving out the

Bible, you would judge so and so. But do I leave out the Bible? Is not that what the Bible is for, — to help us in making up judgment? And do I object to using it for that purpose? If I should descant upon your cub, " Leaving out the revelations of the Natural History books, and of the professors of that science, I should say that it has a simple, playful, kindly nature," would you immediately cry out, " O, now you are going over to the lamb-and-kitten theory of bears!" or would you answer quietly, " That is true as far as it goes; but in finally making up your mind you must not leave out their revelations, nor the revelations which your own eyes will make, when your cub has become a full-grown bear. All who have made a study of Bruin's life from infancy to old age, agree that a bear is a bear by nature and not by education "? I declare expressly, that I am not able to account for the abounding wickedness in the world, except on the theory of innate depravity; but, on the other side, I am equally certain that I recognize no marks of depravity in Jamie. His infancy has completely masked it from me. And I am talking about what I see, not what you assure me is there.

H. But directly afterwards you begin to modify the creed, and reduce depravity to disease, thereby virtually abolishing it.

I. Abolishing a great deal of it to be sure, but not the whole. What I maintain is, that the evidence is not all in until healthy human nature has had a chance to testify.

H. But you are ready to deny that to be human *nature* which is diseased. Yet morally it has become so by sin, and you must take it as it has become since the fall.

I. I do take it, fall and all. By disease I do not mean any mysterious kink caused by Adam, but such moral and physical disease as we see contracting around us all the time. I mean, for instance, that parents neglect their children's teeth, and so the children have toothache, and toothache makes them cross. Parents suffer their children to eat improper food in an improper manner, and so impair their digestion, and this again makes them fretful and unhappy. They permit them to sit up too late, to go out evenings while they are still children, — and when a child ought to be in bed, it does not matter much whether it is a children's ball or a Sunday-school concert that keeps him out of it, — and so the nervous system is injured. They do not enforce prompt and perfect obedience, and the character is permanently weakened. They thwart unnecessarily or scold capriciously and the temper is soured. Now I say, this is our own fault, and nobody else's. A mother can send her child to bed at seven o'clock just as regularly as if no apple ever grew, and to turn all the wrong off upon Adam, and call it human nature and original sin, is a great piece of injustice.

H. O yes, it is original sin — with all who commit it.

I. You never lapse from logic into puns, till you have exhausted every other resource.

H. Possibly the very weakness which cannot command obedience, and the ignorance which does not see its necessity, may be owing to the fall, if you trace it back far enough.

I. Whatever it is owing to, away with it as fast as possible. Rend off all the wickedness that comes from palpable mismanagement, and let us see what manner of being we have on our hands. I, for one, have not the least apprehension that it will be a creature too bright or good for human nature's daily food, or that there will not be sinfulness enough left for faith to fasten on. But some of you people seem to stickle for depravity, as if it were a precious legacy, and you feared lest an avaricious world should seek to rob you of some part or lot in it. You make an idol of it, and guard it against profane approach. You cry out, with the old lady, " When you have taken away my total depravity, you have taken away my religion."

H. Very tart and smart, my dear; but as an argument, to borrow the phraseology of our "wayward sisters," not worth shucks.

I. No, but at least you need not be so anxious, lest humanity should not be painted in colors dark enough. Why, your own cubs here turn and rend you. They grow up into ravenous bears, not because they are neglected and mismanaged, but because their nature is ravenous. The most healthy and the best-bred cub is savage and bloodthirsty. But a child healthy and properly trained is expected to become a well-behaved man. If he proves anything else, we call it strange, inexplicable. Therefore it seems his bent to badness is a different thing from a bear's bent to blood.

H. Of course the human being is more susceptible to training than any other.

I. And that fact ought to be brought out more fully. Whatever theory we hold as to how we came to be so weak and wicked, or even to what degree we are weak and wicked, the vital thing is to make the most of Christ's help in becoming strong and good. This we scarcely begin to do. We scarcely know there is such a thing to be done. We talk about our strength being in the Lord, but we let it be there. We do not lay hold of it and use it economically. We have inexhaustible treasures laid up in Christ, but we rarely draw upon them. Where do we look chiefly for accessions to the Church? Why, to revivals.

II. Where would you have us look?

I. To the children of the Church for the steady supply. Public opinion should be so formed that the Christianization of children shall be considered as much the duty of parents as the clothing of children. Children shall grow up into Christianity just as they grow up into manhood and womanhood. Their spiritual strength shall go hand in hand with their moral and intellectual strength. They shall become members of the Church as regularly as they become citizens of the State. It should be as unnatural and uncommon for the children of Christian parents to grow up not Christians, as it is for the child of honest parents to grow up a thief, — something to be remarked upon and looked into. It is intolerable the way we have of considering wrong as right. If a boy of sixteen becomes a Christian during a revival we call it early conversion, an answer to the prayers of faith, and give glory to God, and are abundantly satisfied. But in truth it is late conversion, and only just better than no conversion at all. As if one could go on sixteen years in sin with impunity, if at the end of them he repents of his sin! The sixteen formative years, the very years that make the man, are reckoned of small account. I think that is one reason why Christian character is so defective; it is because the Christian principle comes in so late. A man after years of wrong-doing, wrong-thinking, wrong-feeling, may become a sincere Christian, but his bad habits are so strong that he can hardly break them off. He has been so long in the clutch of sin that he cannot wrench himself free. His selfishness has become a sort of mould, his soul has been fashioned in it; and though he would now break the mould, it is only with the utmost difficulty, and after years of patient struggle, that this distorted shape will be changed into the image of Christ. And this struggle he is too weak to make with vigor; often he is so thoroughly debauched by sin that he does not perceive the necessity of making it. So the religion of Christ is constantly falsified by his shortcomings.

H. But he does break off his habits. If he does not see the need of making effort to become better, he was never truly a Christian. You make no account of grace. Paul says he can do all things through Christ strengthening him.

I. So can any of us, but we do not. What is the use of talking? You know perfectly well that people's bad habits cling to them long after they have become Christians. You have seen self-willed, prejudiced, domineering, miserly, gossiping church-members enough to know that. I am not accusing them, but excusing them. I suppose them to have gone on gossiping and domineering so long that they do not know they do gossip and domineer. Grace does not make a man reform in those respects in which he deems himself right already.

II. But it does often open his eyes to see the wrong in that which he thought right. And if such a man is to be changed at all, so much the more there must be a revival to change him. His childhood lacked the forming hand. The ordinary ways of God have failed to move him. It needs the extraordinary, the sympathy and excitement of a revival. He may never be so symmetrical a man as if he had served the Lord from his birth; but he will be a better man than if no revival had touched him. As things are, I do not see how we can get on without revivals.

I. As things are, but things ought to be different. I do not object to revivals as an adjunct, as a sort of aggressive movement upon the world; but we content ourselves with them, we count upon revivals to do our work for us. We have a long period of indifference, then an excitement, numerous meetings, a good deal of religious emotion, some awakening of religious principle; much hasty, ill-considered, unintelligent action, some real benefit. Perhaps a revival is better than indifference. Sometimes a religious life is begun which brightens on into the perfect day. Sometimes a man is lifted out of the mire of gross sins into clean and fair habitations, and sometimes selfishness gets itself baptized in the name of Jesus of Nazareth, and goes its way as complacently as if it had been changed into love.

II. But I think a revival generally leaves those who have been brought under its influence a little better than they were before.

I. But I do not see that a community living midway between a second and third revival is on a higher plane than when it was midway between a first and second revival. Good and shrewd Mrs. Blank was saying the other day how much revivals were needed. I answered, "Yes, I wish we could have revivals, — such as would keep us church-members from telling lies, and breaking promises, and enjoying our neighbors' troubles, and not paying our debts." "Never," said she emphatically, — "never will you live to see that day."

H. Very likely, but there is one comfort; we are not quite so bad as the early Christians. They must have been a hard set, those Gauls and Corinthians, judging from the way Paul took them to task.

I. I wonder he was not wholly discouraged.

H. So, though you cannot see improvement from year to year, you can see it in eighteen hundred years. And eighteen hundred years is not much in the world's history.

I. But I really think if we cannot put revivals more into the background it would be better not to have them at all. If we are going to spend all our force on them, call them the harvesting of the crop, we shall have the work to do over again from generation to generation, and shall never get on. But let Christian parents be taught that they are responsible for their children; that they are not simply to pray for the child's salvation, but to work it out; that the formation of his Christian character is not only their duty, as much as the establishment of his physical health, but is equally within their power; that every child who grows up unconverted is a living monument of parental ignorance, or unfaithfulness; and then —

H. The first twenty times I heard you say this I thought it was all right, the second, I kept silence, but now that you have begun on the third score, I begin to think I don't believe it. I admit that the parent's power over the child is great, but I question whether it is supreme. Where is your authority?

I. In the Bible, in nature, and in the character of God. The Old Testament —

H. Heavens! Have I upset another basket of theology on my poor head?

I. No, only a thimbleful if you keep quiet. The Old Testament recognizes absolute power of the father over children. The Lord said, I know Abraham, that he will command his children and his household after him, and they shall keep the way of the Lord. The New Testament promises everything to the prayer of faith. By expecting good parents to have good children, by being surprised when the child of bad parents turns out well, we confess the law of nature. And knowing the goodness of God, can we believe that he would give to human beings the power of evoking a soul without also giving them the power of saving it alive?

H. Yet you see the children of the most careful and prayerful parents going wrong.

I. Not without seeing also a sufficient predisposing cause,—that is, where there has been opportunity to see the process; and this in so many cases, that where I see only the disastrous result I infer that there has been a cause. From my observation I judge that cause and effect are just as closely connected in families as in farms. Wise culture in both brings good harvests. We no more gather grapes of thorns or grow thistles on fig-trees in the one case than in the other.

II. But the trouble is in knowing what wise culture is. One Isabella grape-vine is just like another Isabella grape-vine; but of five children in one family, no two will be alike. Every one needs a different management from every other. The young parents strive conscientiously and unweariedly to do their best, but the result is anything but happy. Perhaps you can see where they make a mistake, but they do not see it. Perhaps in their place you would do no better, perhaps far worse. What are you going to do about it?

I. I am going to be confident that the great God who formed both parent and child is more considerate than you or I, and will make every allowance when he makes the final decision. But I really do not see how it is possible to make a fatal mistake, when the Apostle James says in so many words, "If any among you lack wisdom, let him ask of God, who giveth to all men liberally and upbraideth not, and it shall be given him."

Why not take God at his word? Do the very best you can, and *demand* of God wisdom, according to his promise. Do as Manoah did, entreat the Lord to "teach us what we shall do unto the child that shall be born." "How shall we order the child, and how shall we do unto him?"

H. Yet "the child" turned out to be anything but an exemplary man.

I. I know he was no better than he should be. Perhaps they did not follow it up. At any rate, the child grew and the Lord blessed him, and he became a great man. From the answer which was given to Manoah's prayer, I should not infer that his parents were thinking about his moral character when they asked guidance. However, there is the promise. I am not responsible for it. If it is not kept, you must settle the matter with the Apostle James, not with me. And really if it were so, that God would give a child to parents, and would not grant with him, to their earnest prayers and best endeavor, power to train him so as to insure his salvation, I could not say that God was good. Your child is nothing to be thankful for, if he may be lost in spite of you.

H. It is a remarkable fact, however, that the children are pretty well along in the world before their fathers and mothers have reflected very deeply upon its evils. The light-hearted young people are loving and housekeeping and baby-tending without much abstract thinking. Great moral duties and dangers occupy very little of their attention. Knowledge comes late, and wisdom lingers, but the little souls are on time. If you could make some arrangement by which the "idols in white frocks" should be given into the keeping of sensible, experienced, reflecting persons of a philosophical turn of mind, instead of silly young things who know nothing of life, perhaps you might accomplish something.

I. That remark is not nearly so sarcastic as you meant it to be, because it has not that basis of truth without which even caricature has no point. The great need is, not to have people know the right, but to do it. It was sin that first offered us the fruit of the tree of the knowledge of good and evil, and as far as we can put away sin we can put away that fruit. If boys and girls are brought up to do right as boys and girls, when they come to be parents they will naturally and easily do right as parents. Love is powerful as a corrective, but it is all-sufficient as a stimulus. The happy, charming young girl may have had little responsibility or experience; but if her principles are right, her feelings true, with the infant soul come the love and wisdom necessary for its sustenance. It is only because we have so sunk into wrong, so forgotten God, that there needs so much preaching. The highest health is unconscious. Perhaps after a few generations of effort we shall get into that happy state that we shall never think of these things at all. The idea of parental responsibility will be so thoroughly inwrought into social life, that one shall no more dream of inculcating it than of exhorting parents to love their children.

H. Somebody's occupation will be gone then.

"Fly swiftly round, ye wheels of time."

I. And then I shall look upon revivals with less misgiving. I shall not feel that a spasmodic interest is taking the place of that steady interest without which the world can never be brought under the dominion of Christ; without which we may overrun, but can never redeem it.

H. After all, I suspect that half a loaf is better than no bread.

I. Not if the half-loaf is going to content you, and so keep you from vigorous endeavor to earn a steady and plentiful subsistence.

H. It is vigorous endeavor that some people find the most fault with in connection with revivals. The use of machinery is preferred against us as a charge by our opponents and as promptly repelled by ourselves.

I. That is not the kind of endeavor I was thinking of. But it is a very good kind, if it supplements and does not supersede the daily, constant endeavor to make one's own character and habits good, and to bring up one's own children right.

H. Certainly. My sole objection is, that we do not employ enough of it. So far from condemning machinery, I condemn only the neglect and the abuse of it. The Spirit of God will not reform the world without the intervention of men. Spiritual harvests can no more be reaped without machinery than agricultural harvests. Doubtless unwise means are often used to promote revivals; I know that there are not unfrequently impertinence and intermeddling. But these infelicities are entirely local. They do not inhere in the use of means. They do not indicate that we are to sit with folded hands and expect God to do all the work. If union meetings, or readoption of creeds, or renewing of covenants, or a united celebration of the Lord's Supper, is deemed useful in kindling the zeal and strengthening the love of Christians, and so inciting them to fresh efforts in redeeming the world, then they are not only right in taking these measures, but they would be wrong not to take them. And to attempt to stigmatize such modes as "artificial," and to denounce such movements as machinery, and to depreciate such a revival as "deliberately excited," is very questionable in point both of philosophy and courtesy. Revivals ought to be deliberately excited. Poor and shallow and meagre as they are, their faults lie in another quarter than such complaints point to. The Holy Ghost does not need counsel and direction, but Father, Son, and Holy Ghost bless us with fulness of blessing according as we adopt wise counsels and walk in the right direction. We might just as reasonably scorn machinery in politics or in social science as in religion.

I. I agree with you entirely, though I think the excessive multiplication of meetings is unwise, and tends to increase what is harmful in revivals; and do you not consider, too, the insinuation that clergymen have special ends to answer in "getting up revivals" very unjust and in very bad taste? It seems to me that I know everything bad there is in revivals, but I never saw this.

H. The insinuation is far more injurious to the persons who make it than to the persons of whom it is made. There is no question that ministers have their littlenesses; but if absolute purity of motive may be predicated of any man in this world it may be predicated of the educated, quiet, well-bred Christian clergyman who is working and praying for a revival of religion in his church and congregation. If a disinterested desire for the highest good of his fellows actuates any man, it actuates this man. And even in the few cases where learning and quiet and good breeding are not obvious, where the *modus operandi* savors of intermeddling, and want of tact does more harm than zeal does good, the fault is not of motive, but of manner, not of ends, but means. But there, luckily for me, is the sun coming out, and out I am going. Any farm drudgery will seem play to me now.

I. O, but the grass is yet wet. The plantation

is all turned into water-courses, and I wanted to say —

H. Plantation!

I. Yes, plantation. Why not? What is a plantation, pray?

H. I can tell you what it is not, — a plot of land where you do your carting with a tin pan, your planting with a teacup, and your haying with a pair of scissors.

There was a stratum of fact underneath this statement, so I let the case go by default.

WELL DONE.

T is very often urged against American writers, that their productions are ephemeral, that they write for the times, not for eternity. It may be proper, therefore, to state distinctly at the outset, that the present paper is prepared exclusively for eternity. No contemporary need apply. When the existing order of things shall have passed away, when the New Zealand traveller shall have finished his sketch of the ruins of St. Paul, laid aside his portfolio, and drawn from his haversack his simple repast of doughnuts and cheese, then is my time! His eye wandering dreamily hither and thither, will light perchance upon a bit of paper fluttering from beneath a stone. Eagerly exhuming it, he will discover it to be a stray copy of this book, preserved in the desert sands from the tooth of time for many thousand years; and on his return to New Zealand, he will have it laid carefully in the Museum beneath a glass case, while several copies of this paper will be printed for the use of the New

Zealand Historical and Genealogical Society by reason of the flood of light it throws upon the manners, customs, and rural life of a people once brave, humane, and in a degree civilized, but now, alas! utterly extinct. I quote from the New Zealand Evening Gazette.

On one of the first cold mornings in the winter of 18—, there might have been seen a young man of some seventy or eighty summers — I need not remind the thoughtful reader that it was myself — with his head bowed, one eye securely shut, the other determinedly open, gazing steadfastly into a pump. It was indeed an occasion that called for the utmost concentration of purpose, for the kitchen fire was waiting, and the pump-handle refused to move. After mature deliberation, which none better than this young man knew how to compass, he came to the conclusion that the pump was frozen up. A wedge of ice through its centre reaching nearly to the top confirmed him in this conclusion. The first thing to be done was to dislodge the intruder. To effect this, he possessed himself of the parlor poker, and attempted to chip away the ice. It was a brilliant device, and would have succeeded perfectly had there been time enough to carry on the experiment; but after ten minutes of assiduous toil, a close mathematical calculation enabled him to judge, that at the present rate of progress, he would reach the bottom of the wedge on the fifteenth of July ensuing, by which time there was every reason to fear the kitchen fire would have gone out. Some swifter remedy must be applied. He had recourse to the tea-kettle; but the scalding water, while showing every disposition to settle on its lees and become ice, showed no disposition whatever to induce the ice to go into liquidation. As a last resort, a crow-bar was heated seven times hot, thrust into the pump, and pressed firmly down. A great commotion ensued. A fierce volume of steam ascended to the skies. A furious hissing attested the violence of the elemental war within. But the fiery iron kept on its sizzling course, and suddenly with a great gulp it lost its lightness, it became a heavy weight, and the pump was thawed out.

To prevent a recurrence of the trouble, the pump-handle was carefully tilted up o' nights, the pump steadfastly swathed in old quilts, and a dóse of salts administered before the cold evenings set in, but every cold morning showed that all effort was vain. The pump-handle rested on its reserved rights and refused to budge. If it had been left up, up it froze, or if down, down. Every valve was stiff. True, the work of thawing out was not without a pleasing excitement. It was like watching a fairy scene to see the cold, dull iron changing in the glowing coals to liquid, scarlet fire, no longer of the earth earthy, but a child of the skies, sparkling and spiritual. It was like an adventure of knighthood to bear it speedily yet daintily over the twenty rods of icy path without slipping or scorching, and then came the inner rage as of some volcanic battle underground, and the tightening clasp of freezing, senseless fingers when the ice foundations promised to give way and there was danger lest the burning bar should fall down the pump and set the well on fire. Still every ingenuous mind must see, that it will not do to suffer a crow-bar to usurp so large a place in the household economy, and, with the great Jewish lawgiver, the unhappy young man often asked his affectionate but thirsty family, "Must I fetch you water out of this rock — of ice?" So the problem of the hour became a question of hydraulics. Solomon says the beginning of strife is as when one letteth out water. But Solomon, with all his wisdom, lived in an unenlightened age and died young. Had he been a denizen of our happy country, had he pitched his tent on our knoll, and shared the secrets of our housekeeping, our, meaning the young man before referred to, his heirs and ancestors forever, he would have offered an amendment to the previous resolution, namely, the beginning of strife is when one letteth on water. For with that attempt came all our woe. The point was to have easy access to water. Should a ditch be dug, pipes laid, and the old well brought into the house, or should a new well be sunk by our own hearth-stone? The old well was an unfailing fountain of soft water. The new well was in every respect an uncertainty. We decided upon the first plan, and thereupon ensued the Conflict of Ages.

O you dwellers in [New Zealand] cities whose silver-throated naiads spout endless Croton and Cochituate, O happy sons of the mountains, who have only to drop a log anywhere, and a brook immediately leaps through it, there are more things 'twixt the cup and the lip than are dreamt of in your philosophy.

However beautiful and healthy is country life, it is a very serious matter, when you have any great undertaking on hand, to be living at a place to which the nearest point is twenty miles away. However, in the fulness of time a man skilled in pumps and pipes was brought over the twenty miles to train up our wayward Undine in the way she should go. To our dismay, she refused to go at all. Water will not run up hill unless by strong persuasion, and up hill we indubitably were. A spirit-level, improvised from a board and a glass of water, in strict accordance with the Maine Liquor Law, being brought upon the witness-stand, deposed and said that in our lowest estate we stood upon a level with the second story of the next house, and that no water would come for our pumping, pump we never so indefatigably. Seeing is believing, but I must confess I was incredulous, and to this day I find it hard to persuade myself, that every time I go into the garden, I walk out of my neighbor's chamber-window. However, the weight of evidence was against me, and the old well was pronounced out of the question.

Then a new well appeared upon the field with a cistern for its opponent. A cistern? Drink rain-water that has been standing in a tub six months? By no means. But what hope to find water in this gravelly knoll, without boring an Artesian well? A meeting was called, to which delegates came from a sweep of thirty miles. Science said, "You are on the uplands indeed, but springs are as likely to be found in them as in the lowlands. There are higher hills behind you, whence the water may flow down, and be no farther from the surface here than elsewhere." Experience scowled at Science, and affirmed, "You can get your well, but you must dig for it, and keep digging, till you get as low as the bottom of the other well." Who shall decide when doctors disagree? A marvellous man who lives in the blessed woods of Wycombe, and has underground eyes to see springs of water beneath the dry land. Thus up spake noble Faith, and as soon as our Parliament prorogued we ordered what is technically termed "a team," and started for the blessed woods of Wycombe, and the man with the underground eyes, James Knox Onlis by name. Nobody knew the road, except that it ran in a general way to the northwest, so we set our faces steadily towards the northwest, till we reached the outskirts of the unexplored regions, where we halted to take an observation. "In yonder cabin," spake the patriarch of the party, "there once lived a family by the name of Onlis. Perhaps our Seer may be a descendant at the fifth or sixth remove. Suppose we inquire." I at once alighted and approached the front gate. It had apparently never been opened since the lamented decease of the original proprietor, and was not to be opened now. A side-gate was fastened by an ingenious arrangement of sticks and strings, so complicated that it seemed easier to scale the wall than to attempt to loosen them. Gaining thus the freedom of the yard, I trod tentatively and cautiously around the house to the back-door. It was open, but a chair lying lengthwise barred the entrance, and a very ancient and fish-like smell melted on the autumn air. A respectful rap brought out a pretty young woman in a somewhat tattered gown, but with gold beads around her neck. "Can you tell me if Mr. James Knox Onlis lives here?" No, he did not, — to my great relief, — he lived about three miles farther, beyond the river. Three miles were cheerily passed, the river crossed, and again we tarried in pursuit of knowledge. A horseman was watering his horse at the running river, — brook perhaps it might be called, if one were not ambitious. "Can you tell me where Mr. James Knox Onlis lives?"

"Just about three quarters of a mile from here. You must turn to the right, then to the left, then go into a lane and up the hill, and you are right on it." Following his directions we soon found the house.

"Does Mr. James Knox Onlis live here?"

"Yes, he does."

"Is he at home."

"No, he is n't."

"Can you tell me where he is?"

"Well, down on the Agawam road. You must go back to the main road, then turn and go past the ropewalk till you come to a yellow house on the left-hand side. He is there."

"You are quite sure I shall find him there?"

"O yes, he is there. He was going to be there all day."

So we plod on, passing the ropewalk, but there is no yellow house, and then another ropewalk and another half-mile, and the yellow house shines in the slanting sunlight. A stalwart, honest-looking man is just driving a loaded wagon into the yard. I alight and accost him. "Is Mr. James Knox Onlis here?"

"Well he has been here, but he went away about half an hour ago."

"Do you know where he went?"

"No, I don't exactly. He did n't know whether he should go home or to Agawam."

Aroused by the voices, two heads appear above

a high board fence half a dozen yards away. One belongs to a young man, and one to an elderly one, whereupon the colloquy takes on a fourfold character.

"Did you ever hear that Mr. James Knox Onlis can tell where water is to be found?" A suppressed giggle from the young head above the fence.

"Well, he does do that business sometimes, when folks want him to."

"Is he generally successful?"

"Well, he most always hits on the square."

"Is he a good deal engaged just now?"

"Well, no, I do' know 's he is partic'l'ly."

"Would there be any probability of my being able to engage his services at once?"

"Well, yes, I think like 's not you might."

"As I did not meet him on the way here, is it not probable that he is gone to Agawam?"

"He's gone to Egypt to buy corn," says the young head above the fence.

"And where is Egypt?" I ask.

"'T an't nowhere. There's no such place," says my stalwart friend confidentially in an undertone. "He's gone to Agawam to get stores. That's where he was going."

"Perhaps I could find him at some of the shops?"

"Well, he most generally goes to Knightman's or Wheelill's. Likely enough he'll be in one of them very places."

" And we are to keep on this road ? "

" Yes, this will take you right to Agawam. He will be there or on the road somewhere, — unless he goes down by Lampboy's to buy some hay; though he said, I remember now, that perhaps he should come round the other road to see his sister."

" Can you tell me any way by which I shall know him ? "

" Well, he has a black horse and buggy."

" And looks just like me," says the elderly head over the fence.

" And has a young man with him," says my stalwart friend.

" With black hair and whiskers," says the elderly head.

" And two firkins and a can in the wagon," adds the young head.

Thus replete with valuable and exact information, we resumed our journey, setting our faces towards Agawam, three miles farther on, and keeping a sharp lookout

1. For all black horses and buggies.
2. For all black hair and whiskers.
3. For all heads like the elderly head above the fence.
4. For two firkins and a can.

So we rode and rode and rode through the beautiful Indian summer, the warm soft air falling and floating around us in a haze of dreamy delight, all the roses of June deepening in the ruddy woods, all the violets of May purpling in the distant hills, Spring pouring her tender promise and Summer her perfect splendor into the lap of this gorgeous autumn queen, till, betwixt the glory of the skies above and the glory of the earth beneath, this whole round world became a palace of dainty delights. Kind Heaven! that is ever mixing honey with the bitter draught of life, that makes the path of our lowliest duties a *via sacra* for our souls.

So we drove lordlily into Agawam, as beseems monarchs of so fair a realm; and there at the door of the first grocery-shop stood the black horse and buggy that had hitherto so persistently eluded us, and there, too, the cabalistic words brought to light the ever approached yet always receding James Knox Onlis, whom we had begun to regard as some shadowy myth, cloud-born and cloud dissolving, but who appeared before our eyes, a man of mortal mould, and promised in very human fashion to unravel for us the riddles of the deep earth betimes the next morning, and in very un-human fashion kept his promise.

Herein is a marvellous thing; for this man affirms that he possesses a power whose nature he does not understand, of whose origin he knows nothing, over which he exercises no control, whose working he only partially comprehends, whose existence he but accidentally discovered. The assumed facts are, that water flows through the earth in veins at unequal distances from its surface, and when he crosses one of these veins, a little upward curving rod in his hand is forced and twisted by some occult influence till it bends downward. The material of the rod is unimportant. Witch-hazel is the best substance, but any common wood obeys the hidden law. Our experimenter brought the fragment of an ordinary barrel-hoop, and began at once to walk around the house, clasping it lightly in both hands at each end, his palms turned upward. I followed him steadfastly to see what was to be seen. He paced slowly and watchfully hither and thither, and presently the hoop gave an indubitable twist. "Here is water." He crossed and recrossed to find the general direction of the vein, since, according to his theory, no effect is produced when walking along its course, though he may be directly over it. But the water did not flow to suit our convenience, and he resumed his search, soon discovering another vein which branched off from the first, and made directly for our kitchen in the most obliging manner. Here he planted his stake and took measurements. His scale not being yet perfected, he is unable to give exact results, but after sundry manœuvres with pebbles and paper, he pronounced our spring to be from twenty to twenty-two feet below the surface. This was so favorable a view of the case, that we were inclined to adopt it.

"For so to interpose a little ease,
Let our vain thoughts dally (even) with false surmise."

Having then made his professional discoveries, he made a few more "for fun," and pointed out several places where water could be found. So that, if we should ever become addicted to well-digging, we should know just where to begin, and in fact could turn our farm into a sponge on very short notice.

His power, or his passion one might perhaps as well say, for he seems to be less acting than acted upon, is not confined to water, but extends to metal. By it he can discover gold and silver money hidden on floor or in field. Unfortunately for our experiments at the present time, the gold must exist, before he can discover it, which very seriously restricts active operations. A half-dollar, under one of twenty sheets of paper laid on the carpet this lively little wand points out. According to his theorizing, lightning always strikes above these water-courses, so that a house standing between two of them would be safe without lightning-rods. He once visited a house where a person had been killed by lightning, and after making examination he said, "I do not know whether he was in the front or back room, but he must have been standing somewhere on this line," and the bystanders confirmed his decision. His discovery of the possession of this faculty was, as I have said, accidental, if we may use the term. A number of persons were discussing the possibility of this power, which, if it exists, is very rarely possessed, and were trying experiments with the witch-hazel rods. He refused to try, believing it to be mere superstition, and even declared that he should be ashamed to be seen walking around with a stick in that way. But several days afterwards, he happened to see one of these rods lying on the ground, and, as *nobody was in sight*, from mere curiosity he took it up and tried the experiment, which, to his astonishment was completely successful, showing that he possessed the power in very large measure. He had been called upon several times when persons had dug in vain for wells, and had never failed to make their dry lands evolve springs of water. Out of twenty wells, whose depth he had previously reckoned, he had been told the average variation from his measurements had been less than one foot. But he acknowledged frankly, that he did not always estimate so accurately. This was his own story.

We had taken our measures so promptly, after having decided upon them, that we had quite stolen a march upon our neighbors; but the thing was not long hid under a bushel, and the little currents of remark soon began to flow quietly but significantly. It was a very nice study in mental philosophy to mark them, as they varied from a gentle compassion to open ridicule, — open but not very violent, even from those who were most disposed to use it, for the conclusion of the matter was so near at hand, that even those sublimely superior to superstition thought it not wise to make any marked demonstration which might by chance—of course it could be by chance alone—redound to their own discomfiture.

"You have been consulting a diviner, I understand," drawls Elegant Leisure,—on whom I now wreak revenge. "Do you design to preserve the wand of enchantment for future generations to venerate as Aaron's rod was laid away for the Jews?"

"Going to have your well stoned, as well as dug, by mesmerism," haw-haws practical Common Sense, who is to be imposed upon by no old-wives' fables.

"I don't believe in it," says Metaphysics, stoutly,—Metaphysics, who accepts any quantity of incomprehensible sesquipedalian theory about the mind, and very safely too, since nobody can say whether it is true or false,—"I don't believe in it. If it is ever true of any man, he is to be pitied. He is an unfortunate man. Send him to the Lunatic Asylum, or to the Massachusetts General Hospital. It is disease."

Convinced that success would be the best refutation, we held our peace and longed for the advent of the well-digger.

It was Saturday when the "diviner" left us,

and Monday the well was to be begun. But Monday came and another Monday, and Monday still again, and brought no well-diggers. We were not surprised. The only thing that surprises us is to have workmen come when they say they will. If our experience is at all indicative of the state of public morals, there is a lamentable infidelity to engagements among manual laborers. They do not recognize the sacredness of their word. They do not comprehend the nature of a pledge. They make it and break it with equal readiness. Whether it be to build a house or trim a tree, or mend a door, or make a window, or pay a debt, or bring a load of wood, or finish a dress, you cannot depend upon its being done at the appointed time. They will agree to your plans with obliging alacrity and carry them out at their own sweet will. I do not see in this respect, the smallest difference between the church and the world. Six years ago a church-member promised to haul us a load of coal before Thanksgiving, and it has not yet appeared, nor been heard from. Five years ago another church-member entered into a similar engagement with similar results. Yet both these persons still continue to adorn the doctrine of God their Saviour by a well-ordered life and conversation, so far as ecclesiastical eyes discern. I know one unhappy man who belongs to two churches, and between them he does not seem to have any moral sense left. He cannot wait for temptation, but hastens to forswear himself spontaneously. Apparently his perception is quite bewildered, and he sees no distinction between "I go" and "I go not." He might with great propriety adopt the Brahminic riddle, which is no riddle to him, —

> "Far or forgot to me is near,
> Sunlight and shadow are the same,
> To me the vanished gods appear,
> And one to me are shame and fame."

And we sound Evangelical Christians talk about the "merely moral man." *Merely* moral! As if morality were a common thing, to be lightly estimated in the general sum of human character, and not rather the solid earth beneath our feet, without which the heavens above would be of no account to us. Merely moral! Happy the day when the world shall have grown so rich in Christian graces that it can afford to leave morality out of the reckoning; but the infant born this hour will not live to see it. Meanwhile, and to hasten its advent, let us preach morality side by side with religion, and preach it with such clearness and fervor, that, if men will sin, they shall sin with malice aforethought and their eyes open, and not from ignorance and a befogged vision, as they undoubtedly often do now. Pulpit teaching ought to lay hold on a man's conscience with so close a clutch, with so unyielding a grasp, that he cannot escape from them without rending his conscience and leaving it all torn and bleeding with an eternal wound, — only let them be the teachings of the Gospel, not of prejudice or ignorance. Justification, sanctification, election, atonement, — let them all be discussed, but especially let their connection with a man's business character be made clear. It is not enough to lay down abstract propositions. Men will assent to them promptly, and go straightway and violate the law that is in them, and disregard the principle that underlies them, without even knowing it. The preacher ought to make the applications, to bring down the Gospel to life, to bring up life to the Gospel; to show exactly what the first demands, and where the second fails; to instruct workingmen and women, as we all are, or ought to be, how to make the whole week bear fruits to God in our most common words and ways. And especially let all clergymen and teachers whatever recognize and teach, that truthfulness lies at the bottom of character, without which none is utterly pure, with which none is utterly corrupt.

Does this seem to you a digression, Messieurs New-Zealanders? Not in the least. It is a way we had in those old times of speaking a word in season and out of season; and as this, moreover, is but a brief recapitulation of the thoughts which shortened a long walk to the well-digger's, the most enlightened of you cannot fail to see that even artistically it is quite in the line of my argument. Not that I proposed to deliver any such lecture as this to our delinquent gnome. In the first place, illness or a misunderstanding might show that there was no delinquency. In the second place, it is not so easy a matter to tell a man what you think about certain things which he may be supposed to have done or have failed to do. It is all very well to put ministers up to doing duty, but it is quite another thing to do it yourself. Besides, in our free and beloved country one must walk warily if his progress shall be unimpeded. However eloquent he waxes in the bosom of his family over the right-hand fallings off and left-hand defections of his brethren, he will hardly find his account in obtruding his eloquence, for his own satisfaction, upon those brethren. So, as I walked over the hills and far away, I improved each shining hour in improvising some inoffensive speech which should satisfactorily account for my appearance. The crops, the weather, and the fears of future rains which should spoil our well by swelling the shallow springs, were all dismissed in favor of an anxiety lest illness might have prevented the undertaking. In this defensive armor I presented myself at the well-digger's house; but his house took no cognizance of his whereabouts, only recommending the barn as a hopeful place for further research. To the barn accordingly I turned, picking my way carefully among the great heaps of corn not yet stripped of its swaddling-clothes, under the withered grape-vines that had borne their rich burdens bounteously, and were now resting from their labors, fragrant still and not without a certain crisp loveliness, as the yellow sunshine floated softly through them and the tender breeze rustled them in cooing melody; and sweetly sung to my charmed ear those rich lines of old Andrew Marvell, —

> "What wondrous life is this I lead!
> Ripe apples drop about my head;
> The luscious clusters of the vine
> Upon my mouth do crush their wine;
> The nectarine and curious peach
> Into my hand themselves do reach," —

past huge piles of wood, rough enough to such as should see only their straggling outline, nor know the blessings that lay deep hidden in each rugged pile, — warmth for chill and rest for weariness, fireside talk, the crooning of old stories, the prattle from child-lips, the purr of the comfortable cat, foam of cider and fragrance of apples, home-comforts, neighborly cheer, and boundless hospitality for the wayfarer against the long frost-bound evenings that lay in ambush behind golden sunshine and dusky grapes, and could not discern in each shapeless mass the beautiful, insidious foe that should steal away their sharpness ere they were aware, and thrill the heart of December with the glow and gladness of June. And still as I trod cautiously the hens stared at me and stepped aside, not too far. And the gray gander left his harem and pursued me valiantly with level neck and ferocious hiss, and the turkey-gobbler strutted and sidled up to me, scraping the ground with the tips of his bristling wings, and boasting his prowess with most unmusical gobble. Thus attended, I came suddenly upon the harvesters. The broad barn doors were flung wide open to the flooding southern sunshine, and the laborers sat half hidden among heaps of stalks and unhusked corn, sturdily stripping off the shrivelled glume with steadfast, brawny hands, — all but he whom I sought. Inquiring for him, I was directed aloft; and there, half-way up the high ladder, well on towards the great beam, was the hale old man, bearing his eight and seventy years as blithely as a boy his dozen summers. My questions died on my lips in mute surprise. You cannot anxiously inquire after a man's health when he is frisking like a squirrel before your eyes, so I changed my tactics on the instant, and only made some commonplace salutation to attract his attention, supposing naturally enough that he would descend on seeing me to a convenient table-land for conversation, and so give me time to collect my resources. But he had no notion of permitting the serious business of life to be interrupted by a little whipper-snapper like me; he just glanced back over his shoulder, went on up his ladder, and scrambled over upon the scaffold as unconcernedly as if but a little brown mouse had startled out of the corn, and the men from their mounds below began to pitch up great forkfuls of stalks which the old man caught and arranged deftly, and all the while we talked the dust of the lively corn-husks came floating down into my eyes and face upturned at an angle of about eighty degrees to the dimly outlined figure upon the scaffold. But as soon as the gander ceased to hiss, and the turkey gave over gobbling, I managed to insinuate a question about the future prospects of the well. "You do' want no well at present," spoke the handsome, black-eyed son from his cereal pile, and extinguished me at once. I had thought all the time that we did want a well very much. In fact, it was solely owing to this mental hallucination that I had taken my walks abroad that very morning. But the old man above benevolently came to the rescue with an assurance that the well should be dug all in good time, but his hired man had been sick three weeks, and his work was all behindhand. You could dig wells when you could not get in grain, and of course he must harvest his crops. But, I said, I feared the rains would come so heavily as to fill the springs and our well would fail in the dry season.

"O, don't you worry," he sang out cheerily, never pausing in his work, "I know all about it. I 've dug more wells than any man in the county. A shallow spring might rise, but deep wells like yours won't be touched this month. By the time we get down three feet you 'll see. Did n't you ever make dough for your chickens?"

"Yes, indeed," brightening up with pleasure at touching on familiar ground.

"Well, you know how the meal drinks up the water. Now the earth is an ash-heap, and swallows up the rain just like Indian meal. That last storm we had did n't wet down an inch in my field."

It would have been a very remarkable rain if it had. Farmers will often allow that a timely shower has freshened the grass, but in the whole course of a long and eventful life, I do not think I ever heard a farmer in a dry time admit that any rain, however profuse and protracted, had wet down to his potatoes! So cavalierly do we receive the good gifts of the Good Giver.

Then I told him that I had met his son on the way, who had begged me to ask him to make a new pump for a wayside well, that had been long disused, but was now needed in the general drought; but I added, with miserable selfishness, I hoped he would dig our well first, we had been waiting so long.

"O, I know that pump, I made it myself. It was the first one I ever made. I sha'n't hurry. They 've done without twenty years, I guess they can wait a spell longer. I sha'n't meddle with it till I 've dug your well. My folks don't want me to dig wells. That 's what the talk about the pump 's for." It could hardly be wondered at that his "folks" should desire him not to engage in this hard and hazardous work, but it was plain to see that he had no design of gratifying them. His eye was not dim, nor his natural strength abated. Life and health and heart were stout within him, and he scorned to give up his firm foothold on the active world. Wise man! Work is the sole preservative. I came away reassured, though it is hard to say on precisely what grounds, for the most definite report I could take home amounted to no more than that he would come when he got ready, which we suspected before.

But come they did, man and horse, pick and pulley, shovel and scoop,— how wonderful it is, the time and trouble and tools, the science and skill it takes to do things. Certainly a well is nothing remarkable, yet you must know how, or you can no more make a well than you can make a world. But these people knew how. They just drew a circle on the greensward, and cut out a deep round hole as clean and regular as the hole in a doughnut before it is cooked; no jagging into the turf, no scattering about of stones and soil, but a round hole constantly deepening, a pyramidal mound constantly rising. Merrily, merrily went they down, burrowing in the earth like so many moles, and came up all smeared with sand and loam, kobolds, goblins, with a human trick of the voice, and many an underground jest; down and down thirteen feet the first day, and then they struck the hard clay and made only three feet the second day, and three feet more, and still three more, — twenty, twenty-one, twenty-two; and, O heavens! there was no water! and slowly, slowly, with pick-axe and platform, down, down —

Twenty-three feet, twenty-four feet, twenty-five feet, still dry land. O Science, O Philosophy, O Mystery, where were ye, nymphs?

Twenty-six feet, — O that we had not been so strenuous for a deep well, but could have contented ourselves with a shallow one!

Twenty-seven feet, — to think how fearful we had been lest autumn rains should swell surface streams to fallacious size, and now my kingdom for the shallowest stream!

Twenty-eight feet, — and a thread of water comes trickling tardily in six feet behind time, a little better than nothing, from the predicted quarter, true; but anybody would know if it ran at all it would run down hill.

Twenty-nine feet, and the merry rills come dancing in from all sides in a frolic of freedom.

Thirty feet, and there is a basin of water, yellow, thick and clayey, but soft and promising to be plenteous, and we will go no farther.

O, but then did not the wiseacres glorify themselves over us poor slaves of superstition, dupes of a wily adventurer? Now where is your diviner, where your magnetism and your electricity? Water is there truly, but water is everywhere if one but digs deep enough. Might *know* there was nothing in it! Absurd to suppose a man could tell what there was ten feet under him through the solid earth!

I have thought much lately about Friar Bacon,— the light that shone out of the darkness six hundred years ago, and could not dissipate it because its time was not yet come; the great sad soul that wrought in speechless solitude, wooing Nature in her fastnesses, studying the secrets of the mind, and trying to fling somewhat of the brightness of his mountain heights down upon the glooming valleys below, — and himself flung into prison for his pains. O, I hope that somewhere, somewhere in some pleasant, strange, curious world, Friar Bacon is still studying with all heavenly helps the mysteries of the universe, and that love and friendship, and every tender, human solace, and every Divine benignity, make amends a thousandfold for that short, cold, and bitter-sweet earth-dream of his! But the spirit that imprisoned Roger Bacon is still abroad upon the earth. It came down our way last fall, toothless and fangless now, thank Heaven! but grinning horribly with its old hate, and showing what it would do, had not time destroyed its power to hurt. Yet it ought to be dead. There was an excuse for the men who imprisoned Roger Bacon. How should they know that the sulphurous and sonorous gunpowder was not set on fire of hell? Living a life of the senses, and that in its grossest forms, how should they believe in unseen, unheard, impalpable material forces? But Friar Bacon has lived, and labored, and died. The earth has been weighed, the moon measured, the clouds plundered, the sea spanned, the depths uncovered. Hidden powers have been tracked to their lairs and forced into human service. We have gone but a little way into the kingdom of our inheritance; we have, as it were, but crossed the threshold of our palace, and every step has showed it to be a treasure-house of mysteries; yet now we are to recoil with contempt from one mystery the more! Believing so much as we do of physical science, how passing strange it is that the trained reason of any man can reject without examination, and ridicule without misgiving, anything which claims to belong to its domain! What is the element of absurdity in this water attraction that does not equally inhere in electricity or magnetism? Who that believes in the American Telegraph or the Mariner's Compass can afford to scoff at the hazel-rod? We have seen, or might have seen, that the greatest and most beneficent discoveries and inventions have had an apparently puerile origin. A falling apple, a steaming tea-kettle, a dead frog, a child's kite, have not done so little of our drudgery for us, and so little added to our sum of knowledge, that we can safely despise even a barrel hoop. Contempt, contumely, violent opposition, have been the foster-mothers of some of the most useful arts that now bless the human race, and it would seem to be the part of a wise man to wait before pronouncing adverse judgment. I am speaking now, not at all of evidence, but of intrinsic probability; and I affirm that, apart from any evidence, there is no more absurdity or improbability in Bletonism than in Magnetism or Galvanism.

But though the theory is so strong that we can discard the evidence, on the other hand the evidence is so strong that we can dismiss the theory. When our world pointed its slowly moving finger of scorn at us, we bore it awhile patiently, and then bestirred ourselves to make defence. We found that the matter was one of sufficient scientific research to have received a name. *Bletonism* stands in Webster in equal honor with the other *isms*. That is surely a fair introduction to good society. Admitting that our own experiment was a comparative failure, — an entire failure in respect of the distance computed and not a certain success in respect of finding water, — knowing, too, how untrustworthy are mere stories and reports, we determined to ascertain for ourselves whether there was any tangible proof, anything that could be relied on, in making up an opinion. We ascertained names and places, and cross-examined the witnesses. One intelligent farmer, who had spent his life under our own eyes, that is, not more than six miles away, told us how he had begun to dig a well, and after two fruitless trials a friend came by and said to him, "I would not dig at random in this way. Go to Mr. Onlis, and let him tell you where you can get something besides your labor for your pains." Whereupon he proceeded at once to Mr. Onlis, who said, "I do not wish to go. I have just had two failures. I would rather not go."

"Never mind," said the believing farmer, " but jump right into the wagon and go with me."

So they went together, and the little rod pointed to a spring just nine feet under ground, which, when they had dug nine feet, they found bubbling up to meet them. The farmer then called upon Mr. Onlis to point out a spring for a well for one of the farm laborers, which he did with equal accuracy, and subsequently another for the barn. In the latter case a very slight excavation showed the site of an old well whose existence was remembered, but whose location had been forgotten. A few repairs brought it out as good as new, thanks to the little Puck of a wand.

A second man gave in his experience also for our edification. He dug down in a certain spot, according to directions, and came upon a ledge. The laborers blasted till they were tired, and were upon the point of giving it up; but, as they had gone nearly to the depth indicated, they determined to make a complete trial. Their perseverance was rewarded by their finding an unfailing supply of water in the solid rock.

A third testified that he had taken Mr. Onlis upon a solid ledge to a distance of about ten feet from the precipitous front of the cliff, and asked him for water. He found it, after a short search, a dozen feet perhaps below the surface.

"Do you mean to tell me that there is a spring of water in this ledge of rock?"

"I think there is."

He then took him around to the front of the cliff, where, at about the designated spot, a little trickle of water could be seen oozing from the rock.

"I have noticed that there is always water weeping there through drought and summer," said the gentleman, "and have thought whether it might not be made available."

"Undoubtedly it could," was the reply; a process of drilling was at once commenced, and a spring of water found there which has never failed, though several years have since intervened.

Another witness told of an exhibition of the power in a public hall, in the presence and under the scrutinizing gaze of a hundred people, members of a scientific association. The president of the association was an avowed disbeliever, yet the rod turned unerringly when brought over a piece of gold, and with such force as to take the skin from the palm of his hand.

Another man had dug two wells only a rod or two apart, and to the depth of forty feet, but found the water so insufficient that he filled them both up. Some time after his death his son heard of Mr. Onlis, and engaged his services. The rod indicated a vein about midway between the two old wells. On digging there, an abundant supply of water was found at somewhat less than half the depth of the other wells.

In the Report of the Commissioner of Patents for the Year 1851, Part II., is a statement made by Alfred Burnson, of Prairie du Chien, Wisconsin, over his own signature. He says: "In 1812 I settled on a springless farm in Ohio, expecting to obtain water by digging a well. A neighbor of mine, who had on an adjoining farm obtained good water only fourteen feet from the surface of the ground, by means of this Bletonism, urged me to try the same means. But, being of the class who could not, or rather would not, believe in what I could not comprehend, I declined resorting to what to me, as to others, appeared to be consummate nonsense, and I spent my leisure time in the dry time of *three* years in digging, but found no water. At length, despairing of finding water in this way, and having the curiosity to test this new science, I invited a 'water philosopher' to try his skill for me. It is proper to observe, that this man was an independent farmer, a man of intelligence and high moral worth, and, as he performed in this matter without fee or reward, I had no possible ground for suspecting any design of humbuggery on his part. And further, he told me that he knew no more of the reason, the why or wherefore it worked in his hands, while it would not in those of others, than I did. By mere accident he ascertained that he was 'one of 'em'; and on discovering this he experimented until he discovered the fact — that the rod would be attracted at an angle of 45°, and that from the point at which the attraction commenced to where the attraction was perpendicular, would indicate the depth to dig to reach the water.

"All this, however, — his high character and his explanations, — did not remove my doubts. He prepared his peach-twig fork, and I placed him over a well which I had dug, and was at this time full of surface or seep water; wishing, if possible, not to lose the labor thus expended. But this seep-water had no effect whatever on the rod. The operator then travelled slowly, I keeping my eye upon the rod and his hands, to see if the turning of the rod was not from the motion of his own hands. At length the butt or fork-end of the rod went down; the operator holding his hands upon the rod so tightly, to prevent its slipping, that they turned purple, and I could plainly see that the twig ends of the rod did not slip or turn round in his hand, but that the twigs actually twisted so that the bark broke and gave way. When I saw this I gave it up. What I saw with my own eyes, and that, too, against strong prejudice, I could not doubt. He selected the point where the dip of the rod was the strongest, and measured the depth by the 45° rule, and I stuck the stake to dig by; and in the ensuing autumn, when all was dry, I dug, and found the depth, quantity, and quality of the water just as he had told me."

It is natural and to be expected that the uncultivated mind should reject or neglect evidence at its own will, and satisfy itself with calling names; but it is difficult to perceive how the intellect, trained to distinguish between truth and falsehood, between reason and prejudice, between probability and absurdity, between science and charlatanry, can reject without evidence or after evidence, statements so interesting and so well supported as these. The philosophy of the thing is a question of opinion or conjecture. Its existence is a matter of fact, as well fortified by testimony as any of the miracles recorded in the Bible. That is perhaps an unhappy remark, as those who seem to think themselves the divinely-appointed sponsors of the sacred teachings will at once be up in arms to defend them from fancied danger, and those who reject the sacred teachings altogether will think it a weakening rather than a strengthening of the case. For the latter, it is neither the one nor the other; it simply leaves the thing where it was before, but I should like to have the former adduce any evidence in support of Christ's miracles different in nature or stronger in degree than this. This does not either tend to explain away the miracles into common occurrences or to cheapen them by a new dispensation of miracles. Even though ultimately Christ's miracles should be shown to be the using of simply natural forces, still his use of them was as miraculous as if he had contravened nature. To have known perfectly and have commanded supremely what eighteen or eighteen hundred centuries would but obscurely discern and partially control, was as godlike an attribute, was a more godlike attribute, than to wrest a law from its normal working and force it to oppose itself. Our modern " diviner," as he is most improperly called, makes no such pretensions. He says frankly, " I do not know. I can make no promises." He arrives at what knowledge he possesses only as a private in the great army of progress. The names of " magic," " witchcraft," " divining," are entirely out of place and mischievous. They prejudice the common mind against what promises to be a useful discovery. There is no assumption of mystery or anything of the nature of incantation. And the educated man who countenances any such belief misuses his education. If he cannot or does not choose to investigate the subject, let him hold his peace.

It is objected that though a man may designate a spot and water may be found there, yet to infer that the man knew anything about it is to jump to a conclusion. Very true, but it is such jumps as we are taking every day. A ruffian strikes you a blow with a club and you fall to the ground, and judge and jury jump to the conclusion that the fall is in consequence of the blow. A very evil case should we be in if they did not. A certain regularity in the succession of events is allowed by the most enlightened science to constitute cause and effect. You plunge your burnt finger into cold water and the pain ceases; you justly infer that the water effected the easement. The only question is as to the character and the number of the cases required to establish the relationship of cause and effect. If the hazel-rod points to water only on land where springs abound, and wells can be easily filled, or if only now and then it points to water, its claims could be reasonably disputed; for in the one case it could only by chance fail, and in the other it might by chance succeed: but if it invariably points to water, and as well on land that has been repeatedly pierced in vain as on fresh fields, we must jump to the conclusion that there is an understanding between the rod and the water, or we must relinquish all claims to reason and write ourselves down as members of that class of beings which mistake stubbornness for sense!

It is said, also, that if these persons had true faith in their alleged power they would avail themselves of it as they do not now. They would go into the oil districts and the mining districts and make their fortunes. I suppose, then, men always do what it is for their interest to do. Industry, honesty, sobriety, tend to happiness and wealth; therefore of any particular man who believes this it may be predicated that he is industrious, honest, and sober. He who knows that the wages of sin is death, scrupulously keeps himself in the paths of righteousness. On the contrary, idleness, trickery, and drunkenness abound even in the most enlightened sections, and many a man works hard with open eyes to earn his wages from his father, the Devil. It is not safe to depend on what men would naturally be supposed to do. But apart from this, if one may judge from the incredulity which prevails in his own neighborhood, a Bletonist would have little encouragement to leave his certain occupation, his quiet, and his family, to encounter the unbelief and ridicule of strangers, and the roughness of a new and but half-civilized life. His habits do not sit so loosely on a man of middle age and New England life that he can lightly change them. Moreover, the whole matter is as yet too little understood and valued to inspire great confidence. The scale of measurements is far from being perfected, and though the depths of the water is but a collateral matter, entirely distinct from its locality, and depending more on a man's judgment and skill, and therefore of minor import as affecting the physical discovery, yet it is of great importance in a practical point of view.

But while the power itself is so little comprehended that the conditions of its existence, or those upon which it may be acquired, retained, or controlled, are absolutely unknown, no man of conservative years or character can be expected to stake his fortunes on it. "If I should advertise," said Mr. Onlis, "and set up an office, and then should fail, it would be a serious matter. But now if people want me they must run their own risk." Electricity is the most probable agent that has yet been advanced to account for the phenomena. A silk handkerchief on the ground prevents the dip of the rod. Indeed, Mr. Burnson says that a great variety of experiments shows that all the phenomena of the rod are governed by the laws of electricity. When men of science have completed their investigations of the subject, have discovered its connections, and established its domains, we may hope that it will be fruitful of benefit in ways of which as yet we have not dreamed.

Meanwhile I submit that to believe that a man accounted honest, and certainly respected, comfortably placed, and dwelling among his own people, should falsely declare or vainly believe himself possessed of a power, the proof of whose existence is within any man's reach, and should be upheld in this declaration and confirmed in this belief by men of judgment, intellect, and high moral worth who had tested his power and declared themselves satisfied of its existence to the full intent and extent of his declaration, — to believe this, I say, requires, in my judgment, a credulity as far removed from intelligent caution on the one side as it is from an intelligent boldness on the other.

While we have thus been turning the defeat of our foes into a shameful rout, the well has been swallowing stone wall by the cart-load, and now the kobolds near the surface; they are tunnelling through into the cellar, prying out its big rocks and powdering its hardened cement, and I think of Colonel Streight and the Andersonville moles, and wonder if the Chicago tunnel under the lake is a work of perceptibly greater magnitude than these water-works of ours; for faith fails me to see how they are ever going to bring order out of this chaos or get that hole in the wall filled up, and even while I muse, forlorn, a hollow log is shot into the hole, and anon all the wreck clears itself away and the cellar is in apple-pie order once more, and the well takes another gulp of stone wall, till at length its rapacious maw is lined to the lips with rock. How finely they are fitted in, these jagged fragments! How round and regular the rough work looks! How beautiful it is to know how to do things well, and to do them well, and to take pride in doing them well. Why do not mechanics and all workmen set themselves to be skilled workmen, and not rich men? How much better is sincere work, than a little money, or a great deal of money, gained by sleight of hand. And now, *pugnis et calcibus*, to speak after the manner of Webster's spelling-book, down goes a boy into the well, to clear it of all rubbish, — very speedily and bravely it seems to me, watching him with beating heart, but the old man, following him with his eyes, frets at his slowness and caution, and but for a wholesome fear of his "folks," would, I am persuaded, cast aside his seventy years, and go down into Tartarus himself, — and then all is pronounced complete, the well is covered up, the ropes and picks and shovels and buckets are piled into the cart, the old man sits down on a board, and with his own unaided eyes and hands makes out his bill as properly as any clerk. Then westward ho! a dozen miles we go to prowl among pipes and pumps, and come home laden therewith, — pipes not of lead, for they poison you, not gutta-percha, for they crack, but galvanized iron, possessed of every virtue under heaven. And already imagination fondly stoops to trace the pictured splendors of water in the house, when of a sudden we are brought to a stand-still. The hollow log through which the pipe must pass is not placed on a level, but slopes upwards, and the pipe-joints screw only at right angles. So another three days delay, and another dozen miles journey to get the joints retwisted, while we feed our faith by calling up the manifold difficulties that beset the great Atlantic Cable, and a miserable man, feeling feebly around for bugbears, as if they do not come full swiftly enough of their own accord, asks querulously, "Suppose when the pump is set up it won't pump? Why should it, if this well is as deep as the old one?" and for all answer gets the idiomatic, highly figurative but emphatic response, "Hold your tongue! It will pump!" But clandestinely I consult the philosophies, which say comfortably that pumps will pump at from thirty-two to thirty-four feet, and this water is only twenty-eight feet underground, and of course it will pump. Here come the pipes again, up through the floor, down through the log, plump into the well, and every screw is screwed tight, and every crack stopped with pretty pink liquid lead, and the carpenter comes and builds a box for protection, and rounds the top into elegant curves, and fastens the pump firm upon it, and we are ready for the inauguration.

I make the first trial, — by favor, — expecting a great parabola of water, with a single touch. There is a silent expectancy in the bystanders. I lift the pump-handle once, twice, thrice by main force and bear it down; then ignominiously give way for the carpenter's strong arms. Up and down, up and down, swiftly at first, more slowly at last, he plies a melancholy see-saw. There is no response. One and another change guard. Water, water, everywhere, but not a drop from our pump. Round we throw our baleful eyes, that witness huge affliction and dismay, mixed with obdurate pride. "Let 's wet his whistle for him," says some one, and pours a pitcherful of water down the iron throat. See-saw again, for an indefinite period, till the sun comes out in a little faint stream, straggling from the pump-nose, evidently having lost its way, — not a parabola, bold, full, and furious, but a little split vein that falls flat into the sink, exhausted. Still we hail it as the harbinger of better days. "That 's it, that 's all the trouble," says the carpenter. "The leather is dry, and the pump leaks; keep using it from day to day, and keep the leather wet till it swells, and it will work. There 's most always trouble with new pumps," with which solace the foreign population withdraw, leaving us to our fate.

So we treated the pump hydropathically, giving it a great deal more water than it ever gave us, pouring it down plenteously and pumping it up painfully; and every time we stopped pumping, we could hear the water scudding back into the well, but never, no never could we hear it scudding up. We were indeed a little worse off than before; since formerly we had been obliged to bring water only for our own use, while now we had to quench the thirst of this parched pump. It was robbing Peter to pay Paul at a fearful outlay to the robber. "We shall have to buy a horse and build a treadmill if this is going to last long," said a person who is not fond of manual labor; but it did not last long. One fine morning all pitcher persuasions proved useless. The poor pump wheezed and groaned and squeaked and moaned. I heard the noise, but could not decide what it was, and called out from the head of the kitchen stairs, "How does the pump work this morning?"

"Works like a Trojan," and so indeed it did, but in vain. Halicarnassus said he would examine the pipes. He went down cellar with a candle, and then down the well, and was gone so long that I forgot all about him. Presently he came in and threw himself on the lounge. Then I recollected, and asked eagerly, "What have you done with the well?"

"O, I left it there, — out doors," he replied, indifferently, as if I had supposed he might have put it in his pocket, — but no water followed his explorations.

In the midst of our perplexities came a new and startling development. The mountain of earth that had been dug out of the well was to be sold to the town surveyor at six cents a load, for mending the highways, — which seemed to me so good a bargain, that I advised Halicarnassus to have the whole farm dug up and carted off at that price, as the most profitable mode of farming we could adopt. There was delay, of course, in removing the pile, and presently the frosts fastened their fangs in it, and it became a fixture till spring. After a while, a man who was examining the well in pursuit of knowledge, ascertained that it was filling up. The rains had slyly washed the soil back again. It was already five feet deep in the bottom of the well, and at this rate it would not be long before we should have to dig it all over again. How the little underground imps must have clapped their hands in malicious delight, at the practical joke they were playing on us! But worse still, the rains in one spot had washed away the background from the rocks, and left a hole which every rain enlarged. Another rain-storm might be fatal. In short, the well threatened to cave in. It might as well have been in as out for all the good it did, besides it was absurd to think of mending a well before it was fairly made; nevertheless, for the name of it, we concluded to heal the breach. Speedy measures were urgently enjoined. It was Saturday night, and a rain-storm imminent. I suggested stuffing the hole with cotton wool and rags over Sunday, and was looked at for my pains. Perhaps the plan was hardly feasible, as the hole, on examination, turned out to be large enough for a man to hide in. No, we must go at once, and bring laborers to fill in stones and pack clay, — even to work on Sunday, rather than encounter another rain. There are two livery stables in town owning a horse apiece; messengers were despatched to both to make sure of a conveyance, but though the clouds lowered, and the drops pattered, no man's conscience was tampered with by any inducement to work on Sunday. It turned out just as well, for the clouds thought better of it, and after giving us a sad fright and a few "love pats," floated away and left us a bright Sunday and Monday; and the well, after a little wise correction, relinquished its purpose of caving in, and surrendered at discretion.

So here we are. If it were a mere matter of human mechanics, something might be done; but how contend with the great wild atmosphere fifty miles above our heads, and the solid earth beneath? The stars in their courses fought against Sisera; and Sisera was conquered.

> "Who shall contend with his lords
>   Or cross them or do them wrong?
> Who shall bind them as with cords?
>   Who shall tame them as with song?
> Who shall smite them as with swords?
>   For the hands of their kingdom are strong."

In calmer moments, in some soft twilight hour, we conjecture that possibly our little lodge chances to be perched on a water-shed, and that is the reason all the streams run away from us. We recount the history of the old world, the irrigation of the East, the wondrous masonry of the Roman aqueduct, and resolve that the remains are no remains, but mark the spot where the builders gave up their work in despair, and we know how to sympathize with them. I read to my friend one morning the vainglorious boast of the Cincinnati people over their monster pump, which they declare to be the largest pump in the world, for it draws a stream five feet in diameter from the river.

"We can match it," he responded; "we have got the smallest pump in the world, for it draws just no stream at all!"

We are gradually recovering from the stupor of exhaustion consequent upon our prolonged and incessant efforts. When we have nothing else to do, we take a turn at the pump, rather, however, from force of habit than hope. There have been even faint attempts at wit. Halicarnassus beguiles the tedium of pumping by calling it practical high-draw-lics. I suggested mechanical aid one morning, a steam-pump or a force-pump. But no, said he, we will let well enough alone. Once he aroused himself from a long and brown study sufficiently to remark, in a dreamy sing-song, "They say, 'all's well that ends well.' Would n't all be better if it begun well and ended water?" Or perhaps he exclaims, his eyes heavy with unshed tears, "We love not wisely but two wells." I smile, not having the heart to refuse him such cold comfort as may be found in bad puns, and just as we are beginning to be a little reconciled and settle down into our former ways, Mr. Olefogee is sure to call and say, "Better have a witch come and see what's the matter in the pump," and the old wounds bleed afresh.

There is one comfort, however, in the general wreck. The pump and the log and the well are of small use, it must be admitted; but the top of the pump-box makes a very handy shelf.

"Yes," says Halicarnassus, "but rather expensive. Tell me now, you who are accustomed to fine distinctions, on the principle that ''t were well done if 't were done quickly,' shall we consider our well done, or is it ourselves that are done?"

I have never disquieted myself to answer that question, nor shall I carry this record further. If subsequently Genius came to the rescue, and gave us a happy deliverance from all our troubles, why recount the tale? It is not victory, but struggle, that makes the happiness of noble hearts. And not the victory, but the struggle, shall have a history.

Friendly reader, if by this time any such is left me, have I with a winning word or two at the outset of my book, lured you into rough and unexpected paths? *Mea culpa!* Do you remember the story of the Queen, who had once been a cat, — how, sitting in state, she forgot herself, and popped under the table in pursuit of a mouse, to the consternation of her lords and ladies? *De me fabula!* Learn hence, my dear young reader, to be on your guard against the first symptoms of polemics, lest your whole life become saturated with it, and when you would fain utter only the pearls and diamonds of peace, frogs and toads of controversy leap forth unawares; lest even the melody of birds have a twang of Sternhold and Hopkins, and in the midst of bloom and beauty that which should

"Turn out a song,
Perchance turn out a sermon."

Cambridge: Stereotyped and Printed by Welch, Bigelow, & Co.

www.ingramcontent.com/pod-product-compliance
Lightning Source LLC
Chambersburg PA
CBHW020234240426
43672CB00006B/527